WHEN 'WILL' IS MORE THAN 'WON'T'

YOUR JOURNEY CONTINUES

BOOK 2

JAYNE WILKINSON

WHEN 'WILL' IS MORE THAN 'WON'T'

YOUR JOURNEY CONTINUES: BOOK 2

Published by Magic Flute Publishing Ltd. 2024
ISBN 978-1-915166-17-3 paperback
ISBN 978-1-915166-30-2 epub

Copyright © Jayne Wilkinson

Jayne Wilkinson has asserted her right under the Copyright, Designs and Patents Act 1988 to be identified as the author of this work.
All rights reserved. No part of this publication may be reproduced, stored in a retrieval system, or transmitted in any form or by any means, electronic, mechanical, photocopying, recording or otherwise, without the prior permission of the copyright owner.

Magic Flute Publishing Limited

231 Swanwick Lane

Southampton SO31 7GT

www.magicflutepublishing.com

A catalogue description of this book is available from the British Library

To everyone brave enough to bare their soul.

BIOGRAPHY

Jayne, an identical twin, from a council estate in Birmingham, was born into a family of four, to a factory worker father and a housewife mother. Travel for her was the local park or a coach trip to the seaside, not driving around the world in a Land Rover.

As an identical twin, she came out of the womb, firstly pissed at having to share an egg, and secondly with half a personality. Her's competitive and artistic, Jenny's studious and always on time; neither had confidence nor self-belief. By the age of twenty-five, married, with two children, she realised alcohol and debt were not what she wanted, and found her feet.

Then she met David and they decided to drive around the world. She was told she was going to live the dream, but soon realised living two feet from her other half, twenty-four hours a day, was no dream.

PREFACE

There are moments in all our lives when something changes it forever, when we walk down a path that becomes 'our' path, our destiny.

This book came about when David, my partner of ten years, and I decided to 'buy one of those Land Rover things' and drive it around the world, starting with Africa. From the very first moment I stepped foot on African soil, I wrote a revealing personal account of the impossible being made possible.

I've been asked many times to publish my journals about our journey, from those on their all-inclusive holiday, to those hitch-hiking, cycling, driving, or simply living vicariously, so here it is. It's for all the women shuddering at the thought of digging their own toilet, or changing a tyre, and the men looking for just this sort of woman. For those sat in the garden to a setting sun sipping wine, soaking in the bath, tucked up in bed, or out chasing their own horizons.

It's not a travel book as such, but it does take you on an epic journey, through countries and continents, but mostly through life. The reality of living that dream, the relationship, sex, hygiene, illness, corruption, pollution, poverty, despair, loneliness, wonder, laughter and total utter joy.

This is Book 2, from South Africa to Australia, told with complete honesty, in the moment, as it happened, by me, Jayne. I am not a writer. I've screamed, cried and questioned my abilities daily, but somehow, like the journey, I did it.

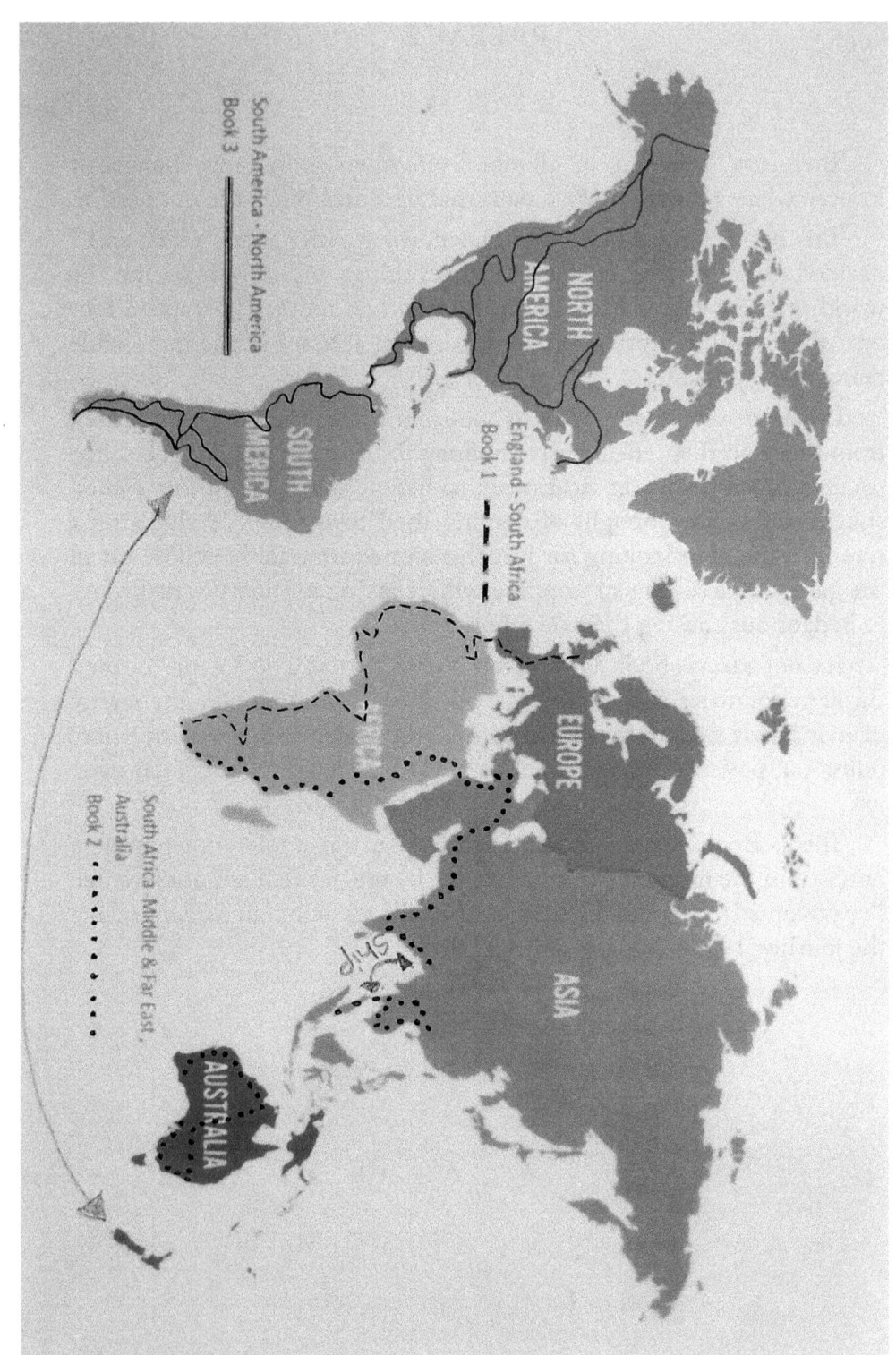

CONTENTS

Map of the Journey   vi

Chapter 1	And so it continues....	1
Chapter 2	Reunited like swallows	9
Chapter 3	Its life, just how we knew it	21
Chapter 4	Survivors of the last frontier	38
Chapter 5	Poisoned on the way to Kenya	50
Chapter 6	Africa works her magic	60
Chapter 7	The revelation of Ethiopia	67
Chapter 8	Feeling part of something	79
Chapter 9	On the edge of insanity	90
Chapter 10	Armed rebellions and civil wars	99
Chapter 11	Anarchy on the streets of London	112
Chapter 12	Who needs fuel anyway?	124
Chapter 13	Convoys and sickness take their toll	139
Chapter 14	Waddling like a duck	148
Chapter 15	Impounded in Bangladesh	156
Chapter 16	Freedom comes to those who wait	161
Chapter 17	The desire and need to explore	169
Chapter 18	Rotting in the jungle	183
Chapter 19	A gin sling in Singapore	194
Chapter 20	G'day Australia	198
Chapter 21	No worries, mate	205
Chapter 22	One word – VAST	212
Chapter 23	The Gibb	218
Chapter 24	Where the '****' is Alice?	228
Chapter 25	The realisation	239
Chapter 26	The Calm before the storm	253
Chapter 27	It´s time to face the music	256

INTRODUCTION

In the pitch black of night, I hear a gnawing sound. Switching on the single hanging light bulb, I see a scrawny rat eating our bread. This would usually freak me out, but right now I´m more concerned we won't have any breakfast. I zip what remains of it into our backpack. With the light back off, in the dark and quiet of the night, I can still hear scuttling feet. In my semi-sleepiness this becomes a stampede of yellow toothed, monster feasting rats. I'm so glad we have been upgraded, who knows what the cattle class is suffering?

It started from an idea whilst backpacking in Chile to buy a Land Rover and drive it around the world, an idea verging on insanity. With David working in criminal law and myself in a call centre, or any job that paid me money. Never having owned or driven this kind of vehicle before or, if we're honest, held any lifelong desire to do so. It was a flawed plan from the start.

In a time when Tunisian street vendor Mohamed Bouazizi, frustrated by the oppressive system, the humiliation and harassment he suffered by the municipal officials, had set himself on fire in protest, to die later in hospital. Thus sparking protests and revolts that spread across the Arab world. I would listen to reports like this on the BBC news whilst ironing David's shirts for work. Not once thinking it would be part of my life.

This book takes you along the east coast of Africa into Asia and on to a country so big it is its own continent, that of Australia. The reality of life at its most raw and at its most incredible, written with candid honesty on the journey as it unfolded, by me, Jayne.

CHAPTER 1
AND SO IT CONTINUES….

It's strange to be stood here in the queue at Birmingham airport seeing Johannesburg South Africa as our destination, a country almost as familiar to us now as England. Looking around me, I see the collection of happy holidaymakers and sad farewells. It will take just over a day to return to a place that took over a year to drive to. I suppose I'm different now in that I'm a grandmother and a mother-in-law, but these are life events that can happen to us all. What has really changed is us, David and I. Changed because everything that we ever knew - house, job, language, showers - was taken from us, voluntarily it's true, but nonetheless gone, and replaced with the unknown.

We're returning to a life that has become our life. The next chapter in this never-ending story of 'driving one of those Land Rover things around the world'. Which came about after a throwaway comment whilst backpacking with David, my partner of fifteen years, in Chile. From a day trip in vehicles that just so happened to be Land Rover. With me being so impressed with what they could do, saying to David: "We should get one of them Land Rover things", and David replying: "Yes, and we should drive it around the world". There and then making it a thing.

The fact that neither of us, David working in criminal law, and me in hostels and call centres, or any other job that paid me money, had ever driven an off-road vehicle before was insignificant. To us, the biggest obstacle was money oh, and getting a vehicle.

It took two years from that day to buy a Land Rover we called Lizzybus, to kit her out with boxes off eBay, a long-range fuel tank, a roof tent and our luxury item, a fridge. To sell, donate, and trash all our worldly possessions, and rent our houses out. This giving us sixty dollars a day to live on, with a pot of cash saved, so at the very least we could get back to England if it all went disastrously wrong. It's odd thinking about it now, as once we had voiced this, it became set in stone, and felt like a sentence we had served on ourselves, rather than an idea, and one we had little choice in.

Until that rainy overcast morning, we set off from Birmingham, destination world, for no reason other than I had heard it was hot, we headed for the west coast of Africa. A year later, we made it to South Africa, through some of the most corrupt, unstable, civil war-torn countries in the world. It's there, we left Lizzybus and returned to England to renew David´s passport and the Carnet de Passage (a bond that allows you to take a vehicle in and out of these countries). To visit my mother lost to me two years ago to Alzheimer's, and most importantly, for the birth of my first and only grandson.

There are seven continents in the world:

Europe, Africa, Asia, Australia-Oceania, North America, South America, and Antarctica.

We are one and a half continents, twenty-six countries, and one hundred thousand miles into our journey with, I'm just going to say, "a lot further to go". The ultimate goal is to drive Lizzybus around the world, but this is such a loose plan it's not really a plan at all, more a desire. It also depends on what you see as the whole world, top to bottom, crossing lines of longitude and latitude, or pole to pole, who knows? It's not so much about driving around the world, it's just that that sentence put it into some sort of box, giving it a goal.

From South Africa, we will continue east, crossing continents and the countries within them. We would love to go to every one of them, which we'll try to do, but it will be the logistics of getting Lizzybus in, or running out of money, or the stability of the country that will decide this. Oh, and the small matter of if we have murdered each other or not.

Our biggest challenge has been, and still is, getting ongoing visas. On very rare occasions, they can be bought at the border, but normally many hours, days, even weeks, can be spent trying to secure them in capital cities where the embassies are based. We focus only on the few countries ahead, in the general direction we're travelling, which seems to work. For now, we are heading along the east coast of Africa to:

Mozambique, Zambia, Tanzania, Kenya, Ethiopia, Sudan, Egypt, Syria, Iran, and Turkey.

Some of these countries are on the brink of civil war and very unstable - Syria and Iran for a start, but there is no point whatsoever in thinking about that until we get a bit closer and know for sure. I live in Jayne World and too much knowing or thinking is not good for me.

I'm just incredulous that it's me, from a council estate in Birmingham, who thought Jamaica was in Africa, who'd never even been on a plane until the age of thirty. Is the one who's not only talking about unstable countries but is driving around them with David in Lizzybus.

Arriving back at Johannesburg airport, we find Lizzybus, washed of her African dust, waiting for us with the man who stored her. It all feels so familiar driving back to the same backpackers we left three weeks ago. We are welcomed back and upgraded to an en-suite room, where concrete blocks support the home-made wooden bed frame, and wire springs protrude from a hair stuffed mattress. It takes a while for our eyes to adjust to the single hanging light bulb, before dumping the bags, eating noodles, and sleeping away the trauma of another goodbye.

We want to get going again, but it takes a few days to re-organise kit and fit the much-needed stuff David has brought back for what has become his mistress, Lizzybus. I can think of many vehicles that would be far better to live in than Lizzybus; we chose her as she not only looked the job, especially for Africa, but being all mechanical you don't need a laptop to fix her, just a hammer and a big pot of grease. Grease and greasing are, and I'm sure will continue to be, a full-time job on Lizzybus, specifically nipples, which can only be greased whilst cursing, due to them being underneath her and always pointing in the wrong direction. But isn't that what nipples do?

Whilst Lizzybus is filled, rather than fitted, with all this extra kit, I focus on what I have always seen as the essentials in life: shelter, water, and food. Lizzybus is our shelter, although by sleeping in a roof tent, accessed externally, our security is and has been compromised. Water comes from rivers, streams, or standpipes to pump through the ceramic water filter system from two twenty litre Scepter (plastic military grade) jerry cans. Food, with the one drawer that is not filled with Lizzybus spare parts, now filled with pasta, rice, noodles, tuna and the likes.

We're woken through the night by gunfire, which apparently is normal here and to be ignored, so we do. Whilst David works on Lizzybus, with my Afro frizz hair needing re-plaiting, I get the bus to a 'hair salon' I've been told about. After my last experience of having been taken on a bus by the cleaner to a local 'hair salon' in Nigeria and left by a block of broken buildings in the middle of nowhere. Where I stood crying until the local children put me on the bus back, telling the driver to drop me off at the backpackers, I am most reluctant to go alone. Comforted by the fact that they at least speak English here, I take a deep breath and go. It's hard to imagine that taking out plaited hair, even Afro frizz hair and re-plaiting it, takes one whole day, sometimes two, but it does. With the plaits now ripped out of my head and washed, I´m instructed to return tomorrow for re-plaiting. Most of my time was spent sitting and waiting in a chair, as breastfeeding and eating by the stylist took priority. Africa is all about Inshallah.

In the communal kitchen there are sealed boxes to store our food stuff. When I went to make breakfast, ours had been pinched, so tonight I take what is left of the bread and coffee into the room. In the pitch black of night, I hear a gnawing sound. Switching on the single hanging light bulb, I see a scrawny rat eating the bread. In the past I would have totally freaked out, but right now I´m more concerned we won't have any breakfast again, so zip what remains into our backpack. With the light off, in the dark and quiet of the night, I can still hear scuttling feet; in my semi-sleepiness this becomes a stampede of yellow toothed, monster feasting rats. I'm so glad we have been upgraded - who knows what the cattle class are suffering?

Sorting through the expensive external grade vinyl flags I'd had made in England; I find over half of the countries are missing. These credit card sized flags, stuck in chronological order along each side of Lizzybus, have become invaluable where language is such a barrier. They bring with them very special moments in time when, having made it to our next country and crossing its border, we have the 'flag sticking on ceremony'. It's so disappointing and colours the mood for the rest of the day. As does trying to squeeze in the much-needed Lizzybus spares: drive shafts, ceramic water filter candles, nuts, bolts, tools, every gasket, and seal you could ever imagine needing. They'll never ever stop the oil or water leaks, just redirect them. I do now understand the importance of these things, but it doesn't stop the irritation of trying to fit them into Lizzybus.

Once we are on the road and moving, we never want to stop. If or when we do, it's incredibly difficult to get going again. Our friends call it the overlanding disease. The freedom and excitement of the unknown is superseded by the part in all of us that wants to ´nest ´. To me it's about wanting to ´rest´, to rest from the constant of moving. We know many who never got to where they were going and settled where they ´rested´. I feel like the hibernating bear; you keep sleeping, until one day you wake with this urgency to get moving.

You're ready for the challenge of the unknown. Yes, it's with trepidation of what you're heading into, but that's thrilling. I ponder the significance of how one thing, one action, delivers you to different destinations. The action of turning the key that fires up the Lizzybus engine, the beating heart of this journey. An action that for three years took me to work, shopping, and the gym. Unable to afford two cars, she was my transport. Now this action is propelling us back into the life that has become our life, our goal, our dream.

Hello world. Today we are coming to explore you once more - we are off!

It's not long before the euphoria ends in this driving rain, we're unable to see through the steamed-up windows and water is puddling at our feet heading for Durban. As Africa's largest port, once covered in mangroves and inhabited by pelicans, flamingos, and hippos, it is now a vast urban sprawl. With huge sugar, cotton and tea plantations, since the abolition of slavery in South Africa and the need for cheap labour, Indians were brought over on Indenture. A contract that was little more than slavery, resulting in South Africa's largest Indian population. At Harrismith, a town framed by mountains, we camp at the municipal campsite, with its squat toilet, sink hanging off the wall, and single pipe shower. It's filled with black highway workers. Having been warned to check we are in a mixed-race area, seeing the owner is white, to us that makes it mixed race. Sitting in the setting sun obscured by gathering rain clouds, ants crawl up my legs, mozzies oblivious to the thick layer of deet bite, and a chorus of panicked birds announce imminent nightfall. I look up to see a solid line of mountains frame a star-filled sky, I am where I belong. I am home.

We had such a peaceful night back in the roof tent. In our sleeping bags we slept fully clothed as we have no form of heating in Lizzybus. Well, I did. David, never too cold nor too hot, slept in boxer shorts and t-shirt. Surprisingly this morning, the single hanging pipe in the shower has gloriously hot water coming out. This, along with our new coffee pot, cheers me up no end and makes for a day we're ready to face driving through the heart of the Drakensberg mountains. Forced up over millions of years, the mountains lie like shards of shattered ice, menacing and rugged in any direction you look. For now, we're on perfect tarmac roads, driving through the lush basin plateau. The fields are full of bony African cows twitching their muscles to rid themselves of irritating flies. The blustering clouds keep the sting of sun away as a cool breeze pushes through the open Lizzybus windows.

At Amphitheatre Backpackers with sauna, jacuzzi, swimming pool and fully equipped communal kitchen, the very gay guys who run it tell us it's a 'flash packers'. In Lizzybus, we check out Cathedral Peak Park. It's late in the day, too late to hike to any of the spectacular lookout points, but they still ask us to pay two dollars to go to the Lodge Restaurant. On the veranda we're seated at one of the ornately painted wrought iron tables with pure white linen tablecloths, by a waiter wearing a bow tie and gloves. We feel obliged to order something, so order coffee, which comes in a silver pot with hand painted porcelain cups and a little plate of biscuits. We gaze out over this natural amphitheatre, with a carpet of vivid green velvet encircled by shattered mountains - it's simply stunning.

When the bill arrives, the two-dollar entrance fee has been deducted, leaving just one dollar to pay.

In life, certain things burn into your subconscious forever. One of them for me was the Michael Cain film 'Zulu', based on the successful defence of the Rorke's Drift mission station, when just one hundred and fifty British soldiers faced nearly four thousand Zulu warriors. And today, quite incredibly, we are here. As I look out across the rolling hills of the savannah where the chanting Zulu warriors surrounded them, I'm with my parents at the cinema, watching this epic battle in glorious technicolour. I can hear Michael Cain's immortal words 'bloody thousands'. I learnt something today: shivers down your spine is an actual thing and complete silence is far more powerful than noise.

My mother is back in hospital. I'm struggling with my feelings as I just want so much for all this to end, for Mom to pass away peacefully in her sleep. Someone stole her from me long ago, her mind destroyed by Alzheimer's and her body crippled by a stroke. Even her familiar smell and once soft cheeks have gone; my mother has been reduced to a shell. I wake up every night with the most vivid beautiful memories of her. I can taste the fresh bread and cakes she baked every Sunday; I can feel her hand in mine skipping and dancing over the park, I can hear her voice reading our bedtime stories. I knew Mom loved us unconditionally, and now in her prison of fog, with a broken body and mind, the pain of losing her would be nothing next to the pain of this twilight world she now exists in.

It is with a heavy heart we press on. I know we are making progress as the South Atlantic Ocean that followed us down the west coast of Africa has become the wild coast of the Indian Ocean. At Howick Falls, with its single ninety-five metre drop into the Umgeni River, having claimed the lives of many swept over its crest, is now fenced off and the municipal campsite is closed. With most of South Africa being fenced, this constant battle of finding camping spots or sites every night has become an ordeal. Late afternoon is the hottest part of the day. Your backside, well my backside, is complaining loudly at having been sat on all day, and everything is radiating heat. It usually ends with us bickering in our frustration when, unable to find a good place to bush camp, we take the easy option of paying to camp, which eats into our tight budget.

We're splashing away in a swimming pool with three dogs and their owners Jenny and Ron. English Jenny, on visiting South Africa thirty years ago, never left. She got married and then divorced, before settling down with South African Ron. The pair, both mildly eccentric, were shopping in town when they saw us and Lizzybus, who having decided to sod the expense were having a beer at a roadside cafe. I often wonder if people realise what these chance meetings really mean to us. The generosity offered to us complete strangers and the life rafts they are in a journey, a journey that at times we are drowning in. What a fantastic evening with homemade boerewors cooking away on the braai, and us swigging Castle Lager, but the most fulfilling thing of all is the conversation - glorious, wonderful conversation - chitting (my word) and chatting the evening away.

It's a much-needed tonic, enabling us to put this journey back into our hearts where it belongs. It is so much more than what we see - it´s our experiences through it. We have many times been so overwhelmed we wanted to forget all about it.

Jenny phones her ex-husband Hilton and his new wife Alison to say we are heading their way, and they must put us up. I need to mention here my English reserve and the struggles I've had in letting it go on this journey, which to some extent I have managed, but this truly pushes it to its limit. I would much rather Jenny didn't ask, but my protests are dismissed with assurances he will love us. We are now driving through The Valley of a Thousand Hills which roll up down and around the

Umgeni River where we find Hilton in his rambling house nestled on one of them.

In 1906, Hilton's grandfather became the first Park Ranger in the area, and the room we are now sitting in is a true reflection of that. The coffee table is an elephant leg, the ashtray an elephant foot, faded pictures of a bygone era when big game and Zulu inhabited the plains hang on every inch of wall. It's a very special honour to be chatting late into the night with Hilton. I sit listening, in wonderful silence as another shiver runs down my spine.

We wake to an empty house; Hilton and his wife have gone to work. Gordon, the maintenance man, makes us a pot of coffee and breakfast. I leave a book for them on the migration of the swallow from England to South Africa. I feel we have so much in common with these tiny birds who migrate from England following the west coast of Africa to avoid the blistering Sahara Desert. Something even more incredible is that they do this twice a year. I imagined those little swallows, flying high above us, as we migrated here.

Spirits are high as we follow the wild coast of the Indian Ocean. The sinking clouds plunge us into a thick fog we can see only a few metres ahead in on our way to Port St John, a small peaceful town on the banks of the Mzimvubu River. Dropping back down out of the fog, the Africa I am familiar with is back. Pyramid piles of vegetables are sold at the roadside, children are once more strapped to their mothers' backs, or trail behind carrying bundles of firewood. David sets up camp beside the muddy Mzimvubu River, I take our yellow bar of African soap and, in the earth-coloured water, scrub our clothes which I lie on the boulders to dry. It´s with a sense of belonging we sit in contented silence drinking a beer as the glowing ball of sun disappears into the horizon.

My mother has died. The peace I thought this would bring has not arrived. I feel cheated and resentful for her and for me in her not knowing I´m on this journey. It leaves an empty hollowness within me. We only arrived back in South Africa less than two weeks ago, even though she was lost to me, it's of some comfort I said what I wanted to say to mom then. But right now, I need to be with my family.

It's the same sky, with the same clouds, in the same hills, but for some reason it all feels different. I wonder where the swallows are now.

CHAPTER 2
REUNITED LIKE SWALLOWS

The shutter of my eyes close once more, to open here in Durban, South Africa having gone back to England for my mother's funeral alone. While sitting in the church, listening to family members and friends sharing their memories and funny stories of my mother, I looked around at our children. Ours as in Jenny's, my twin sister, and mine because for most of their childhood it was the four of us. Jenny having got out of her abusive relationship and me, after alcohol took the life of my husband and left me destitute. What I call the wilderness years. Merely children ourselves, we eventually figured it all out, worked day and night to pull the remnants of our lives back together, managing to buy a small house each.

It is with a huge sense of pride in the adults they have become, each affected by losing Nan-Joy (their name for Mom) in different ways, having spent time with her during school holidays. I smile when I remember Adele at age six, home after a week with Mom, counting to three before getting off the toilet after peeing. I asked why she did that. "Nan-Joy said I have to count to three, so I don't drip".

So along with skills like cooking, gardening, reading, writing, tying shoelaces, and how to hold a knife and fork, I know with certainty that our children will never drip! This also gives you a very good idea of how my newfound toilet arrangements, of digging holes, no toilet doors, and audiences have been a massive personal battle for me, when 'dripping' is something to avoid.

I had missed David and Lizzybus, but not quite as much as he had apparently missed me, not spoken through words - that would never be a thing - but in how distant and lost he was. But passion, despite the 'absence makes the heart grow stronger' crap, didn't happen as it's words that are needed to make me feel wanted and desired. Oh, and I almost forgot, personal hygiene and grooming. As once more I smell of soap powder and shampoo, not engine oil and African dust, and it being even more noticeable. Our commitment to each other and this journey has never faltered. We are puppy-dog loyal and fiercely protective of each other. I'm sure if couples were to be honest with each other and specifically themselves, they would prioritise differently; a night of steamy sex, a one-night stand, or an affair as being way down the list of priorities. To having an ally, a confidant, someone you can and do put all your trust in as right at the top.

On that subject, there was a group of girls at school who had done 'it', and thought it hysterical to ask out loud in the changing rooms, in front of everyone, who else had done 'it'. I wasn't exactly sure what 'it' really meant. Was it a kiss, a grope, showing your bits, but to get in with them, whatever 'it' was, I was adamant I had. This worked until they wanted details which, of course, I could not provide. I can feel the humiliation now. I swore the sooner I did 'it' the better, so a career, qualifications, all that stuff, was not what I aspired to. I wanted to have 'it'. In my adult life, that all changed. I hated anyone in my space, being close to me and I became very picky, prickly, and selective.

David, from an all-boys school, the confirmed bachelor with no children, had lived with people, mostly Jane's oddly enough, was living alone when we met. He was at his happiest among all his chaos, sitting in his leather recliner chair, surrounded by boxes of vinyls, listening to his music on an old school turntable, or out on his motorbike. Unlike me, David had done crazy adventurous things like drive to France with his mates in his Ford Escort Popular company car with gallons of free diesel in containers in the boot, and with one of the Janes in an MGB called Ebie. Little did I know that what we were about to do would make this all seem like a walk in the park.

To say David had what I lacked, 'intelligence', and I had what he lacked, 'social skills', is a bit of an insult as we each had both, but we brought these qualities out in each other even more.

Having been apart for three weeks and into the third year of this journey, sitting twenty-four hours a day next to each other, we know every detail, not only of the day, but also the personal habits of each other, details I'd much sooner not know. It's wonderful to now have things to talk about. David's things are mainly what he's repaired, replaced, or upgraded on his mistress and what he's eaten. I listen with interest, ignoring the chaos he has created. Knowing my mother is no longer suffering has allowed me to take a deep breath, to find a sort of peace. But like an open wound I am still healing. All this living on in spirit and time is a great healer stuff seems hollow to me right now, but I'm sure it will come to comfort me one day.

Two days later, with everything back where it should be and wiped of its thick grease covering, we head off once more. I have no fear or trepidation as to what might lie ahead, just pure relief at finally being able to get going, to be back on the road driving Lizzybus around the world, one country, one mile, one road at a time.

The 'tracks for Africa' programme in our Garmin, given to us by Klaus, a German man we met in Windhoek, allows us to follow minor roads free of traffic with confidence. The rattle and noise of Lizzybus soothes me, allowing my mind to relax. I think back to my first real holiday with David to Orlando Florida. I was going to Disney! For me this would be the holiday of a lifetime, and although David had been twice before, he was just as excited to show me as I was to be shown. On arriving in Orlando, we picked up the hire car and headed not to our hotel, motel, or even a room, but to the newsagents where David picked up the local free ´Florida Traveler´ newspaper looking for discount tickets for local motels. What, you mean we have no booked accommodation, something, anything, but nothing?

My holiday of a lifetime started stood in the reception of a shabby motel used as temporary accommodation for homeless families and waif and strays, with David asking if they honoured discount coupons. I was incredulous we had flown halfway across the world, to be stood here bargaining for a half price room. Of course, they honoured the vouchers with the grottiest room available, not, I might add, for the whole three weeks, but for just a few days, so the whole humiliating process had to be repeated. The suitcase full of new holiday clothes stayed in the suitcase - why bother unpacking when we had to keep moving?

Despite this I was totally and utterly beguiled and bedazzled with Disney. With 'economically challenged parents', okay, poor, only on very special occasions as a family did, we go to the cinema. Seeing Tinkerbell, Mickey Mouse, Snow White and the Seven Dwarfs, in glorious technicolour, I didn't dare even blink in case I missed anything. As an adult child, with my memories brought to life, it was quite wonderful. I even began to find flitting from motel to motel a bit of an adventure. Thinking about this now I realise how much I´ve changed. Places to stay are now judged on how secure Lizzybus is and the price, not what the room is like.

South Africa has vast fenced off areas for disease control, isolating wildlife from cattle and poaching. This makes bush camping difficult, we tend to stop at camp sites which are cheap and good. We don't have specific mileage goals. I drive the first two hours; if there is something of interest to visit or see along the way, we stop. What we have found is the need to set a finish time, to avoid driving in the dark. To stop at the first place that looks okay and not to keep going in the hope of finding something better or end up driving into dusk and arguing.

Pulling over at an exclusive spa and camping lodge, I'm the first into reception asking if we can camp in the grounds, use the facilities, for at best nothing, or at least very little. I´m a little triumphant when they not only let us camp for free but join the few out-of-season lodge guests in the warm sulphur pools to watch the sun set. Off the back of Lizzybus, David fries chicken livers with spinach, adding the half tub of cream he had apparently saved just for me. I know being grateful is warranted, and as we're seeing the positives in each other right now. I am most appreciative, giving him a kiss on the cheek, despite the horrid wiry grey beard he has grown.

Lizzybus, as much as Lizzybus can, sparkles having been washed. At least the limited view out of her windscreen, due to a great big spare wheel on the bonnet is clear. We're driving on through miles of managed forest, either stumps, or saplings, or half-grown trees, with gigantic logging lorries thundering past. The cooling breeze is heavy with the intoxicating scent of pine. We set up camp deep in the forest and eat the remains of the chicken livers without any cream, swilled down with a cold beer. Now my mother has died, were both full of hope, that we can continue this journey without compromise. There has always been and always will be a certain amount of selfishness in following your dream. Losing people is not just something that happens through death, but through life and the choices we make. We had no choice in this ordeal - of course, I mean adventure! It just became a thing, our destiny and now we see nothing to stop us. Or so we think.

Kruger National Park is the size of a small country, a vast area. What makes it special is that over the years, fences between neighbouring private and state-owned parks and reserves have been opened up to allow for the more natural movement of animals. The Kruger also has several rivers running through it; animals no longer need to congregate around managed water holes but have access to natural water sources. Africa feels real once more, as its spirit settles upon us; it flattens out and we see the vast savannahs. Lion, elephant, buffalo, rhino and leopard are known as the 'Big Five' of the Kruger, and as the animals most hunted for their ivory, horns and skins, they are now protected. It's mostly photographs that are taken, although illegal poaching still exists.

What is just as incredible to me are the Big Five trees. Without them, life would not exist in this hostile environment. The baobab 'tree of life' with its fat body and root like crown; the weeping boer-bean single trunk tree; the jackalberry tree, so named because its fruits are often found in jackal dung; the Natal mahogany, an evergreen shadow-casting tree where prides of lions sleep away the heat of the day; and finally the sycamore fig. Totally dependent on the fig wasp, the tree attracts the insect by the scent of its flowers and entices it through a tiny gap in the forming fig to pollinate, lay its eggs then die. Some of the flowers become seeds, and others form a kind of wasp nursery - how incredible is that? What all these trees have in common are the life and cycle they give to the Kruger.

The Kruger is well signposted, with good tarmac roads set up for self-drive or jeep safaris. On the next bend we find a park warden with a radar gun enforcing the fifty-kilometre speed limit. That's never going to affect us, we only do those sorts of speeds downhill with the wind behind us, and why would you want to go any faster? For now, the vegetation is making spotting anything that didn't fancy a stroll across the tarmac rare. We do see giraffe heads above the tree canopies, with their incredibly snakelike long purple tongues curling around the succulent new shoots. The giraffe's tongue is like the monkey's tail, adapted to grasp and hold, allowing the monkey to swing around and the giraffes to hold onto its juicy buds. We also see herds of elephant and zebra. As majestic as this all is, sitting for several hours in a boiling hot Lizzybus means by late afternoon we have had enough and want to camp up. Of course, you can't have people just 'bush camping'. You need to have designated secure campsites, but they are not included in the entrance fee (conservation fee), making for a very expensive day.

We are up at six this morning and off by seven for two reasons: game apparently is at its most active early in the morning, and we need to be out of the park by midday or pay another forty dollars. Once more I feel like that child with my parents at the cinema, watching Elsa the released-into-the-wild lion cub. Seeing is about so much more: it´s brought to life by hearing, hearing the noise of Lizzybus when the smooth tarmac becomes graded gravel, the trumpet calls of elephants heard up to six miles away; feeling, feeling the dust settling on your skin and the furnace heat; smell, smelling arid dryness and dung. All the senses submerge you completely into these moments.

We see herds of elephants wallowing and thrashing about in muddy rivers; the eyes of crocs amongst the reeds; the ears and eyes of hippos. On the plain's herds of zebra and antelope, even the endangered white rhinoceros, and a lion with its kill draped in the branches of a tree. I can't take it all in. It's so very special, and a much-needed distraction from the pain in my bottom and the stinging heat of the sun.

You could drive around this country, I mean park, for days and still not see everything, but not wanting to pay for another day, we head out. I can't think of a more fitting end to our time in South Africa, as tomorrow we are crossing into Mozambique. After setting up camp for the night at a public campsite adjacent to a river, David spends the afternoon working on Lizzybus and I clean. To a setting sun, we take a walk along the riverbank to a car-wide concrete weir spanning it, where locals wash their tuk-tuks, cars and motorbikes, and women, with hips swaying to the blasting music coming from suitcase sized speakers in the cars, scrub clothes and children.

The current is strong, creating a drop off where tumbling water traps and spins fallen tree branches and garbage. Apparently tomorrow we need to drive over this to the border, so we decide to test it out by walking over it. Holding hands on the basis if I was going in, David was coming with me, find it slippery as hell and the current incredibly strong. We only made it halfway, until David now wishing he had never told me as I'm freaking out at the prospect of driving over it, comes up with another plan - to sit it out and see if any other vehicles cross. Half an hour later, realising its beer o´clock and everyone had gone, we give up and head back to camp.

Mozambique, sitting between South Africa and Tanzania, official language Portuguese, capital Maputo. On its flag is a Kalashnikov crossed with a hoe over an open book. In the late 1990s civil war broke this country, taking it to the brink of bankruptcy; a time when villagers were rounded up and anyone with skills shot, along with other atrocities committed on a massive scale. Entrenched corruption is ongoing. Kidnappings still happen but are criminal rather than terrorist led. This is a relief as we have no intention of doing, or getting involved in, any criminal activities. Landmines are still a concern in remote areas. It's a country with endless coastal plains, plateaus, has three of Africa's major rivers flowing through it and six national parks - a paradise despite its troubled past, and we're looking forward to it.

(In four years' time, Mozambique will be declared free of landmines, thanks in part to the work of British charity The Halo Trust.)

It's morning and no longer can we ignore the crossing of the weir; our plan to wait and watch until someone else crosses is still a flawed plan with the absence of any other vehicle. Despite mornings being my 'shift', I nominate David to drive over as one of us needs to take pictures. Recording this journey through pictures has been sadly lacking. With only the two of us we're busy getting on with the job, one spotting, the other driving. It didn't help that we had an in-your-face brick of a camera; taking pictures of people in their daily life felt intrusive. And the fact we were almost arrested for taking pictures in Nigeria of a bridge. A lot has changed now with the smart phone, people are happy to have, even want their picture taken.

Firstly, I walk across the weir on my own. I wanted to do it on all fours, but I could see a group of women watching me, so on two feet, at a snail's pace I finally made it to the other side. Things are always worse when you imagine them. I imagined David and Lizzybus slithering off the weir into the tumbled mass of garbage and fallen trees, but although the water was door height, Lizzybus stayed in a straight line. It looked such fun I wanted to have a go. Driving back over to the group of women doing their washing whilst swaying their hips to the music once more blasting out of the speakers in the boots of the cars being washed. I park alongside them to wash Lizzybus. It's wonderful being amongst them, doing such a normal everyday thing, like washing. I start swaying my hips and bottom in time to the music, but it doesn't have the same effect since our African diet and my already little bottom is now non-existent. Still, it amuses the locals who reward me with beautiful smiles, and we have a cleanish Lizzybus who, I realise, still has elephant dung used as fire lighters on the roof.

In South Africa we had bought a new 'clam shell' roof tent, as our old one leaked, was a pain to fold up every day, and had holes in it from a mice infestation. We were assured we could claim the VAT back for it along with the spare parts we had bought. We are now shuffling along in the blistering midday heat in the queue of women, with sacks full of cheesy puffs balanced on their heads, backs and a few more dragged behind them, claiming their VAT. We're pushed sideways, forwards and backwards, cushioned by bottoms and bosoms. With no shelter from the midday sun and the heat from all the bodies, I faint. It doesn't really matter as we are so tightly packed, I stay upright. David empties the remains of his bottle of water over my head, and pours mine down my throat, I begin to come round, choking on the water. This fainting has been a problem for me on the journey. We are now monitoring how much water we are drinking and putting salt in our food.

Still light-headed, we reach the customs office, a wooden hut with an opaque scratched piece of perspex for a window. We see only the fuzzy outline of the two customs officers behind it who want to see the goods we are claiming for, but as they have already been fitted or used, we can only point at them and show the receipts. They ponder this for a while before agreeing to a refund but advise us the amount, we are claiming for is too much to give us a cash refund here at the border. They will issue us a cheque, but it will need to be certified and posted out to our English address. We have no faith whatsoever that we will ever receive this cheque. I´m past caring - I just need to get out of this midday sun. (we did receive this cheque six months later)

We're stamped out of South Africa and are now driving through no man's land towards the Mozambique border. Mozambique is one of the few countries you can buy a visa on the border; painless in that you don't have to spend days securing one at the embassy, but painful in that they cost 90 dollars each. We're trailed by the usual groups of waifs and strays that hang about at borders, all wanting to take you to the various offices for a fee. This is our twenty-third border crossing - it seems like a lifetime ago since that terrifying crossing from Morocco into Mauritania with its mined no man's land. We are different people now, but despite knowing the process it's always a test of nerves, as many things can and do go wrong. We understand the system, the scams and the need to be patient whilst persistent. It's a small victory and a huge relief when everything is stamped, and we get through.

What a difference a strip of land between two countries makes, from the roads to the buildings to the way people dress. We were told we would take a huge sigh of relief on reaching Namibia and South Africa. I never understood what that really meant, but on leaving these two English speaking countries, I want to go back. I have a feeling of dread as to what lies ahead. Seeing the stuff for sale is no longer behind glass fronted shop windows, but behind metal grilles, or in pyramid piles along the roadside. The men are hand mixing cement blocks, which are laid out in the sun to harden and used to build the small square corrugated steel roofed homes. It's unbearably hot in stationary gridlock traffic, the road is reduced to a single lane, whilst workers with shovels and brooms fill the enormous holes with gravel, which wash back out in the next rains. There are no barriers or cones to protect them; the traffic weaves in and out of them regardless, as they breathe in the toxic fumes all day in this traffic. I end the day with a nose full of snot and soot.

We arrive at the capital Maputo with its Mediterranean style architecture, tree lined avenues, pavement cafes, and bistros, supposedly one of Africa's most attractive capitals. I can't see it, but in fairness for us on this journey our budget restraint has always forced us to seek out, let's just say, the cheaper less desirable areas, which every city has. What I do see is a city rebuilding itself, with glittering shimmering steel and glass shopping complexes, office blocks and apartments, sitting between derelict shells, mounds of rubbish and the obligatory peanut and roasted sweetcorn sellers. Inching our way out of this 'attractive city', we stop at the first campsite to find a group of American students on an organised two-week tour. The small pool is a murky milky colour, but after the heat of the day, it's far too tempting, we all pile in regardless to chat the night away.

We have been taking Mefloquine Larium anti-malaria tablets for over six months now. The side effects of long-term use include: headaches, ringing in your ears, dizziness, loss of balance, problems with coordination, anxiety, depression, paranoia, hallucinations, thoughts about suicide, and hurting yourself. I´ve often had thoughts of throttling David, with his paranoia of worst-case scenarios - could this be why? In South Africa, talking to a group of doctors doing aid work we asked them what they take. They told us they take nothing, but if feeling any of the effects of Malaria self-test with the kits available from the chemist and treat if necessary. So we bought some of these kits and stopped taking Larium. David realises how much he was hallucinating at night now he has stopped. I wonder if it might also be one of the reasons I kept blacking out. We will see, but it has done diddly squat to stop my urges to strangle him!

On another level, that of contact, we have a basic pay-as-you-go mobile phone with my English SIM card which my sister tops up from England. This is for text messages or an emergency call, assuming we have coverage, which most of the time we don't. The best thing we have is SPOT (Synchronized Predeployment Operational Tracker) which sounds fancy, but just a GPS tracker. It allows you to send a text message with your GPS position to a telephone number or email addresses This at least, lets family know as we are moving, we are not dead. It also has an emergency button that once pressed activates a search. They have become widely used now and are a lot more advanced. Still, for us, it was all we had, as a satellite phone was way out of our budget.

It's a wonder, with everything now relying on smart phones and access to the internet, how we functioned. Once a week we would hunt out an internet café to send or collect email. I was surprised and, if I´m honest, a little sad when I was back in England at seeing how attached people had become to their phones. Sat in cafes and on public transport no longer chatting to each other, but with heads down and earphones in. This reliability and love for their phones was a gradual thing for them, but we missed the programming. My time had done more than stood still - it had gone backwards.

At this point in our journey, David and I didn't do any form of social media, like Facebook or twitter. We did have a very basic website written by David, but it was months out of date. I loved writing, so it was my journal every evening that was my focus, my friend, my confidant. Something I sent only to personal friends and immediate family. On my last visit to England, I had been talked into joining Facebook by an old work colleague, but as none of my family did it, or in fact do it now, and the sporadic internet access, it was another year before I posted anything. As for twitter-twatter-all-night-natter, it's on the don't-do-it list.

I'm incredibly miserable this morning as last night, in the sweltering heat and in my long-sleeved shirt, trousers, shoes and socks, covered in one hundred percent DEET, I was bitten mercilessly by mosquitoes on my bottom. I have realised that our chairs with their mesh seats allow the bastards to bite through it. It was so painful I had to sleep on my stomach. David's description was that I had a pair of breasts under my buttocks with the bite being the nipples. I don't even laugh at his supposed attempt at humour. I slather myself in antihistamine cream, take antihistamine tablets and, for the first time, pain killers, knowing

I will be sitting on my derriere with fake boobs all day in a boiling hot Lizzybus. On top of this, the drizzle that fell all night has coated everything in ochre red mud. After cleaning my teeth and washing my bits with my cupful of water, I drink my coffee in the silence of my very own perceived pit of misery, pain and filth.

Eventually, as the antihistamine and painkillers kick in, driving along under a billowing cloudy sky which keeps the sting out of a rising sun, my mood lifts. Blood red dirt roads become blonde sand as we arrive at the small, picturesque town of Axi-Axi. After following a sandy road amongst the trees set back from the beach, I leave David setting up camp and go for a walk. One of the hardest adjustments to make on this journey has been the freedom to do, to go, or to be alone. I sit letting the tide gently wash around me, shivering in the breeze; it´s soothing to my 'second pair of breasts'. There are hundreds of tiny little pink crabs and just like an orchestrated symphony they scuttle in and out to the flow and ebb of the tide. In the setting sun, they cast elongated shadows making them look gigantic. They're funny and I laugh. It's not just the salty water and breeze that washes over me, but a sense of real freedom. I´m completely overwhelmed in this moment and at peace.

When I get back to David and Lizzybus, he is chatting to a group of local divers, who invite us to go diving with them tomorrow. One of the most ridiculous things we brought along with us was our diving kit (minus the tanks) and this would be the first time we might get to use it. Diving was an idea David got into his head when he booked a backpacking holiday to Australia, as Australia has the Barrier Reef and diving it is supposed to be spectacular. For some reason, mainly that I didn't want to be left out, I had agreed. There was a small flaw in this plan - I could barely swim. In fact, I wasn't even that keen on getting water on my face in the shower.

Once I had agreed, in order not to waste any of the three weeks we had in Australia on learning to dive, we, or should I say David, arranged for us to take a diving course in England. It started in the classroom, going over the basics of pressures and equipment, moving on to the written test, then the actual water stuff. At a local swimming pool, they had us doing things like jumping in, floating, duck diving and swimming in a snorkel. Never having snorkelled in my life, I bought a mask and snorkel and at the gym, whilst my mates were doing spin and body pump classes, I nearly drowned in the waist deep pool, trying to learn how to use it.

Somehow, I completed and passed the classroom theory, the swimming tests and even a bit of diving in the swimming pool with all the kit on, but I hated it. Now it was time for some 'open water' - thankfully not in the actual ocean, as we lived in landlocked Birmingham, but in a quarry. It was November and bitter cold, as we waddled to the wooden platform to do our 'giant stride' into the quarry. I was the last one. I could see through the bubbles the group below freezing their nuts off, waiting for me to jump, but I was paralysed with fear. Shutting my eyes, I took the giant stride, but with the shock of the cold water and all this stuff in my mouth, I panicked. When only a few feet under the surface, I hauled myself out using the safety rope, much to the relief of the others below me.

I don't take failure well, I sat dejected and, most unusually for me, crying, humiliated, but worst, broken, thinking of all those little fishes I was never going to see. Despite this, my desire to learn remained and once in Australia did a four-day dive trip. David, now a qualified diver, joined the advanced group I joined the group who were doing their open water bit. No longer giant striding into the confines of a quarry, this time into the actual ocean. It was aqua blue, crystal clear, and warm as toast, full of lots of incredibly colourful fish and corals. I was simply mesmerised and completely forgot to be terrified.

So, learning to dive was, and still is, a huge achievement for me, and has become a shared passion. But the diving on offer with these men was to go out on their rib (small rubber boat), fall backwards off it and have fun. I refused; despite my insistence that David go alone he decided not to. We're both disappointed, me with myself, and David in that he didn't go alone. Waffling on about ribs, giant strides, and diving like I know what I´m on about, from a girl who aged ten, was taken with the class to the outside pool. We were all lined up at the deep end and instructed to 'jump in'. The teacher was going along the line pushing the ones in who wouldn't jump. I wanted to run but was frozen to the spot. Once shoved in, I surfaced twice, then suckered myself onto the boy next to me. I don't know what the biggest shock was, the freezing cold water, the near drowning, or being so physically close to this boy. We both had to be dragged out as I absolutely refused to let go.

CHAPTER 3
ITS LIFE, JUST HOW WE KNEW IT

Every morning brings drizzle. Packing up has become easier with the new clam shell roof tent, but even so the bedding is damp and going mouldy. I'm getting agitated about the lack of internet, isolated once more by the language. I think I'm feeling home sick. This is such an odd thing, as coming back felt like coming home; home for me now has become Lizzybus. I'm comforted by her smell, her sound, her temperamental ways, the sense of adventure, being free from domestic chores like ironing, vacuuming, dusting and polishing. Free from dressing for work or a night out, basically free from conforming. But there is a hunger for conversation, for being with and around people I know and love. I feel it like a huge void within me.

We're passing through mile after mile of coastal grassland. It has a music to it as the offshore wind blows through it, bending and swaying this way and that it shimmers, the few palm trees giving it a tropical feel. Despite my refusal to be thrown off the back of a rib, David's desire to do some diving has been ignited. As it's been a few years since we last dived, we need to update our certification. Making enquiries find it would cost five hundred dollars. David finds it hard to hide his disappointment, I find it hard to hide my relief. He is like a sulking child, which amuses me no end.

This journey has been a mix of wild/bush camping to keep costs down, and backpackers or dodgy rooms, where we can have a shower and wash kit. Here at Fatima's backpackers, we meet Irish couple Donna and Dave, newly married teachers on a twelve-month sabbatical. Donna and Dave have just driven the east coast of Africa and are on their way up the west coast, the reverse of our route. A little later around a campfire, a Swiss couple arrive, who we met in Ghana, it's like meeting old friends. What a great evening, swapping tales of derring-do, and how we are all adjusting to this life and each other. I have always been aware of the incredible privilege to be doing what I'm doing and ashamed of myself in the moments when I don't exactly hate it but am finding it tough. Knowing others feel the same allows me to understand this a little more.

Donna and Dave left this morning. We know they have a tough road ahead on west coast Africa but say nothing. What's the point? It won't change what they are about to face. The internet café is closed today but with the promise it will be open tomorrow, we decide to stay another day. We don't find the abundance of fish we thought we would at the local market. It could be as you need to be up early to buy from the local fishermen off the beach, and we never are. We find a man with a polystyrene cooler box half full of ice selling a few prawns and ask to buy all of them. He weighs them with the ice, we laugh. Back in camp we're told the water is not safe to use, only the water in the urns filled by the staff, which have no lids and are full of floating insects.

One of the best things David fitted was our water filter system. Water pumped from our two jerry cans through it makes it safe to drink and the ceramic cartridge just needs to be scrubbed once a week. We also have boxes of sterilizing tablets, which diluted we soaked vegetables in, but had given up on that realising cooking is good enough. We use them now to kill off any bacteria in the jerry cans and for soaking the clothes and bedding.

Tonight, David barbeques the prawns on stones over a fire pit. With a chunk of bread and the sachet of tomato ketchup a friend had given us, both agree it's one of the most delicious things we have eaten. We bought with us a fishing rod, with romantic ideas of fishing for our supper Robinson Crusoe style. Armed with this fishing rod we head off to the beach. Stood on the rocks David launches the line with the prawn carcasses as bait. The line snags on his shorts, ripping a huge hole in them, but undeterred he tries again. The line becomes heavy, David thinking he has a fish gives it a big tug, but it's caught on something, and the rod breaks. My cheeks ache with laughing and I drop to the ground, legs crossed to stop myself peeing. One thing in Africa is, you are never alone. We are being watched by a group of children, selling shell necklaces. We give them the broken rod, the box of hooks, fly things and extra line. Back in camp I sew David's shorts, whilst we determine our new mission is to buy more prawns!

It's six-thirty in the morning and we're sat watching rain pour from the thatched roof of the hut we're sheltering under. It's been three days since our friends left and neither of us is in the mood to pack up or push on. David wires up the batteries to the new battery indicator thing. Batteries, and the state of them, has been a constant topic of scintillating conversation during this journey, but reaches a whole other level with this digital flashing light indicator thing sitting in full view on the dash. Immediately an alarm goes off, indicating the second battery level is low (due to having the fridge on whilst camped). David is ecstatic it works and will become something to fixate on. I leave him to it and go off in search of prawns.

Tonight, on the beach barbecuing prawns we realise it's Valentine's Day; not that we have ever celebrated it, apart from the time David bought me the tangerine orange cement mixer which I loved. David acknowledges it by giving me his last prawn. Who said romance was dead?

Today the sun shines, the battery indicator bleeps and, as the staff have not filled the urns and the water to the showers is off, we leave. Small collections of brick or reed-built houses sit amongst a barren landscape, each with a patch of sweetcorn and a few banana trees. Along this broken tarmac road with no car traffic, just people traffic, we see piles of deep red sand ready to fill the gigantic holes, that will just wash back out in the next downpour. The area is full of the comical baobab trees, we pull up at the most magnificent one with a trunk wider than Lizzybus. It offers no protection as its top is like tangled roots, but its presence gives us a sense of belonging.

Last night's monsoon rain continues into the morning, in these oppressively hot countries, it's such a welcome relief, even in a leaking Lizzybus, I dance around David, celebrating the rains. Then we wash us and our clothes with our bar of yellow African soap. We know in this humidity we will always be wet with sweat, so being wet with clean is refreshing. Back on the road, the heat rises to form a shimmering heat haze before us. Our air-conditioning, the two flaps below the windscreen, blows air hotter than the Lizzybus heater can. I resort to wetting and wrapping my sarong around my exposed flesh for a few minutes' relief from the burning sun. It's exciting to be back on the road, heading now for Malawi, but the distances are vast and with the road conditions progress is slow; some days we barely make fifty kilometres.

It's early afternoon, when we pull down a track to a gravel quarry, the recent rains having filled it making a picturesque pond with reeds full of birds. As dusk descends, it brings a crescendo of insect noise - and a cloud of mosquitoes. David, at the water's edge, is peeling and cleaning our bag of prawns when a young girl appears. She is ebony skinned with huge chocolate-coloured eyes. She is shy but laughs and giggles whilst filling her yellow plastic bucket before balancing it on her head and leaving. I give her the tin with my last two shortbread biscuits Jenny had given me. With camp set up, and close enough to beer o´clock to crack open a beer, she returns, this time with all her friends who form a circle around us, staring like we are an alien species from Mars. We smile and point to the flags along the side of Lizzybus, stuck on in chronological order each time we cross a border, the first one being the English flag. We also have the outline of the world map on the door with our route, they all smile when seeing their country's flag. We give them a two-litre bottle of ice-cold water to share; they can´t believe it's so cold, passing it between them, not drinking it, just feeling it. Like our life now, theirs is governed by day and night, so as the light fades, they fade, back to where they came from.

Last night's full moon reflected in the pond is replaced by that of the rising sun. Two worlds touch as my day starts by writing on Mini Me, the name given to my laptop, and the locals going about the collecting of water, a simple, basic uncluttered life. Northern Mozambique is one of the continent's last wild frontiers. We take a detour to the Isle of Mozambique which can only be accessed across a four metre causeway during low tide. It just sounds so romantic, but of course this is from a person who finds romance in someone's last prawn, or cement mixer. I'm not sure what a wild frontier should look like, but for now the scenery becomes tropical along with the sweetcorn and banana patch is a rice field patch. Along the roadside, petrol is sold in old coke bottles, next to flapping held-by-the-neck chickens, or bush meat. We had long ago decided strangling and gutting a chicken or eating strips of dead meat, covered in flies or no flies, (not wanting the fly covered ones, and certainly not the ones the flies wouldn't touch) or rodent looking animals was something we would not be doing or eating. Had become virtual vegetarians.

We're running low on fuel and fresh food so take a sixty kilometre detour into town to fill up with diesel from a fuel station, not coke bottles full of it at the side of the road and shop at a supermarket. I get the wild frontier bit now as the road becomes an unnavigable swamp; even Tracks for Africa has nothing listed. One thing we've learned is not to push on regardless, but to retreat to a point we have a rough idea of where we are. We're in the middle of a tropical storm when both windscreen wipers stop; the motor rotates, but the arms just spin in the socket. We try gaffer tape and zip wire, but nothing works. We have no choice other than to drive on without them.

Somehow, we make it to a graded gravel road. David, whilst driving, leans out of the window with one of the removed wiper blades, trying to clear the windscreen. We both crease up with laughter as he does this with the dialogue and the action of a robot. We can barely see a metre in front of us or avoid the crater-sized holes. Exhausted and not wanting to inflict any more damage on Lizzybus, we pull off the road to the cleared flat area around a pylon. The grey skies make for an eerie dusk; we think it's still raining but it's just the humidity dripping water rather than rain. Switching on our head torches, we see what we think are bats flitting around, only to realise they are moths the size of bats, their marble eyes reflecting the light from our headtorches. With David's revulsion to moths, he sits inside Lizzybus and refuses to move. I´m forced to switch off my head torch to avoid the kamikaze moths and by feel peel the rubbery potatoes carrots and onions, adding a stock cube to make a vegetable stew. Thirty minutes later, David is coaxed out of Lizzybus by the aroma, hunger, and the promise I won´t switch any lights on.

Up and off by seven am. The rain has lost its appeal with the realisation we have no wiper blade, can barely see a few metres ahead, and have no idea how we are going to get them fixed. Averaging less than twenty kilometres an hour, being constantly stuck in this heavy clay-like mud and trying to avoid the wheel-swallowing holes, is a real test of everything we have learnt, including teamwork. Using the sand ladders and winch, we are taking a real pounding. Eight hours of this later, totally and utterly exhausted, we follow a track to a small lake surrounded by skeletal trees. The area around the lake is solid granite and perfect to park on. With camp set up, we crack open a beer - feeling incredibly fulfilled and victorious to have made it. The fact we have not made it to anywhere, and face a lot more of it tomorrow, is immaterial. It's all about one day and one challenge at a time, and on this day we are triumphant.

We hear giggles and chatter. A man on a rickety old bike appears, trailed by a dozen raggedy dressed children carrying a scrap book each. It's the schoolteacher taking his pupils back to the village. They sit cross legged in a circle around us; we become the teacher and Lizzybus the blackboard. I loved being able to point out on the map where we'd been and where we were going; they sit wide-eyed and fascinated. I have a box full of pens and whistles on lanyards, given to me by my daughter who works in the corporate world, merchandise left over from the football world cup. I give the children a pen each and put a whistle around the neck of the teacher. As darkness descends, the teacher leaves on his bike, trailed by the children, like the Pied Piper of Hamelin, but instead of a flute he blows a whistle. Its shrill noise is heard long after they disappear - a very special moment. Getting into the roof tent, I see stuck to the side of Lizzybus a beautiful tiny vivid green frog with bright yellow dots. He looks just like a fridge magnet; I hope he stays forever.

I think I hear a whistle in my semi-consciousness of dawn. Unzipping the tent, I look out to a sea of smiling faces - the barefoot faded t-shirt clad children, gripping their book and now a pen each, with their teacher. Morning means one thing: I need a pee. Peeing with strangers is nothing new to me since Liberia when all the women and children followed me into the bush to see if my bottom was as white as my face. I have learnt wearing a skirt gives me a modicum of dignity. As the children and their teacher are now sitting cross legged watching David prime and light the Coleman petrol cooker to brew the morning coffee, off the side of Lizzybus I pee discreetly. With the coffee brewed, I fill our two white expresso china cups, giving one cup to the teacher and the other to be passed around the children. It's hysterical as they hold their little pinkies in the air to drink from this cup, screwing their faces up as it's bitter with no sugar. It's barely a sip each, so I make up the sachet of powdered blackcurrant with ice cold water - they like this a lot more.

The whole village arrives to watch us pack away; even cleaning my teeth is fascinating to them. They line the path cheering and waving as we leave. I know this is a very special thing to have happening in their village, but I just wonder if they realise how very special it is to us on our journey too.

Finally, we make it to the main road, only to be immediately pulled over by the local police. We're not doing anything wrong or committing any offence, such as speeding, overtaking, or not stopping at a stop sign, we're just here. West Coast Africa taught us well; being stopped up to thirty times a day, we're not fazed. We just put on our fixed smiles and show no irritation whatsoever. Once again, looking through our documents they notice Mr T Senior's leather wallet with the West Midlands Police Crest in one side and an identification card with a picture of someone the image of David in full police uniform (David's alter ego) in the other. Assuming it's David, they welcome a fellow comrade, an officer of the law, to their country and wish us a safe journey.

At the fuel station, we fill the main and spare tank with diesel, the two jerry cans with water, and the third with a gallon of petrol for the Coleman cooker. From the roadside, rather than a supermarket, buy a bag of fruit, vegetables and a dead, plucked, cut into pieces chicken, which is now in the fridge. We feel like jungle survivors.

We're driving now over the causeway to Ilha de Mozambique, Mozambique Island, a crescent-shaped island just three kilometres long. Once the Portuguese East African capital, it's now part ghost town, part fragile fishing community. A UNESCO registered island for many years also has a programme for its protection. What we see is so much grandeur with so much decay. Locals scratch out a living from the sea, living in reed houses dotted along the shore overlooked by the most magnificent, ornate and mostly derelict, mansions. We can feel the tide of change here with a few buildings renovated into guest houses or restaurants, but for now we view it in all its dereliction, which only adds to its mystique.

We see the impressive Fort of São Sebastião, the oldest complete fort in sub-Saharan Africa, taking over fifty years to build. The Chapel of Nossa Senhora de Baluarte with vaulted ceilings. In the heart of all this splendour, we book a room in a recently renovated colonial house. Our room also has a beautiful, vaulted ceiling, a four poster bed and spectacular views out over the Indian Ocean. Lizzybus is parked on the cobbled street below. Across the oak floored hallway is a huge bathroom, with freestanding roll top bath, flushing toilet, fluffy white towels, bar of soap and toilet roll. It feels like someone has shown us around an historic building and we have hidden in the cupboard, to sneak back out once the curator leaves. I cannot believe we are here and not digging Lizzybus out of the mud or a toilet hole, or avoiding bat-sized moths, stinking with sweat.

Breakfast is served in a separate room where ceiling to floor faded pictures hang lopsidedly from rusty nails, and a grandfather clock stands silent in the corner, ensuring that time really does stand still here. On the long banquet-sized polished solid wood table, our breakfast has been laid out: fresh bread, butter, jam, a slice of delicious papaya, jug of café and refreshing fruit juice. We're not sure how it all got here, but it just adds to the feeling we're trespassing; apart from the person we spoke to on arrival, we're alone. We literally have been frozen in time, in this truly haunting and desolate place. I don't dare blink in case I wake up.

Walking through the now empty streets, which long ago echoed with the footsteps of Arab traders, I feel the despair of those incarcerated in the dungeons at Fortaleza de São Sebastião before being sold into a life of slavery. Stone archways lead us through into once exotic gardens, the ornate balustrades framing intricate pink and white mosaic marble paths, shimmering in the sun. Where grasses and whole trees grow through them, splitting them into mini earthquakes and slowly destroying them all. At the far end of the island, we find a rickety old hut where locals drink coffee. We join them, sitting on plastic crates looking out over a rugged sea. It's not a desire to stay put for now, but a desire to stay here forever in this magical place, but with our visa for Mozambique running out in two days, we need to find internet to check the status of our next country, Malawi.

We're both sad to leave. Our time here has been bewitching, giving us the most precious memories that will stay forever and a much-needed respite from such a tough few weeks. Back on the road, with eight hours of torrential rain and no wipers, the choices are endless due to the amount of pot-holes. Your choice is which one to hit and which one to miss without taking the wheel off. We drive as close to the middle as possible; anywhere near the verges and you're swallowed up in thick red African mud. Diminishing light and exhaustion forces us to pull over next to a reed shelter. Everything is wet and the evening brings its usual number of mosquitoes. I sweat it out in long trousers, shirt, socks and boots. Sitting under the shelter eating tuna pasta with a soggy wet tent and everything caked in mud matters diddly squat. I am still full of the magic of Mozambique Island, and having found an internet café in town, I have emails from home to read.

We hadn't noticed at first that we were camped right next to a village. Just after we'd eaten, a group of villagers arrived carrying a kerosene lantern, bringing tears to my eyes for two reasons. First, they were offering us their precious lantern and a plastic bottle filled with hot water, and second, the split second when I thought we were about to be at best robbed, or at worst murdered. We gently refuse the lantern showing them our head torches, but the bottle of hot water we graciously accept and was glorious for washing pits and bits before getting into the roof tent. This morning they're back, with another flask of hot water and a juicy sweet mango. I´ve struggled on this journey with my English reserve and accepting things with the kindness and generosity they have been given. Finally, I understand - giving can be as powerful as receiving.

Packing up, I notice my adorable vivid green tea bag-sized frog, glued to the side of Lizzybus, has become four; she's had babies. Of course, I know frogs aren't born as frogs, but tadpoles, but to me they are her babies.

Back on the road, children are selling piles of delicious pineapples, five for a few meticais, but we only want two. This is very confusing for them - they can't work out the cost of two - so we pay for five but take only two. Our journey gives us a freedom we never imagined possible, but at the same time it is a logistical nightmare for things like local currency (metical in Mozambique). I had an email from my bank to say my Visa debit credit card had been cloned and the account suspended. I was refunded the fraudulent six hundred dollars transaction, but the only way to reactivate the card is by visiting my branch in person in England with proof of identification. How the hell am I supposed to do that here in the middle of Africa?

Despite our secret agents, my sister Jenny and Mr T Senior, we are quite alone in all of this with no sponsors or back up crew. Online banking is not yet a thing, and even if it had been, internet access ranges from sporadic at best to non-existent. Getting local cash from ATMs incurring admin charges and a piss poor exchange rate is our only option. We do have the very significant wad of American dollars, thanks to the seniors who having spent their winters as Trailer Trash in Arizona for several years, had made it their mission to amass a small fortune in small American dollar bills for us, as well as a large amount of Euros. Not in a safe, but hiding in plain sight, which we can easily access if needed without arousing suspicion. It's not ideal, but this journey is not ideal. You cannot dwell or think too much about security. It was suggested we get fake documents, two wallets and bolt a safe inside Lizzybus, but the reality is, it's hard enough keeping on top of the documents you have. If ransacked or broken into, a safe might help, but you could be held at gun point until you hand over the code or key. We have photocopies of all our documents and the cash is hidden, but I'd have to kill you before I could tell you where.

It's nothing short of a miracle that both us and Lizzybus have not been broken by this journey. I know a lot of this is down to David's constant maintenance of Lizzybus, the huge number of spare parts we carry, like water and fuel pumps, clutch plates, bearings, filters, oils, gaskets, and all the greasing he does. A fact lost to me at the start, when my priorities focused around personal stuff like bras and knickers until I realised that underwear is so overrated. It's just another layer to rot, rub and wash, as is having any more than two sets of clothes - one to wash and one to wear - avoiding a bag full of laundry that requires a lot more than half a bowl of water to wash. This sounds crass, but honestly our best weapon has been to try and enjoy the journey. That's not an 'all the time' enjoyment, but an 'on the whole' enjoyment, as this directly affects how we deal with each other and situations.

Being moody or wallowing in the discomfort, even though at times it feels unbearable, and I succumb, does not change it. I know I have more of these moments than David, but it's more to do with the lack of conversation, of hand holding or him joining in with my childish whims, and you all know how I struggle with personal grooming, of caveman beards and grease filled nails. David's black clouds all relate directly to his mistress. When she is playing up, nothing can be said or done to lift him; it's personal. In these moments I just let him regurgitate worse case scenarios, until just at the point of me thinking Lizzybus is terminal and our journey is over, he figures it all out, leaving me mildly traumatised.

Today both our hands and feet are covered in a bright red itchy rash. I'm wondering if, like the jungle around us we're rotting. There's not much I can do other than spray more insect repellent over us. I´m getting more reluctant and a little repulsed by being in the roof tent as it smells of mould, but worse it smells of a greasy David. My struggles with intimacy and personal space since he went feral reaches new levels. It's such a difficult sensitive subject; I insist David washes his feet before getting into the tent, but I´m sure I don't smell or look that good either. I´m cross with myself and not sure why I´m finding it so hard.

I know the last thing I want is to be asking or telling anyone, let alone my partner, to cut nails and wash feet, but having to be so close it's the part of the journey I feel will destroy me, us, and it has to be addressed somehow.

After the abundance of food and supermarkets in Namibia and South Africa, we're back to buying from the roadside or shacks with iron grilles. Getting eggs, Laughing Cow cheese triangles, potatoes, onions, overripe tomatoes and any fruit, usually bananas, always makes a great day. We can have egg curry, Laughing Cow cheese omelette dinners and egg sandwich lunches. Back on our almost vegetarian diet, getting chicken is a splendid day. Oddly, we do somehow always manage to find beer and cracking open a cold one at the end of a long hot day is essential and sometimes the only thing keeping us going.

Under a cloudless sky today, we put up at a local campsite, for me to clean and David to get on with greasing. In a huge round metal bowl with two biological detergent blocks, I put the sheets, pillowcases and our clothes, treading them like you would when crushing grapes for wine. It stings my blistered feet, but feels fantastic. I swill them in a solution made with not one but two sterilising tablets and a good slug of citronella oil, before using it to scrub Lizzybus and the tent. With a line of washing drying in the midday sun, I snooze the afternoon away in my hammock as a gentle breeze pushes the intoxicating aroma of clean up my nostrils.

It's been over two years since we set off. I know at times both my twin sister Jen and I struggle with this enforced separation, losing each other not through death, but through life and the path I chose. Jenny is no longer able to visualise me and where I am, unable to replace what we had, or find an alternative to our days off doing stuff together; I still feel her sense of abandonment. The death of her best friend and work colleague Jane last year only compounds this along with the real prospect I might never come back. For me, in the back of my mind and in the pit of my stomach, this leaves an ache, a void I find very hard to ignore. I also feel a frustration in Jen for not getting out, for not doing her own 'derring do' stuff to set me free me from this hurt and guilt.

Our way of supporting each other now is in the only way we can, by writing with 'me-to-you' emails. These emails are my connection back to the life I hardly recognise, not for discussing the journey - my journal is the place for that - just for day-to-day stuff, like the death of our mother which we both felt in different ways. I try desperately to remember her full of life, hair bouffant, lipstick on, baking bread in heels, in our council house like she was the lady of the manor. But I only see the vision of the shell she became, her mind destroyed by Alzheimer's, her body paralysed by a stroke. I struggle with the bitterness and anger I feel that she was reduced to that. I remind myself of my own words 'losing her would be less painful than seeing what she had to endure'; at least Mom is now at peace. So, for both Jenny and I, this is what our 'me-to-you emails' are all about, a place to connect, to talk, in a way a legacy from our mother, as writing was her passion, her escape, a comfort to us both.

One of the crazy things about this and everyone's journey is the coincidences. We noticed back in camp an old, abandoned Land Rover; it was held together with rust, had flat tyres and a broken windscreen, but what was not broken was the metal clip that attached the wiper arm to the motor. Only the one on the driver's side was intact, but for us, it's a miracle and it's a perfect fit. Pressing on now through marsh, mud and jungle, we're incredibly upbeat, able to see where we're going if only out of the driver's side.

We now know why this is called 'The Last Frontier', having not seen any other vehicle for hours as we head for the Malawi border. We pass collections of wattle and daub huts, where the children frolic naked in muddy puddles, their ebony black skin covered in beautiful mosaic patterns of ochre reds. If we thought we'd been tested so far on this journey, we're about to reach a whole other level as the recent heavy rains have made a tough route even tougher. David is having to wade into rivers and streams to check the water levels and for any debris or boulders below the surface. We know how important it is to keep moving through water to avoid getting sucked into the heavy clay, but it's a fine line. If you do hit something, like a rock or tree stump, you don't want to hit it at speed and break stuff. For the first time, we really wished we were in convoy, just to have another vehicle supporting us, to be able to winch or tow each other out. Despite our heroic efforts, it's suicidal to continue with the constant downpours and rising water levels. With the distinct possibility of being completely cut off, the decision is made to turn back.

Three days after setting off, we're back at the camp site we started from, sort of defeated, but sort of not, knowing it was the right decision.

After a day of rest, this time we take the main road. Yes, there was a main road, but come on - we had to try the off-road route, we're intrepid overlanders after all! Even the main road has its challenges, trying to avoid the potholes and the police. One thing we are anal about (wherever possible) is having the correct documents, and of course we know all the scams - or so we thought.

This police officer, although apparently not speaking English, can read English. Pointing at the number four in the logbook, walks around Lizzybus counting the doors, including the back door, holds up five fingers. He points once more at the number four in the logbook. What he is pointing at has nothing to do with doors, rather engine cylinders, but he just won't accept this. Obviously in the past, he was able to overlook this with a little cash. It's time to bring out David's alter ego. This nonsense has to stop and it does when he assumes David is a comrade and officer of the law. Hands are shaken and we're waved on our way.

It takes a few hours to get back to the point where we'd admitted defeat, only this time on the main road. We pull over at a local garage as Lizzybus needs some maintenance after the battering she's taken over the last week. We negotiate using the ramps so David can do an oil, oil filter and inline diesel filter change, all stuff we carry with us including the oil. David is very particular what oil Lizzybus has and for a few meticais, there's somewhere to discard the used oil. It's also a chance to check out what might be causing the clonking noise from the front offside. One thing I am learning is not to ignore noises, knockings, squealings, squeakings, anything above the norm of a Lizzybus - there's always a reason for it. The hardest thing for David is finding the cause or diagnosing it, which is the case right now.

It's the first of March 2011 and breaking down this journey is the only way I can comprehend it. Our first goal was South Africa, which took us exactly one year to the day, not from setting off from the UK, but from stepping foot on African soil in Morocco. The continent of Africa has a peninsular halfway up its east coast known as 'The Horn of Africa', quite simply because it looks like a horn. As Kenya can be included in this to some degree, in my head Kenya will be our next goal, with just Malawi and Tanzania to get through. Another reason for seeing this as the next goal is that the country after Kenya is Somalia and all advice is 'Do not travel to Somalia due to crime, terrorism, civil unrest, health issues, kidnapping, and piracy, with violent crime, such as kidnapping and murder common throughout Somalia, including Puntland and Somaliland'.

Despite our desire to drive Lizzybus through as many countries as possible, we would quite like to be alive at the end of it. On reaching Kenya, we will make the final decision on whether to avoid Somalia by cutting up through Ethiopia or not.

With the Malawi border in our sights, like all borders, the closer we get to them, the further away they become. It's all about pounding out the miles, pulling over for a Laughing Cow cheese triangle and banana on stale bread, parked under the shade of a tree. A naked barefoot boy walks by using a stick to propel his toy truck made from coke cans. I get some of the spare vinyl flags to stick on his coke-can-truck, but he is shy and runs away, leaving the truck behind. I put the flags with a handful of sweets in the dust next to his abandoned coke-can-truck and drive off. In the rear view mirror, I see him with his friends, sucking on sweets and sticking the flags onto their coke-can-trucks. It's precious moments like these that stay with me forever; they are just like a hug from my life now.

It's late afternoon and the comfortable silence is shattered when we hear an explosion followed by the steering shaking violently. The tyre wall has blown out, exposing a tangled mess of wire. It's a mystery as to how the tyre wall has been punctured, driving along now on a decent tarmac road. I have a sick, horrible, sinking feeling, remembering when I was digging out, I had caught the tyre wall with the pointy end of the shovel. Could it have been me, did I weaken it, did I do it? I say nothing. In the blistering heat, this being our sixth puncture, or as in this case, exploding tyre, we're getting good at changing them.

Due to the time taken up with this little set back, along with the constant police stops, darkness is setting in as we arrive at the frontier town, a chaos of dilapidated broken buildings and vehicles. It feels like a place you end up in when looking to give up on life. We're surrounded by hawkers, beggars and chancers, the sun disappears, the sky darkens and rain pours down on us. We go now on gut feeling and both agree it doesn't feel good, so head back out of town to the campsite listed in the guidebook. Down little more than a mud track, we find ourselves at an imposing set of solid iron gates. If it ever had been a campsite, it certainly isn't one now – today it's a logging compound. The security guard sitting in his little wooden hut with pump action shot gun strapped to him can't believe what he's seeing. We smile, make the universal closed hands at the side of the head with shut eyes sign for sleep. Confused, he just opens the gates allowing us to drive in. There are rows and rows of logs piled higher than double decker buses with a couple of almost derelict buildings – home to the loggers - in the middle. We drive to the furthest point and, in between two walls of logs, park up.

It's times like this I wonder what the hell has happened to me, to us. Thinking back to Spain, when I refused point blank to camp anywhere other than a secure camp site, to now being somewhere on the border of Mozambique and Malawi, in a logging compound, wet, dirty, a little miserable - no, a lot miserable - just glad the day is over and we have stopped moving. Both on edge, we sit in the driver and passenger seat of Lizzybus in the pouring rain and pitch black, deciding what to do. As it's not safe to continue driving, we have no choice other than to stay. Although we had replaced the tent in South Africa by a clam shell affair, making it easier to open and close, it's still positioned on the roof and accessed externally, leaving us vulnerable and exposed when in it, but it's what we have.

Having put up the roof tent, we're now sitting under the awning eating a bowl of pasta and tuna when the security guard returns, along with his friend, armed, and although it's pitch black, both are wearing dark sunglasses. It's a moment in time that hovers. Are we about to get robbed, raped, plundered, shot or any other unmentionable horrid thing? Knowing that not a single other person on the planet knows where we are only adds to this fear. We're momentarily struck dumb before managing to smile, which is more like a grimace, and offer them a beer each. It's like a scene from a suspense thriller, their bulk highlighted by sheet lightning, the rain dropping like pearls from their peaked caps, the reflection from our head torches making fuzzy blobs in their sunglasses. Grinning from ear to ear, they take the offered cans of beer and disappear back into the black of night. We continue to eat dinner as if nothing had happened. I think what a crappy end to a thriller this would have made, with no shoot out, but know it's the best possible crappy ending for us. We even feel a little safer and looked after by our armed security guards.

After having had a safe and peaceful night, I always wish when morning arrives that I'd known beforehand it would be like that; it would take a lot of worry out of the night. Last night's restlessness was not just about our safety here in this logging compound, somewhere in Mozambique, but as I am convinced it was me who sabotaged us with the shovel, I feel like the traitor within. I can't believe I did such a stupid thing and I'm broken! We're both utterly exhausted from the last few weeks; this fatigue, along with the irritating breakages and losses, makes for a sombre mood. Things that are simple fixes back in the modern world become a huge task for us here. David takes the clunking from Lizzybus personally, along with the second wiper arm, the shredded almost brand-new tyre, the lost insulating mug, the sheared bush wire needing a thread nut and mating bolt, and the leaking 'new' roof tent. The most immediate worry is the water pump; not being able to filter water is a big issue in this heat.

Thinking we might make it to the border today, the mood has lifted slightly. Along the way we see plots of sweetcorn, rice and banana plants, and makeshift bamboo frames with huge tobacco leaves hanging from them like washing. The road is a mix of broken tarmac and African mud. The landscape becomes enchanting with 'Tors', torpedo shaped granite rocks, protruding from smooth oval rock. At the end of another long day, with the realisation we won't make the border, we camp on a huge piece of oval rock, high above the mud. Coming our way is an electrical storm. With the tent erect, it's highlighted by the lightning against an inky black sky.

David tries to pacify me by saying that the rubber tyres will absorb any stray lightning bolts. I don't believe him, imagining the metal ladder will act like a conductor. About two thousand people a year are killed by lightning, but it's the ones that survive that worry me, suffering from a variety of lasting symptoms like memory loss, dizziness, weakness, numbness, cardiac arrest and severe burns. Lightning can also vaporise water inside a tree, creating steam that can blow the tree apart. Wow, that would be impressive just so long as we weren't parked under it. On the positive side, nine out of ten people survive with no side effects at all and in a way, David was right, tyres and metal frames can conduct electrical current, diverting it harmlessly to the ground, all provided you're not in its way.

We're so wet and mouldy at this point, we strip off and dance around naked on our rock island, washing ourselves with carbolic soap. It's like being at our very own disco with flashing lights.

CHAPTER 4

SURVIVORS OF THE LAST FRONTIER

We made it - today we cross into Malawi. Despite being a landlocked narrow strip of a country, twenty-five percent of it is water as in the middle is Lake Malawi. It's an underdeveloped country, that has been known to struggle with high rates of AIDS and under-five malnutrition. Malawi has been described as 'Africa for beginners' as it's fairly safe - the cities and driving at night are still to be avoided - but its people are laid back and welcoming. Having been colonised by the British, and now independent, English is still one of the official languages. The best thing of all is that the visa is not only available on the border, but also free. We know from the way that we're treated at a border as to what to expect in the country. It's a simple border crossing with the usual clamour of money changers and beggars and we are the only vehicle. In no man's land are the usual people selling everything from old to new clothes, bike bits, shoes, beads and African carvings.

Welcomed into their country, everything is stamped before we even have chance to ask. Immigration, customs, and even the police, join us outside to stick the Malawi flag on Lizzybus before waving us on our way. We are already in love with this country and, driving along on good tarmac roads, the locals are out waving and cheering as we head for a campsite on the banks of the mighty Lake Malawi. From the snaking switchback road, in the distance we get our first glimpse of this shimmering glistening lake. She is not an aqua blue lake, but a sultry, and in places, muddy blue, and our campsite is nestled right on her banks. With Lizzybus parked on the carpet of grass creeping down to the sandy shore, we leave her and fully clothed join the group of giggling gambolling children in its shallows. David, who dislikes salt water and sand is the first to jump into it being freshwater with grassy banks.

We are staying a few days, so I can dry out the mattress, wash the bedding, and David can strip the water pump down. I hang out the washing on a line strung from Lizzybus to one of the palms framing her against the shimmering lake and distant slumbering mountains. She looks magnificent. I worry I am falling in love with her, or should

I say, I have fallen in love with her, despite reminding myself she is an inanimate piece of metal. It's very special tonight as David has agreed to walk along the shore to a setting sun with me. Followed by the group of rag clad children we swam with, we see a line of people hauling in one long fishing net, full of tiny silver fish. The net is so full it undulates, wobbling like a plate of jelly.

Today we go shopping in the local village followed by our gaggle of children, dancing and skipping behind us. They are not asking for anything; they just want to be with us. At the wattle and daub hut with an iron grille we buy eggs; the bread is apparently sold next door in the restaurant. Our budget of just over sixty dollars a day is doing okay, especially when bush camping and living on bags of vegetables. It's slowing the journey down that helps the most, with the less mileage we do the less diesel we use, and it gives the pot chance to build up. Of course, driving around the world means driving, and our time is restricted by the time allowed on the visa of the country we are in.

Eating out is a special treat and we decide to treat ourselves by eating here. Sitting on one of the two wooden benches that make it the restaurant that also sells bread, we order the only lunch we're told is available: three pieces of gristle in a tomato sauce with rice, served in small plastic bowls for a few local tambalas. I give my gristle to David, but the rest is surprisingly delicious. We're being watched by an ever-increasing gathering crowd. Apparently white people don't eat here. It's not that they can't, it's just that they don't. We love it and have decided to come back again tomorrow.

The South African family that run this campsite, mother, father and son, have invited us to join them for Potjiekos. Potjie is a cast iron three-legged pot which, like a wok, seasons with use and is stood or hung over a fire made of wood, charcoal, twisted grass, or even dried animal dung. It's one pot cooking and each family or region has secret spices and seasonings influenced by the Dutch and Malay to give it its unique flavour. Potjiekos is made with any sort of meat, for us it's goat, but it can even be vegetarian. To me, the best thing about a Potjie is it's a communal way of cooking and needs several hours and several beers to be consumed whilst stirring and tending the fire. We feel very special to be part of this South African family as they are as interested in hearing about our tales and experiences of driving through their country as we are in talking about them.

A few days later, the water pump is fixed and we have clean sheets and aired bedding. We're excited and ready to explore Malawi. Malawi has a fuel shortage, 'fuelled' in part by the president's love of Learjets and not paying his fuel bill, so the suppliers have stopped supplying. Urgh! People in power who could do so much for their countries are consumed instead by greed and a skewed belief that possessions like Learjets are a show of wealth and leadership. I'm often asked how, or if, I've changed on this journey. The physical changes are obvious - David and I have lost so much weight due to our African diet - other changes are not so obvious. Living with local people has been a privilege; our life touching theirs so much was not what I expected or something I'd thought about. If I´m honest, seeing what I'm seeing, I´m a little ashamed of the race we call humans, but at the same time humbled by the human spirit. So if that is changing, then yes, I have.

Before leaving, we have brunch at the Bread Restaurant. This time we have chicken, not exactly chicken but chicken skin and potatoes. It's chewy and rubbery, but tasty, and this time I just eat it, saying how scrummy it is, which pleases the chef no end. We buy what bread they have, to share with the children and keep some for us for later. I feel a little sad to be leaving; I see my children in the rear-view mirror cheering us on our way. But I'm also excited as today we're heading to Fat Monkeys Lodge for a rendezvous with Ana and Paul, a young Dutch couple we bumped into a couple of times on the west coast of Africa. It's not an exact arrangement, just a place we all sort of said we would stay at on our way through Malawi. I can't believe my eyes when we get there and find them, not just them, but an American couple we had also met. We set up camp right next to them and late into the night, we drink beer and recount tales of our journeys and the mishaps we've all had along the way. It's just magical.

In our group of six in the morning sun we stroll along the shoreline. Women scrub children, cloths and pots next to row upon row of bamboo tables where thousands of tiny fish are laid out, drying in the sun. I'm giddy with conversation, but making it is difficult as I can only take shallow breaths due to the pungent nauseating smell of fish. We arrange to take a boat trip together with a local fisherman to one of the islands for a picnic and snorkelling. The boat is moored up at a craggy splat of rock protruding from the lake and after an hour of snorkelling off the rocks in the fresh water, we tuck into our picnic, making it the best island we have ever been on. Heading back, we see a sea hawk circling high above. It swoops down towards us, showing his snow-white breast highlighted against a magnificent black wingspan, with a not so attractive yellow featherless head.

David had noticed earlier in the day chips being cooked in a steel drum over charcoals by the women, and he wants some. Whoever thought chips would bring romance into my life? Under the full moon we walk along the beach on the hunt for them, to be joined by two small boys who make it their mission to take us to the chip lady. Once we reach the collection of mud huts that make up the village, we can just about make out small mounds on the ground. Stepping over them we realise they are sleeping children with muslin sacks over them. Life in the village, like our life, revolves around daylight, not what time it is; with no electricity, dusk is the time to settle down, and that's what the village had done, settled down. I think we should leave, but our little navigators are insisting they can find the 'chip lady', which they do, but she has finished.

She scoops into three plastic poo bags the few remaining chips. I felt bad thinking she was probably taking them home for the family, but they smelt so good we couldn't resist. We had a bag each and the third bag I gave to the boys to share which they covered in salt before running off skipping and dancing, forgetting all about us. We walked back to camp along the shore under the full moon; unlike the ocean there's no crashing of waves, but a shuffling of water and a slight breeze. Chomping on the most delicious chips you could ever imagine, it's a perfect end to a perfect day.

It's becoming harder to leave these pockets of belonging; they have become so important to me, to us. It's also a much-needed chance for David to talk through the Lizzybus worrying clonk with the men. It's interesting how each of the men deals with the responsibility of his vehicle. One thing they all have in common is not ignoring anything, inspecting the vehicle constantly, with a maintenance routine bordering on obsessive. The confidence in what our vehicles can do is clouded by what could go wrong if we push them too hard. We all agree that it's a bloody amazing, once in a lifetime experience, and although we share the common theme of driving, we are all having experiences unique to us.

We arrive at Lilongwe, Malawi's capital, and it feels like all of the

African cities we've seen so far - full of destruction and construction. It has the usual street living and selling and it's a city of two halves, the old city and the new city. We head to a local market in the old city and instantly we're surrounded by people. Despite feeling no threat, it's impossible to get what we want, so give up and head to the new city. Wow! It has a huge shopping complex, selling every luxury item you could imagine, and a massive supermarket. We're overwhelmed at seeing this vast array of food, western food. The overflowing shopping trolleys feel a little vulgar. Remembering how special a poo bag of chips was, we buy only the essentials. What we've prioritised most throughout this journey is beer and make no apologies for it. At the end of any day, no matter what it has in store for us, a cold beer from our Engel fridge always makes it better.

So, here's a thing. Lake Malawi is not just in Malawi, but being an African Great Lake, it sits more or less in the middle of three countries and by doing this, it changes its name to Lago Niassa in Mozambique (where we have just left), to Lake Malawi (where we are now), to Lake Nyasa Tanzania (where we are heading). Clear as water I´d say?

What it is, is gigantic, with lots and lots of shoreline, so it's no surprise that here at another campsite, Big Blue, the stilted bamboo huts straddle the lake. David is still disappointed we have not done any diving yet, despite having our dive kit (minus the tanks). Diving in fresh water would be a new experience for us, so with a dive here costing only thirty dollars we sign up for it. I've forgotten all about the fresh water of the local quarry in the bitter cold of an English October day when learning to dive, a traumatic experience for me, and one that ended in failure and tears of frustration. It's blocked right out of my subconscious, this and the fact it will be in a RIB, where you do the falling backwards off it thing.

Having not dived for a few years, a check dive is necessary to validate our PADI qualifications (Professional Association of Diving Instructors). Unlike passing your driving test which is for life, with PADI if you don't dive for a while, you must do a check dive. But we're in Africa, so the dive itself will be the check dive. It takes a while to adjust to the lack of buoyancy which is found in saltwater. You need a puff more air in the jacket, okay buoyancy control device (BCD) thing that keeps you afloat, or in this case lets you sink, when you don't have enough air and too much lead. This is nothing like reef diving in warm water, with the spectacular corals and vibrant fish to distract you, but a barren underwater undulating landscape of muted rock formations. What is totally fascinating is the Cichlid fish which incubates her eggs in her mouth until hatching. Even after hatching she keeps them in there for a few weeks, protecting them from predators. We watch enthralled as this dinner plate sized fish opens her mouth to release a cloud of little hatchlings and, on sensing danger, sucks them all back in.

Today we make a push for the Tanzanian border. This journey has been the education I never had growing up. Government policy of the day called for twins to be separated to give them their own identity, and there only being an upper or lower class, Jenny went into the upper and I went into the lower. Once in it, having learned to read and write from my mother, I was rewarded by spending my day washing greenfly off Mrs Jackson's geraniums, or in the staff room washing the tea and coffee cups and eating stale biscuits, whilst the children in my class who could not read or write were taught. This more or less is where I stayed for my entire schooling, not in the staff room eating biscuits, but in the bottom class. As the children in my class didn't, or couldn't be bothered to learn, it wasn't long before I followed suit. Now quite literally, I'm not just learning about, but I'm part of a whole world I never knew existed. I'm not the sponge you are as a child; retaining information is difficult, but it's beginning to make sense.

One of David's passions is geology and he tells me the African Great Lakes were formed from a fracture in the crust of the earth. I can make sense of this, but it's when he starts going on about the movement of tectonic plates and mantle plumes, I stop him. Just like the Great African Lakes, the 'trenches' which formed from this evolution to become known as The Great Rift Valley is evident throughout this continent and the countries we are now driving through, in the mountains, canyons, and volcanos.

Tanzania will be our twenty-fifth African country, taking us into our third year on the road living in Lizzybus. I was never looking to find myself, or a purpose, or a reason to my life. I'm not in the slightest bit materialistic, nor is David. We've done our bit; we're both blood donors, I was a volunteer for the twin research programme, I even ate raw pigs' eyes for children in need, I've paid all my taxes and had two amazing children. I'm just an ordinary person who found herself living an extraordinary life, in a Land Rover driving around the world with

David, because?

Because we thought it was a good idea! Now, not only do I know where the African continent is, but the names of most of the countries in it, and even more astoundingly, I know this because we've driven through them. I never even had a driving licence until in my thirties or had been on a plane. Just visiting my mother with the children was a three bus, all day ordeal that felt like the ultimate adventure. My old life feels like the dream and this the reality. Digging toilets, washing in rivers, living in a metal box somehow just feels right.

When we set off through France, I was driving as David navigated us around the infamous Arc de Triomphe roundabout. Apparently when you first choose your insurance cover you can opt out of it covering the Arc de Triomphe roundabout. An iconic symbol of French national identity, it was commissioned by Napoleon after the Battle of Austerlitz. None of this mattered; what mattered was that it totally freaked me out, driving the wrong way around an island with no lane markings in traffic that came at me from all directions honking their horns. I stopped, got out and refused to drive another inch. David, horrified, ordered me back in immediately, but I was adamant. I was not driving anywhere with all these crazy suicidal Frenchmen.

I suffered a complete breakdown of confidence and stopped driving which caused all sorts of problems, not least because my navigational skills were also zero. I questioned why I was even here, or what part I played in this team. It was not until the deserts of Morocco I faced up to it, asking myself how the hell can I say 'we' drove around the world, when all I did was sit in the passenger seat! From that day forward I took the morning shift, no matter what the terrain, be it sand, mud, or just shear rock. Now we both love the challenge of driving the tough sections, almost verging on envy if the other's 'shift' is the most challenging. This resulted in my driving skills becoming good, but navigation was beyond me, so it became my job to drive through the chaos of cities whilst David navigated.

This morning, it's my shift. After last night's camping high up in the forest, the morning dew makes the near vertical drive back to the main road slippery as hell. I engage my point and shoot technique with one eye closed, slipping and sliding to the bottom, inwardly smiling on realising I never got out once.

We hit the border with Tanzania, a country almost four times the size of Great Britain, capital Dar es Salaam, famous for Mount Kilimanjaro, the Serengeti National Park and the birthplace of Freddy Mercury, a singer David enjoys - we can't wait to explore. Having felt so relaxed and safe in Malawi, we're sad to leave it. Crossing no man's land, we are complacent and let our guard down. Stopping at the man waving a wad of local money, we decide to change the last of our Malawian currency. Sitting inside Lizzybus, having negotiated the exchange rate, David hands over the cash. The man takes it then runs off into the gathered crowd.

There is nothing we can do - getting out is not an option. We deserve to lose it for our stupidity when we know negotiating anything in no man's land is a bad idea. This incident and the hundred dollars visa, twenty-five dollar temporary import travel permit, and hundred dollar three-month yellow card insurance (covering all the countries until Jordan) means we're pretty fed up.

Initially, I kept lists of what we spent on food, diesel, visas, camping and suchlike, but life on the road found its own balance. Whether I wrote it down or not, we still had to pay and I hated doing it, so I stopped. Who wants to know every penny you spend anyway? Pushing on through soaring mountains, Lizzybus crawls up and wobbles down them. The clonking has developed into a 'death wobble' vibrating through the steering. After our stupidity in no man's land and now this, the mood is grim. With no local money, we need to find a cash point and a petrol station. We'd only managed to fill up once in Malawi due to the fuel shortage and now the main and long-range fuel tanks are on empty. As soon as we obtain a wad of Tanzanian shillings, we head to the garage, filling both tanks with diesel, and buy a gallon of petrol for the coalman cooker. We chat to a man also filling up and find out that he's one of the parishioners of the local Christian Mission Centre. He gives us permission to camp in their car park with access to the toilets and a shower. This lifts our spirits no end.

This morning we feel a lot better for a safe good night's sleep, hot shower, wad of local currency, filled-to-the-brim fuel tanks, and putting the no man's land incident into the 'lesson learnt box'. We now focus all our attention on getting the Lizzybus 'death wobble' looked at, oh and doing another oil change. On the journey I always felt like we were constantly looking to do or to get an oil change. Writing this now, I realise that was because due to the mileage we were doing, David wanted to do it well before the recommended mileage in this tough environment. We find a registered Land Rover specialist and buy ten oil filters, and not just engine oil, but all sorts of oil and greases, as well as a second hand wiper motor and clips so we will have two working wiper blades.

As it's only a spares outlet, not a garage, we can't work on Lizzybus or get her looked at. At the local petrol station, they let David use their pit to do his greasing and oil change and dispose of the old oil for a small charge, but David still can't see any obvious reason for the Lizzybus 'death wobble'. We need to get her looked at. These days you would just 'google it' but back then, finding somewhere was tough.

It always feels good to work on Lizzybus, but with this 'death wobble' getting worse, the constant downpours and soaking wet feet from a leaking footwell, David, as usual, is taking it personally. It is compensated slightly by having two working wiper blades. We're heading for the capital, Dar es Salaam, five hundred kilometres away. Once again, crossing that strip of no man's land, the change has been instant. With easier access to fuel in this country, the roads are gridlocked with huge, fully laden lorries, coaches, and cars packed with people and their luggage piled high on top like humpback camels, all spewing out black sooty smoke. Progress is ponderous. (I love this word)

After a night in the bush, we're back on the road passing through villages, all with bone-jarring concrete speed humps and police armed with radar guns. The main highway is under construction all the way to the capital, reducing traffic to one lane. It's both frustrating and hysterical as you have twenty minutes of driving and twenty minutes of waiting behind manned barriers where people chat and eat for fifteen minutes, then shout and demand to be let through for the last five. The men, via walkie talkies, check to see if the oncoming traffic has been stopped, but there's always one that has snuck through and gets trapped. With no one willing to give way, they are forced out of the way, even moving the cones to drive on the newly laid tarmac.

It might only be five hundred kilometres to Dar es Salaam, but it may as well be five thousand. At a truck stop, a graveyard for broken down abandoned lorries, we break the day up and treat ourselves to a lunch of fried-in-a-steel-drum potatoes with an egg, covered in a throat catching chilli sauce. Not having much of fried anything in our diet, it's quite delicious. We're opposite what we thought was a derelict building but realise it's the hospital. We see the most elegant, ebony skinned people in traditional dress, with layers of bangles on legs and arms, bone, and wood ear hangings and intricately beaded neck collars. The men, with a piece of woven cloth draped over one shoulder, carry a spear or walking cane in the other hand. Swahilis; they are exquisitely beautiful and majestic in their movements. I can't imagine how many miles they have walked through this desolate land to come to this hospital; it's utterly captivating.

I thought I had got used to being constantly watched, but at times I can't help being incredibly irritated by it and I feel claustrophobic. No matter how remote we are, people appear from the everywhere of the nowhere to watch us. We feel obliged and most of the time want to engage with everyone, ambassadors if you like to England, but it's overwhelming. I have moments of being sick to death of living out of boxes, routing through them for the stuff I want, or need. I question how I deserve to be on such an incredible journey, consumed with irritation and resentment over such stupid things like stuff not being put back or left covered in grease. It's hard to be so physically close to someone twenty-four hours a day, with no escape.

I know I irritate David, as his idea of tidy and mine, along with our priorities, are at opposite ends of the scale. A confirmed bachelor when we met, I was a little shocked the first time I went to David's. In the middle of the room was a leather recliner chair and foot stool, and what I was told was a Linn record player with Ittok arm, and Rega Ela three-foot-high speakers. They looked to me like they were from a past era but had apparently been chosen for their clarity of sound. Stacked everywhere were boxes and boxes filled with his vinyl record collection. Apart from his leather recliner and foot stool, the furniture, which came with the house, was used only to store piles of old magazines, bike parts and empty beer bottles.

For David, this all made perfect sense. He knew his priorities and better still knew where everything was, or should I say where everything 'he' prioritised was. This I realise is how David wants it now, with everything important to 'him' in pride of place. Thinking about it, I quite admired this, possibly because I didn't have to live in it. I want him to have this now, but it's impossible in such a small space. It's not a source of constant conflict, but it is a major cause. I insist we talk this through, to both make compromises, but David hates talking things through. He would much rather just ignore them until he feels I have forgotten all about them, which leaves me feeling even more resentful. It doesn't help that I have another shingles flare up, or that the sting from the jelly fish that had attached itself to me is still sore, and the boil on my fanny is making peeing and sitting on it all day excruciatingly painful. I am feeling very sorry for myself, and that makes me incredibly irritated.

Last night I made bread, such a simple thing I wonder why it's my first time - probably because of the need for flour and oil. Anyway, having bought some I made a dough and dry fried it like flat breads which I loaded with spicy beans for dinner then filled with a tin of tuna for lunch today. Fresh out of the frying pan yesterday, they were soft and moreish. Today they are like cardboard, but we still eat them. It took three days to do the five hundred kilometres, but finally we arrive at Dar es Salaam, the largest capital on east coast Africa. I'm confused as we're now in a three-lane queue of lorries, cars, bikes and puke-green battered three-wheel taxis, waiting for a ferry when I hear my name being called. It's hard to imagine how strange hearing my name is, a once normal thing from family, friends and colleagues in everyday life, but not now. It's the Swiss couple we met in Ghana and Mozambique, coming off the ferry we are going onto, and of course the stationary traffic now starts moving. Both stuck in our own lanes, we can only shout words of hello, but it lifts my spirits no end.

We arrive at an exclusive lodge hotel resort, with laid out manicured gardens and tacky gold painted mirrored glass conference room. It has its own stretch of beach with toilet and shower for the exclusive use of guests. We're allowed to camp on the beach, under the trees and wicker pagodas, and use the toilet and shower for a few dollars, choosing to ignore the signs banning consumption of own food and drink. It's perfect, and if we sit just outside reception, we can access their internet.

For the last two days, we have both felt pretty shitty, with flu like symptoms, blinding headaches and feverish. Malaria is a distinct possibility, having stopped taking the Larium anti-malaria tablets we had taken through west coast Africa. They can do a lot of damage if taken long-term, but it was the advice from the doctors we met working in South Africa - on feeling any malaria symptoms, to test, self-medicate or get help - that was the decider. It might also be the effects of the four horse-size pills for Bilharzia (caught from snail-poo which attacks the liver) we'd taken as a precaution after diving in Lake Malawi.

Speaking to reception, they say it's only five dollars to get tested at the local village clinic, including a return taxi. We get confirmation that we're both malaria-free. Instantly I feel better knowing this, but David goes into full on 'man flu' mode. I just wished it had been malaria - he would have suffered it in silence as a battle wound.

CHAPTER 5

POISONED ON THE WAY TO KENYA

David over his 'man flu' and us both free of the malaria we never had, we leave Lizzybus parked at reception with cameras and twenty-four hour security. We are going on vacation to Zanzibar - I´m so excited! Camped next to us last night was Irish couple Bob and Moira in their top of the range Land Cruiser. Wanting to escape life, Bob set off on a solo trip through east coast Africa where he bumped into Moira, asked her to join him on a friend only basis, and have now become a couple. There's something quite magical about being sat on a beach with a setting sun, the mesmerising dance of a campfire, conversation, and a spliff (them not me but I quite like the smell). I´ve always wondered what makes people do what they do; knowing for us our 'good idea' reason is such a disappointing one, but Bob´s was on finding his wife hanging from the beams of their newly converted barn. He's the same age as my son, still lost in pain, guilt and regret, searching for the peace not yet found and possibly never will. I put my arms around him and just hold him.

Bob is giving us a lift to the ferry from Dar es Salaam port to Stone Town. A sailor with his own boat, had made his dashboard himself out of walnut, with all sorts of gadgets carved into it. I think of how basic our Lizzybus dash is. The only thing added is David's battery indicator thing which bleeps annoyingly, oh, and the engine 'madman' gauge, monitoring water temperature, voltage, engine time, and exhaust gas recirculation stuff, I think. I don't mind it because it fits into the dash, does not bleep, or obstruct the view, unlike the great big sat nav sitting in the middle of the dash. The view out of Lizzybus is limited anyway by the spare wheel on the bonnet, especially when going uphill, something we do quite often. So, although I admire Bob's craftsmanship, I'm glad we don't have a walnut dash with all that stuff carved in it. I'm such a basic simple person, I struggle with the unnecessary. In fact, I'm the ideal person to be living with the bare minimum of life's clutter.

With the boiling temperatures we endure in Lizzybus I'd thought at times how good it might be to have air-conditioning. In Bob's vehicle, it's on full blast with all the windows shut. There's no real connection to the people, to the noise, to the fumes, and it feels sterile, but worst of all, when you get out of your vehicle, the heat hits you like a physical slap. With Lizzybus being so noisy and bone jarring, it makes you part of the journey and the people. I´m glad in a way we don't have it.

Bob and Moira drop us on the docks to get a boat to Zanzibar, to be immediately surrounded by street touts 'papasi' (ticks) wanting to buy the tickets for us, but we just push through them to the ticket office. It's not just one jetty and one boat, it's a chaos of big, little, and in-between sized boats, with lots of jetties. Having bought our tickets and now looking for our ferry, we're stopped by a man looking a bit official holding a clipboard. He announces that he's the port official and here to check our tickets which apparently need his signature to validate them, at a cost of five dollars. I know our old selves would not have questioned this and just paid, but we're different people now. We look at each other, laugh, take our tickets back, and tell him to get lost.

It feels like we've forgotten something - Lizzybus! Carrying only a backpack now, it's like we've become invisible and I like it. But getting to Zanzibar is a whole lot more complicated and confusing than I ever imagined. We take a ferry, a three-wheel puke green taxi, a little boat across the river, then another taxi to get to the hostel in Stone Town. This is only phase one. As archipelago is not a place but a chain of islands making up Zanzibar and Stone Town is on one of the islands. What I do know for sure is Stone Town is an exquisite timeless picturesque collection of whitewashed coral-rag limestone houses, bazaars, mosques, courtyards and squares, a place where ivory, slaves and spices were traded. I feel this in all its walls and cobbled streets.

It supposedly takes three hours to get to Zanzibar, but we're on a cargo ferry, cargo you need to climb over to get on board. The covered lower deck is filled with men and a sooty black haze of fumes from the engine room. We head for the top deck, full of women in burkas with their children. A few hours later, I think the engine fumes might be preferable to the stench of piss and shit coming from the overflowing toilets we're sat next to on the most bum-numbing metal seats. It's gone midnight and we're anchored out at sea as it's too dangerous to dock at night; we need to wait it out. What an ordeal. I want so much to lie horizontally, but the metal floor is so grubby and sticky where people have walked, the disgustingness of urine, oil, grease and fag ends into it. So I spend this endless night shivering on this metal seat.

For twenty-two hours we're on this boat, arriving knackered, sweaty and nauseated from the stink, relieved I have nothing in my stomach knowing it would not have stayed there. David trying to placate me confirms once again that by taking this slow ferry, we've saved twenty dollars. I've made it quite clear it's a saving we won't, under any circumstances whatsoever, be making on the way back. I'll be on the three hours fast ferry. Some vacation!

Finally, we reach Zanzibar. I'm surprised we need to go through immigration and have another stamp in my rapidly filling up new passport to head for a local backpackers. Zanzibar: dominated by imposing buildings, silent in their grandeur and decay and reminders of its colonial past. An important Islamic centre, the majority of the population is Muslim and the women are in full burkas or buibui, covering even their eyes. Children, the boys in pure white shirts, the girls wrapped in shawls, walk to school held in the grand courtyards of these buildings behind ornate wrought iron gates. Sitting in every doorway, street sellers weave palm leaves into bags, baskets and table mats for the main industry here, that of tourism. It's frenetic but calm, safe but edgy, dying but alive, and we love it.

Today we are going for a day's diving with a group from our backpackers. Once in our neoprene rubber shorties with the rest of the dive kit in the trailer behind, we pile into the knackered old minibus. Driving along sandy tracks past mud huts, we see women in full burkas pounding maize and tending vegetables, animals and children in the blistering heat, in stark contrast to the scene in our little minibus where the women, their blonde hair blowing in the wind, are sitting next to the men, and everyone is laughing and joking together as equals. Two worlds, worlds apart.

We arrive at a linen white, icing sugar smooth beach by emerald blue waters where a brightly painted blue and red wooden boat is moored. This underwater environment where humans are not designed for, having not exactly adapted to but have made possible, is a world I thought only existed in documentaries. It gives you a weightlessness and freedom never felt on land, a secret world, full of colour, life and sound - the bubbles of air, the crackling of coral. For me, it's a world that when I'm in it, I don't ever want to leave. I want to stay here forever with all these fishes.

It's the end of the day and we're now sitting in Mercury's Bar, with its faded seat covers, embroidered with images of Freddie Mercury, and bleached dog-eared photos of the singer sellotaped or nailed to the walls. Could life get any weirder? Sat here drinking beer in Zanzibar, the Queen hit 'I Want to Break Free' playing in the background reminds David of the four times he saw Freddie live in concert. I doubt he ever thought he would be in the country where Freddie was born, sitting in the bar dedicated to the singer, having driven all the way here.

The words 'break free' could not be more apt as I am the freest, I have ever been.

I truly feel like we have had a vacation and am more than a little excited at the prospect of being reunited with Lizzybus, especially as this time we are taking the three hour tourist fast ferry that will deliver us in half a day, not the all day and all night ordeal we had to get here. Lizzybus, covered in bird shit, fires up first time with her usual puff of smoke signalling she is ready for some more adventures. And so are we, heading now to our next country, Kenya.

Through the constant speed checks, bone jarring concrete sleeping policemen and torrential downpours, we finally get out into the grasslands of the Serengeti known to the Maasai people as 'the place where the land runs on forever', and it couldn't be more apt. In all this remoteness are the semi-nomadic Maasai, tending their cattle wearing either a red embroidered woven cloth sheet or a basic plain one slung over one shoulder (in their beliefs red drives off lions). Their bodies adorned with beads, bangles, piercings and tattoos, they are as majestic as the land they inhabit. They cover many miles a day, walking or running across open thorny savannah, barefoot or in sandals made from old tyres. Not just any old tyre, but motor bike tyres as they fit the foot better. The front tyre is used for those with little feet, the chunky rear tyre for bigger feet. The sandal is cut out in one piece, with two crossed over straps - so ingenious.

We can't shake this feeling of not having done justice to Tanzania. Something we really wanted to see and be part of was the migration of the wildebeest, but it's well into the rainy season and we've missed it. The main roads are covered in thick clay and mud and every day is a struggle - it's a challenge just to keep moving. But we don't quite give up on it and make a detour to the foothills of Mount Kilimanjaro, the highest free-standing mountain in the world with three volcanic cones. It's a mecca for climbers, claiming about ten lives a year. Ours will not be one of those; we're more than satisfied to camp in its shadow. The mountain is masked by low lying cloud, revealing only its foothills, but we know it's there, right next to us. David had bought some dodgy looking meat in town. As a carnivore on our almost vegetarian diet, the temptation of red meat was too great for him. He barbecues it over the open campfire on a wire rack with a pan of fried onions. It smells delicious and I'm adamant I'm not eating it - but I do.

We're both poisoned!

Heading for the border with Kenya, I take over the driving whilst David dry retches out the window. Every twenty minutes or so, I stop so we can both run into the bush with violent sickness and diarrhoea. Yellow under our African skin, clammy and sweaty, hardly able to stand, we reach the Kenyan border.

Kenya: home of the Maasai, mountains, lakes, game reserves, the Swahili language; capital Nairobi. I don't remember much about leaving Tanzania or crossing the no mans land, but arriving at the Kenyan border and parking Lizzybus, I run to the toilet and David heads to immigration. The toilets are locked; I need to pay to use them. With no local currency, I'm almost in tears pleading with the ladies to just open them, promising I will pay when I come out. I feel a vile liquid running down my legs with a nauseating stench before they agree to open the door. Once open I could cry on seeing a flushing toilet, a sink and a little bar of soap. A few minutes later the woman is banging on the toilet door, saying I must come quickly as my husband has collapsed in immigration. Vomiting into the sink whilst sitting on the toilet, I couldn't care less if he is dead or alive. When my body seems to have evacuated everything, I scoop the disgusting mess blocking the sink into the flushing toilet and wash me and my shorts as best I can, joyous at having soap, but feel awful that there's only a tiny little slither of it left.

Standing in the pool of water dripping off my shorts in the customs office, I see David prostrate on the floor. The shocked but helpful border staff prop us both up on the bench and offer us water, but we both refuse, not daring to put any more liquid inside us in case our bodies decide to projectile vomit it back out. Taking our documents, they go personally to the different departments. It helps that immigration, customs and police are more or less side by side and we are the only people at this border. Once all this is completed, even though Lizzybus is parked right outside, we're not able to stand for the 'flag sticking on ceremony'. We just get in and drive off to the first hotel we can find. We're shown a room with en-suite, flushing toilet, shower, electric, and two towels; we don't even ask the price, just take it. With nothing else other than toothbrush, toothpaste, bar of soap, and four 2-litre bottles of water, we shower, leave our soiled clothes in the shower tray, wrap ourselves in a towel and collapse on the bed. It all becomes a blur - drinking water, sitting on the toilet, sleeping. The manager knocks on the door and insists we pay for the room right now. With David having changed the remainder of our Tanzanian money with the incredibly helpful border staff, we pay.

At seven the next morning, sixteen hours after we walked into the room, I realise that my thumping headache, high temperature, cramps and shivers have gone. With the towels having come off us both, we lie naked next to each other. Looking across at a still sleeping David, I realise I have not seen him naked or been intimate with him for? I can´t remember how long. With desire dying due to stinking pits and bits, cave man beard, wiry nostril and ear hair, not to mention greasy fingernails, but most damaging of all, no comforting words. We're both now so weak and with the lingering smell of sickness and diarrhoea and breath that needs not just a glug of mouth wash, but a bottle of it, it will stay that way. I´m just content we have survived the night and made it to Kenya. We put on the now dry clothes - I don't remember doing it but I'd washed and hung them over the chair back - and having drunk all the water, take only our toothbrushes and toothpaste with us. Guilty at using almost all the bar of soap at the border, I leave our half-used bar. We emerge, squinting in the morning sun.

Hello Kenya, nice to meet you. The last country before we must decide if we go to Somalia or not.

Heading now to the capital, the mud and reed huts become corrugated rusted steel ones. Bony cattle tease strands of grass from baked earth, watched over by proud herdsmen in their vibrant rich red chequered cotton sheets, gathered at the waist by thick leather belts and holding long wooden poles, in harmony with the plains of the Serengeti. The women and children collect water in ceramic urns balanced on their shaved heads, heads like chandeliers as their earlobes dangle with circular wooden discs and the rows of beads form collars around their necks. Still feeling very weak, we look up to the horizon; like a line drawn in the sand, the vast plains become city, the city of Nairobi.

Even on its outskirts, it's a gridlocked fume-filled manic city. The tarmac shimmers with grease and oil, and the honking of horns is ear numbing. We arrive at JJ's, recommended to us for its excellent mechanic. We have everything crossed they can cure the Lizzybus 'death wobble'. We're told it's a good job we didn't arrive yesterday, or we would have been stoned in the student riots gripping the city. So sickness and diarrhoea might have been a good choice. Set behind walls topped with glass shards and twisted razor wire is a rambling two-storey house for backpackers with a communal kitchen and seating area, behind which are the toilets and a shower block. There are camping pitches set on reluctant grass with prickly shrubs, filled with trucks, bikes, cars and people all on their own journeys. We have found a much-needed haven.

It's six in the morning on the first of April. I'm shaking a snoring David. "David you need to move Lizzybus, the owner says we're blocking the path to the toilets!". He climbs down the ladder in his boxer shorts, muttering and cursing as to why no one mentioned this last night. I shout after him: 'April Fool!'. We not only feel better after our food poisoning, but are totally at home here with everyone. The conversation is about what we have all seen, done and experienced, the rookie mistakes, the scams we have fallen for, the total utter joy and wonder of it all. Travel is a great leveller; your chosen mode of transport is not just based on preference, but your budget, time and the point in life where you're at. Be it on foot, a push bike, a motor bike, a little car, a big car, a truck, a bigger truck, a week, a month, or a lifetime, it's all travel and that's what unites us all. We fit in without explanation or justification; we're understood and admired and this feels good. Basically, we belong. Admiration, although I´m not comfortable with it, is something I´m beginning to understand as it allows me to see through the eyes of others what David and I have achieved; to realise it is a small miracle, not only to have made it, but to be alive and still together, especially after the last week.

Since starting scuba diving, as my golden blonde childhood curls became afro frizz wire and knotted every time I took my mask off, I'd kept my hair plaited. On this journey, I've been having my hair plaited by local women. Today I've arranged for the cleaner to take me on the bus to the 'Hair Salon'. We are now sat together, packed in like sardines on the bone crunching bus, winding through the backstreets of Nairobi and thirty minutes later we arrive at a row of derelict looking shops. I follow her up the crumbling concrete stairwell, where the acrid urine stench catches my throat, to the second floor hair salon. After speaking to the hairdresser, my cleaner guide leaves. Sitting on one of the two plastic chairs, all I can think about is how the hell I'm going to find my way back? I see the panic in my eyes reflected in the de-silvered cracked mirror held up by a rusty nail.

The taking out of my plaits begins, or to be more precise, ripping out. I'm not sure by how many, but I've got at least three pairs of pillow soft breasts suffocating me. There are products to ease out tangles in your hair, but these do not exist here. In fact, thinking about it, for me, basic stuff like shampoo and conditioner is pretty hit and miss in life now. Every so often I do treat myself to some shampoo, even at times conditioner, but mainly my hair is washed in water. Another reason to keep it plaited, but this has made it even more brittle, to the point my mouth waters and my eyes run with the pain of it being ripped out. I feel light headed from the body heat in this tiny room and all the people watching this white woman having her hair done. Some of the women waiting start doing each other's hair, others just watch whilst chewing on blackened roasted corn. I'm left as the 'hairdresser' starts another client. I pick up the wooden stick and start taking out my own plaits.

There is a loud drumming and lots of shouting from the street below. I remember the warning about the widespread student rioting bringing the city to a standstill and I just hope this is not part of it and I can get back. Water is boiled over a single gas burner and once the two buckets are full, it's time to be shampooed. Leaning backwards over the sink, pain shoots down my neck at having to hold the weight of my own head just in case the bricks holding up the sink give way. They blow dry my hair until I resemble a candy floss on steroids, saying I have too much of it, hair that is, and finally the plaiting begins. It's not a constant plaiting, but an in-between-other-clients plaiting. It does have a plus in that once the others have been done, they help plait mine. It's several hours later, dusk has arrived. I ask who is taking me back on the bus. A little girl no older than six stands before me, and despite my pleading with her to come with me, puts me on the bus and leaves. With no idea where to get off, I am determined to sit right by the driver. Being bench seats, I just shove the two women sat on the bench behind the driver together, giving me just enough room to perch on the end so I can let the diver know I need to get off at Jungle Junction.

Buses don't stop at bus stops, they just stop whenever or wherever people want to get on or off, with the bus driver slamming on the brakes at the last minute for any fare he can pick-up. My knuckles are white from gripping the handrail and the half butt cheek in connection with the wooden plank is numb. This works well for everyone who knows where they are going, but for someone like me, who doesn't have a clue, it's terrifying. It feels like I have been on the bus much longer than I was when going. I ask the bus driver every time he stops, if it's where I need to get off. Eventually the head shake of no is a nod of yes, so I get off. Standing now in the fading light on streets that have nothing whatsoever to distinguish them, I am alone, having paid no attention whatsoever as to how I got here this morning, expecting to be bought back. I begin to panic. I know I'm being pathetic, but start sobbing, mainly tears of frustration at my incompetence, until I become aware of a load of children surrounding me. All shame forgotten, I´m now skipping along with my children, chewing on corn, until I am deposited at the gates of Jungle Junction. I think of my mate-sealed-with-a-piss Gayle, treating herself to a weekly session at her hair salon to relax. My day has left me needing a very large beer and a lie down.

Nairobi has the unfortunate nickname of Nairobbery; caution is to be taken at all times of day and night, but especially at night. Tonight, six of us are rammed into a knackered old taxi, four in the back, two in the front, on each other's laps as we are going out to Fogo Gaucho an all-you-can-eat Brazilian steakhouse. We're told to make sure we book the return taxi as tourists are being picked up and robbed at knife or gun point by bogus taxi drivers. On arrival, we push the tables together to join the group already here; it's so exciting to be with everyone. The food is mouth-wateringly delicious, but with our shrivelled stomachs we eat very little - I can't even manage the fresh fruit dessert. We would have paid just to be with everyone and for the conversation. All too soon, it's time to leave.

Outside the restaurant, our pre-booked taxi driver greets us and we all follow him to his car. It´s parked well off the main road and down a side street. Rob, one of the men in our group, says "Have you changed your car mate?" He's the only one amongst us to notice that this car was not only a different colour, but a different model and, on closer inspection, the man was not our driver. Rob for ever more is known as "have you changed your car mate". Call us intrepid overlanders? We nearly all fell for it.

It's time to get Lizzybus looked at. Two mechanics and David replace, change and clean anything and everything related to forward motion to rid Lizzybus of her 'death wobble'. Whilst not finding anything specific, bushes and seals are replaced and everything is tightened up and greased. I do the washing which involves cramming as much as I can into the small linen bag you're given, dumping it at reception with a couple of dollars and collecting it three hours later clean, dry and neatly folded. I'm still working on the best way to use squat toilets, a supposed more natural way as gravity aids nature. It seems to me though that the very act of squatting requires leg muscles which impedes the relaxation of them. What I do know is a skirt is far preferable to trousers, and not looking at the dark stained hole before squatting over it helps enormously.

Lizzybus, having been taken for a test drive by David and the mechanic, is I´m told, free of her 'death wobble'. We will see. She smells of new rubber and oil. I strip her out, scrub and re-organise the kit as David tries to seal the still-leaking roof tent. Having been here ten days at ten dollars a night, the five hundred dollars saved on the budget has paid for the parts and labour on Lizzybus, the meal out, my day at the hair salon, and both tanks of diesel. Being here, amongst friends who have become family, has been good for both of us. David has been able to speak at length of worst case mechanical scenarios with the men, which in most cases is all that's needed, and despite his constant protestations that he is ´not a mechanic´, it seems necessity has made him into a very good one and, dare I say it, me into a very good passer of tools.

CHAPTER 6

AFRICA WORKS HER MAGIC

The prospect of getting back out on the road is as daunting as it is exciting: leaving the safety of this compound and newfound friends, free of all the anxiety as to what we will face, constantly questioning the stupidity of saying we're 'driving around the world'. The gates open and a small crowd waves us off. Despite being told Lizzybus has lost her 'death wobble', I don't believe them; it's only when we get out onto the open road I will know. The solar panel is now bolted to the roof, the exploded tyre has been replaced and Lizzybus has had everything greased. Oils, bushes, bearings, seals, all changed where needed; everything has been washed and re-organised, and I have newly plaited hair. We're on the move again. I'm like the proud parent and besotted with Lizzybus. After pushing her hard, David was right, the horrid juddering through the steering really has gone. It's my kind of miracle, giving us both some much needed confidence in her.

We don't usually pick up hitchhikers. Not that we don't want to, but the fact is we just don't have the room with the back filled with kit boxes and the two back seats being our wardrobe with the fridge in-between, But seeing at the side of the road with his thumb out, a silver haired elderly man, his soft grey eyes magnified behind thick rimmed glasses, we decide we will. Gunter, a German watchmaker now the local Pastor, has lived in Kenya for over ten years. He's on his way back from the hospital after visiting his security guard whose hands were macheted whilst protecting the house from burglars stealing the television. He 'preaches' at length to us, on how his healing hands had cured polio, cancer, and various other ailments amongst his congregation. I wonder why Gunter, with all these healing powers, never used them to heal the half-severed hands of his security guard as, apparently, they rotted and fell off.

The deep red African soil turns to a powdery chalky dust which is sucked in through the open windows and front vents to rest on our eyelashes, face and hair until we're a ghostly white. We enter Lake Nakuru National Park. Nakuru means 'dust or dusty place' in the Maasai language which is exactly what it is. Driving on, we realise that in the distance what we thought was a heat haze are hundreds of flamingos. With stilts for legs, bottoms up and heads down sifting through the silt, they turn a sky-blue lake bright pink. Along the shore are thousands of squabbling pelicans, their fleshy pouches trembling in the breeze. On the plains we see the endangered eastern black rhinoceros, and amongst the acacia trees the Rothschild's giraffe with its orange and brown markings. Whoever knew one day, I would not only be here sat in a Lizzybus having driven from England with giraffes in front of us, but realise they are not just lolloping awkward long necked orange and brown animals; their markings or spots distinguish them. I have so many moments of being completely overwhelmed by the enormity of this journey, and that I'm the one on it. This moment is right up there.

Parks in Africa are not for the faint-hearted. They are vast, on the scale of small countries and driving through them takes hours. It's late afternoon when we decide to stay overnight at a designated campsite which is unfenced, remote and deserted except for the troop of baboons. Although it's said baboons are only dangerous when provoked or threatened, they do have sharp teeth and claws and can carry disease. We're worried they might be curious and sabotage the camp in the night so decided to head back to the main gate and towards a more secure campsite. The setting sun elongates the shadow of zebra, giraffe and elephants until it's like the land of the giants. We finally arrive at the campsite and are thrilled to find Simon and John, who we first met in Ghana, sitting around the campfire grilling sausages and drinking beer. Camped on the banks of the river, we're warned to watch out for hippopotamuses and to not get between them and the water. I'm more bothered about the swarms of ferocious mosquitoes.

Waking for a pee in the night and with my eyes only half open, being camped next to Simon and John, I head to the toilet block rather than the bush. Under the full moon I see what I think are huge boulders, but they seem to be moving. You're kidding me! Huge, massive, ginormous up-close, grazing hippopotamus. I remember the warning about not getting between them and the water - which is exactly where I am now. Although round, they seem completely square in their mighty bulk, grunting, groaning and wheezing. I can wait no longer and pee standing up. I walk backwards to Lizzybus and use the bucket of water and soap kept at the bottom of the ladder, for David to clean his feet, to wash the pee off my legs before climbing back into the roof tent. David's awake now and in a stage whisper I tell him all about the moving rocks and peeing myself. He is not impressed and turns over, leaving me wondering if it really did happen.

We're heading for our next country Ethiopia, to the farthest most remote crossing of Banya Fort, along the two hundred and fifty kilometre, notoriously difficult Marsabit to Moyale road. We're told by locals and a group on an organised tour that it's impassable right now due to flooding. I know David and I lost all logical reasoning long ago; it was replaced by some unfathomable notion we are intrepid explorers. Discussing this with Simon and John, we think if we go in convoy we could make it. As neither of us likes convoying, and Simon and John have another game park they want to visit, a loose plan is set in place: to press on alone and rendezvous in three days' time. Even if we had phones or local SIMs, there is no phone coverage. Instead, a town is circled on the map along the route, with an agreement that if we're both there in three days' time, we will continue on together. Wow - it feels like a secret mission!

Simon and John are off early for some big game spotting. We head to the highest point in the park with the remains of last night's sausage between bread for breakfast. The plains before us are littered with black dots of buffalo and beyond are the pastel white of pelicans, the soft pinks of flamingo and an eternity of deep blue sky. It's moments like this you realise that if this journey takes a lifetime, then it's a lifetime worth taking.

The road becomes tyre-splitting volcanic rock with sections of deep blistering hot sand. We need to drive at a speed that avoids getting bogged down in this deep sand, but not that fast we destroy Lizzybus on the hidden rocks. In the distance we see the shimmering jewel of Lake Turkana, the world's largest permanent desert lake with an active volcano island. A desolate place, we see the occasional herdsman draped in cloth with his camels, the tiny wicker domed homes are anchored to the rock against the dessert winds, and women adorned with beautiful beads and bangles grind maize.

This morning I'm woken by the smell of fart and through the mozzie screen I see I am face to face with a camel. I can feel the warmth of its breath on my face; it makes David's breath seem positively floral. Animals are incredibly inquisitive and we are something to be investigated. As these camels are domesticated, they feel no threat. We were allowed to camp in this field by the locals last night, not realising it's where they overnight their camels. I think of all the times I'm asked if I miss a 'real bed'. What, and miss being woken by camel fart breath?

We have, over the last few days, been steadily climbing, and in a clearing overlooking the vast plains of the Serengeti we set up camp. With chicken, potatoes, carrots, onions and a generous dollop of curry paste simmering away, we crack open a beer, the silence broken only by the hissing pressure cooker. Out of nowhere, a vehicle arrives with four men in it. We're a little taken aback when they warn us it's not safe to camp here as the area has many bandits. We ponder this; it's already dark and driving could be as dangerous as being sitting ducks. Ignorance is bliss, but we don't have that luxury now - we have been warned.

Remembering we saw a police car in the last village, we decide to head back to it, throwing the tables and chairs into the back of Lizzybus with our dinner in the pressure cooker wrapped in a towel wedged in the footwell. Driving in the dark, even with the six spotlights on the roof rack, is a nightmare. We regret not just taking our chances, but we're committed to it now. It takes an hour before we see the outline of the village and we're both relieved to see the police car still parked outside the hut. It's in total darkness, but I go inside, in the gloom I can only just about make out a sitting figure. I hear the distinctive rattle of a gun being cocked. There's no electricity so he shines a torch into my eyes which temporarily blinds me. I manage to spit out that I'm English and we need somewhere safe to stay. I am more than a little relieved when he responds in English.

What a fantastic night we have, sharing our chicken curry dinner, chatting about his life in Kenya as a police officer, and our travels. He shows us a tap where we can get water and a squat toilet behind a sheet of corrugated steel we can use. In the morning, another car arrives with three more police officers; one of them, we're told, is the Chief of Police. With our box of West Midlands official police badges donated from Mr T Senior, we give them one each and the silver-plated crest mounted on a wooden plaque to the Chief of Police. I imagine to this day that crest sitting on his desk, a little piece of our life forever touching his.

We're heading now to the world's largest permanent desert lake, Lake Turkana. With the windows open, the fierce furnace wind is sandblasting us, our eyes turning blood red with its grit. If we close the windows, the temperature soars to over sixty degrees centigrade (a hundred and forty degrees fahrenheit). We choose the sandblasting. It's a torturous drive as, for no obvious reason, the brakes are beginning to fail. Using just engine and hand braking, we press on to the village of Loiyangalani, 'the place of many trees' and the supposed rendezvous with Simon and John. It's nail-biting but eventually we hit flat ground then, in the middle of this vast nothingness, we see palm trees and our campsite. We arrive midday but it's late afternoon before Simon and John arrive. David, with two local barefoot, short and t-shirt clad 'mechanics', diagnose the problem as the master cylinder which we have in our spares. Wow, all that moaning I did about the amount of spares David had packed into Lizzybus - once more saves the day.

I see today as the day it becomes a proper adventure, when the reality is the whole bloody fiasco is a proper adventure. Being in convoy with Simon and John, facing the supposedly impassable Marsabit to Moyale road to the border of Ethiopia, should give us some much-needed support, morally if nothing else. I´m just rejoicing the fact we have brakes. Some people prefer to only travel in convoy, but Simon, like us, prefers to travel alone. I worry about keeping up - after all, my nickname from David is 'Driving Miss Daisy' - but it soon becomes obvious we're all in complete harmony, keeping a good distance from each other so we're not eating each other's dust, and at a steady enough pace to make good progress without destroying our vehicles. As the first section of road is the easy bit adjacent to the shores of Lake Turkana a few kilometres in, we unanimously decide to make our own way to the next and final frontier town, then convoy on together from there to the border.

Simon and John push on, leaving a trail of dust stretching off to the horizon. We have stopped because I want to swim in Lake Turkana. Getting across the razor-sharp volcanic rock in my flip-flops is tough, but the thought of having a cooling swim is enticing. Formed from volcanic rock, there is no grassy shoreline or weeping trees, the water's edge is slimy and slippery. I gingerly dip a toe in and remembering the warning to watch out for crocodiles, decide dipping a toe in is more than enough. Back at Lizzybus in this desolate landscape, we find an ebony black, stunningly beautiful girl, her neck elongated with layers of intricately beaded hoops; on her head is a ceramic urn full of water. She points to the far-off distance where we think she has come from, so offer her a lift. Now wedged in the back of Lizzybus, she fills the air with an oily earthy, not unpleasant, scent, her pot of water sloshing about on her lap. Her milky white eyes are wide like that of a startled deer. I give her a bottle of cold water. All too soon she signals we have arrived, at a nothingness which is her somethingness, and then she's gone, leaving just a lingering aroma of body oil and earth.

It's a slow ascent until Lake Turkana is just a vista in our rear-view mirror. I'm concerned - this is supposed to be the easy bit, as it's challenging and endless. Eight tough hours later, we finally reach the plateau and the town for our rendezvous. The streets are a deep red gelatinous goo of mud, buzzing with a mix of traditionally dressed tribal warriors, magnificent in their ornate feathered headdresses, and women in jeans and tight tops. We check into a local hotel, a concrete collection of basic square rooms, as David takes a shower. The two hanging wires create a spark followed by a puff of black smoke, blowing all the electrics in the hotel. A few minutes later, a deafening generator fires up, producing a thick acrid smoke that fills the room. As the hotel doesn't serve food, it recommends a local place that does, so to avoid asphyxiation we go with Simon and John along the dimly lit streets to the bar restaurant. There are people playing pool, couples sat holding hands, music blasting. I can't even remember what we ate, but I do remember thinking it might be our last supper. We discuss everything apart from what lies ahead. Both Simon and John are gentle souls. There is no one else I would rather be going to the gallows with, I mean on this adventure! I know David is as uneasy as me, but he keeps a stiff upper lip knowing I would completely freak out if he voiced any concerns.

We must have drifted off or passed out from the toxic fumes as it's now early morning. We set off in a heavy fog that engulfs the sleeping town. Buildings are little more than blobs and the road, already camouflaged in thick mud, is unrecognisable. It feels right to be in this semi-darkness and thick fog, it's atmospheric like being in a Dickens tale. As I always drive in the morning, all I can think about is not driving into the back of Simon before we even get out of town. Fortunately, the viscous mud holds you in the tracks gouged out by other vehicles, but stopping even with brakes is not a stop but a slither. Once out of town, the rising sun dissolves the fog, the mud becomes sand then rock. It's not long before the bone crunching pummelling takes its toll; the recently fitted-to-the-roof solar panel bolts shear and it flies off and smashes against the rocks. David is gutted. I'm biting my lip trying not to say how ironic it is that it survived all that time shoved in between kit, but lasted five minutes bolted to the roof rack. But, of course, I don't.

With the constant pounding, the bonnet catch shears. We ratchet strap it down to stop the spare wheel bouncing even more. This constant stopping for minor repairs is not all down to Lizzybus; Simon's anti-roll bar mounting bracket breaks. We drive through swamps of mud, just hoping we don't hit rocks or tree stumps, pulled into deep sand and pummelled on jagged rock, every inch of progress is hard fought. We all feel the weight of responsibility for taking this route, for not heeding the warning that it was impassable. There's no recovery vehicle, no phone coverage; it's down to us. United in our fate makes us a team and, in a strange way, we're enjoying the challenge and camaraderie of it all.

Focusing on the few metres ahead and swapping the lead every few hours, it's only from the sinking sun we realise the day is coming to an end. We're not trained military or professional drivers, just four people trying to do their best in fully loaded vehicles, with determination, desire and a touch of madness. In the distance, like a mirage, we see it, the border with Ethiopia.

It's over - we did it!

Like our vehicles, we're all a bit broken by the abuse, but utterly victorious and proud of them and us.

CHAPTER 7

THE REVELATION OF ETHIOPIA

Ethiopia is not just a land of perpetual famine and war, but of castles, invisible monasteries, and solid rock churches. The Queen of Sheba seduced King Solomon here and some believe that at Axum lies 'The Ark of the Covenant', a solid gold-covered wooden chest containing the tablets of stone inscribed with the ten commandments. I am wondering what I was taught at Sunday School whilst colouring with the fat wax crayons that tore the incredibly thin tissue paper, on realising how oblivious to all this Ark history I am.

At the border we're meeting people who are on journeys of weeks, months, even some of a year, but I've yet to meet anyone who is on a journey of forever. I feel a strange envy for those heading home to loved ones and the familiar, to have both a journey and an old life, a mixture of the two. It's not an end to travel, but an end to each journey, a time to recharge batteries, re-group and plan for the next challenge. The logistics, constant worry and fear take their toll, overwhelming us both. I can't discuss or confide this with anyone, as everyone is telling me how lucky I am. I'm thinking luck is winning a few grand on the Lottery ticket you just bought, not giving up everything you ever knew and making something happen. I know we are living our ultimate dream, in many ways, but it also has moments of the ultimate nightmare, when you quite simply have had enough.

Last night, having made it in one piece to Ethiopia with Simon and John, we had a celebratory meal out and our first taste of the local injera, a sour fermented pancake made from teff grass flour. It was laid out like a tablecloth directly onto the plastic table, with different foods spooned on top. You tear off pieces of injera to use as scoops until it's all gone. It tastes very similar to a pancake, but has a sour almost earthy flavour. For me, it is quite delicious, but I´m not sure it's to Simon and John's taste. I just love this communal way of eating - you get to try a bit of everything – because, as hard as this is to believe, I suffer from food envy! I always want what others are eating, to the point where David orders what he thinks I'll like, knowing he will be sharing. This worked well with David being more the carnivore, I swap most of any meat I have for his vegetables, but on this journey it's mostly been vegetables.

Ethiopia is our thirtieth country since setting off. I'm suddenly reminded of mine and Jenny's thirtieth birthday. Broke, we decided to have a house party at hers with a few ham sandwiches, crisps and beer. Mobile phones were not a thing then, but as I had a house phone and Jenny didn't, I called a few of my friends to invite them. On the morning, we took the children to visit our mother. Over a cup of tea, I looked at the local paper and saw an advert: 'Do something different this weekend, horse ride in the Beacon Beacons'. I thought how amazing that would be. We didn't want any boring party, we wanted to go horse riding in the mountains. The fact we couldn't ride or had any stuff to ride in was immaterial. Later that day I phoned the number on the advert and spoke to a George Fern who said to meet that night at the Standard Triumph for the coach to Wales and a weekend adventure of horse riding.

That set off a chain of events that, to this day, I still wonder about, where we got the money from, how the hell we survived it, and what happened to those friends who turned up to a non existent party, which in truth was only a few as we never had many friends. The most incredible part is how we rode horses for two days over mountains the SAS trained in. It's hard to imagine a world without political correctness, blame, or social media reviews, that we could possibly be responsible for our own decision and take a chance, to go on instinct. When, if it was incredible, you would breathe a sigh of relief, if it was horrendous you just laughed about it. This was both incredible and horrendous in equal measures, involving lots of drinking, alarmingly big animals that moved whilst looking down into valleys, navigating over huge rocks or wading through rivers in excruciating pain worse than childbirth, whilst holding onto the mane or saddle, or both, with our eyes closed. But survive it we did and laughed all the way home. Something about it got to us, sealing our love of horses and riding. We continued to ride with George and what became our gang for years. Although over eighty now, George is still taking people on horse riding adventures all over the world and remains a lifelong friend.

Somalia was to have been our next country after Kenya, following the coastal route. The country has been embroiled in civil war for most of the last twenty years and kidnapping of tourists is a real threat. The British government, understandably, does not negotiate any releases. In

2009, the year we set off on our journey, Paul and Rachel Chandler were kidnapped by pirates from their yacht and held captive for a year. In 2011, the year we're in now, David and Judith Tebbutt were kidnapped from a beach resort in Kenya; tragically he was shot and she was held captive in Somalia, released six months later (the family paid a ransom). They were both British couples - it's just too dangerous to contemplate. We're heading inland our route will be:

Ethiopia, Sudan, Egypt and Jordan.

On reaching Jordan, we will make the next decision as to whether to go through Syria, that's if we can even get a visa for it since the escalating civil unrest and what is being called the Arab Spring protests. What? Some wicked witch has cast a spell upon the Jayne I knew and made her spurt out all sorts of nonsense like civil unrest, kidnapping, Arab Springs. What happened to just being able to look forward to 'spring', to the daffodils, crocus and meadows full of spring flowers, not kidnapping, civil unrest and wars?

We are heading now to Ethiopia's capital Addis Ababa, for the embassies of the Sudan and Egypt to get visas. Still exhausted from the trials of the last few days, I want to take the direct tarmac road, but David wants to go cross country following the Rift Valley and its four lakes. It's no secret lakes are formed in recesses of mountains and the route will be spectacular, but it will be tough. It's the first time since South Africa I've voiced a real opinion as to which route we take. David does the planning, which is a good job or we would still be doing circles around Birmingham city centre if left to me. It is, however, one of the reasons we work as a team as the route can be a huge point of conflict in couples, in what you want, expect and need from your journey. David prickles on my suggestions and preferences. He doesn't really want any input, just enthusiasm and support for the freedom to find and decide on the most adventurous route, which in fairness I love, but I am finding it tougher when every day is a battle.

Just over twenty-five years ago, Ethiopia was suffering one the worst famines the world had ever seen. Bob Geldof, lead singer of the Irish band The Boomtown Rats, organised the concert Live Aid in 1985 to raise funds for and awareness of this crisis. Estimated to have raised over one hundred and fifty million dollars, there's no doubt it saved millions of lives, but for us driving through it now, it has left a legacy of aid dependency. Begging reaches a whole other level and we're overwhelmed by it. Camping in the bush is impossible every time we stop. Even in the remotest of places we're besieged by people begging, verging on aggression. We're asked for anything and everything, even the clothes we're standing in. For now, we book into cheap hotels to get some relief from this.

The images I remember seeing during the Live Aid concert, when I was in my late twenties, were of dust bowls full of children with extended tummies from malnutrition. What I see here are rolling green hills with sheep, goats and cows grazing, as the areas affected by drought are in the north of Ethiopia. The word 'famine' is a very sensitive word for the Ethiopian government and is now referred to as 'catastrophe' and categorised depending on the drought conditions. Whatever it is called or however it is referred to, Ethiopia has historic famine and sadly ongoing famine, caused by severe drought throughout the different regions.

We're struggling to find actual shops and are ecstatic when finding a hut with smoke coming out of its chimney, which means someone is cooking. For a few Ethiopian birr, we can get injera with scrambled egg, meat or vegetables, which is just delicious, and we are buying from local families. The road deteriorates as we ascend ever higher, the grass becoming a scorched brown and in the distance see the receding forest. Minimal vehicle traffic is made up for by people and cow traffic, cows that take precedence over vehicles. We also see an army of tiny bent-double women, skin as dark, gnarled and wizened as the huge bundles of wood they carry secured with a hoop over their forehead or cloth straps over their shoulders. The 'firewood carriers', bearing loads close to their own body weight, walk up to thirty kilometres a day for just a few dollars.

Addis Ababa is a sprawling chaotic mess of old and new, tin shacks and modern skyscrapers and smells of urine, diesel and coffee. In doorsteps, under shady trees or plastic bag shelters, the men sit drinking a thick treacle coffee from glass cups. It's a stark contrast from the upmarket shopping district where people dressed in silk suits, designer dresses, western jeans and t-shirts live. On the corner of every street women, children, men, the elderly and the disabled sit begging. In the middle of all this, we find Wim´s Holland House behind the long disused railway station. The Dutch owner Wim, his bulbous red nose and protruding belly, evidence of his liquid diet, is welcoming. It's here we will hole up in hope of getting the Sudanese and Egyptian visas.

Yuk, we have an infestation of bed bugs. Even David has been munched. Unable to wash, clean or dry stuff in these constant downpours, I feel dirty, miserable and red raw. We head off on foot to the Egyptian Embassy. The lady who speaks perfect English advises us that, along with the normal photocopies of all our documents including bank cards, we need proof of cash withdrawals here in Addis Ababa. The problem is as our surnames are different (we're not married), we each need a receipt of withdrawals in our own name, an impossibility since my card cloned by someone in America, has been cancelled by the bank and can only be re-activated by a personal visit to my bank in England.

It's stuff like this that takes us to the edge. It's not like we have many options; we can't drive through Somalia or to the bank. It looks like I will have to fly back to England, get my replacement bank card whilst David drives Lizzybus to Egypt alone where I would meet him. Despite being told I´m an intrepid explorer, I know I will never find my way back to England, let alone get back to Egypt and just the thought of it terrifies me. I feel I´m letting us down until David admits that, whilst he could drive on alone, he doesn't want to. So we really are a team; we both bring something to the table, we are each other's confidant and support. I´ve always known we have a guardian angel watching over us; she is not one to give help willy-nilly and always pushes us to our limits, but just when we are at breaking point, she holds out her hand. Her hand now reaches out to us from the lady behind the counter of the Egyptian Embassy who says she will accept a cash withdrawal on each application, even if both are in David´s name.

Two days later, armed with the two cash withdrawal receipts and knowing how far it was to walk to the embassy, this time we take a taxi. Our guardian angel is stood at the back of the office, propped up against the photocopier, holding her stomach moaning. We realise she is pregnant and in labour. Between contractions, she photocopies the receipts and staples them onto the pre-approved applications, handing our passports back with a wonderful Egyptian visa in them and wishes us a safe journey. We insist on taking her in our bone crunching taxi to the hospital. David, never having been faced with childbirth, is sitting in the front seat, more than a little concerned at the prospect he might now be involved in the delivery of one. I remember the lovingly prepared bag full of toiletries and baby clothes I had ready for hospital. I feel sad seeing her plastic bag with only a couple of square pieces of cotton to use as nappies and a nightie. For once I'm grateful taxi drivers are manic as he gets us to the hospital before the baby arrives. I give her a hug, put a few dollars in her bag and off she goes, our latest guardian angel.

Today in the building behind the bus depot, armed guards search and check our passports before letting us in. It's a chaos of people pushing and elbowing whilst trying to get to the four counters, of which only two are manned. David fills out the two-page form we were given as I hold firm among the people closest to the open counters. Finally, we hand over the completed document along with photocopies of our passports - for what? A local pay as you talk SIM card! Yep, all this for a local SIM, but that is only part one; now we need to get some credit on it, not something they do here. These simple things we took for granted are mammoth tasks of perseverance and persistence here. Many times we want to forget the whole bloody fiasco, but we need a local number for the visa applications. I´m sure that these days, like in the rest of the world, Wi-Fi, phones and phone coverage is a thing and access to it a lot simpler, but for us right now, it is not!

Back at Wim's Holland House drinking beer, we watch on a tiny fuzzy television the royal wedding of Kate Middleton and Prince William. Text scrolls across the bottom of the screen telling us that President Barack Obama has announced that Osama bin Laden, deemed responsible for the 9/11 terrorist attacks on America ten years earlier, has been killed in Pakistan. I marvel at this being ten years ago. Like many of us, I remember the horror of that day vividly, like a moment frozen in time. We know this will only worsen tensions, not just in the Arab world, but across the whole world, the one we're trying to drive around. It's right up there in importance along with visas, food, shelter, water and the eradication of bed bugs.

What we thought would be the most difficult part of this journey, that of finance, has been okay, and what we thought would be the doddle of just driving is proving the most difficult. Not in our driving abilities as we have become quite good at it, but what we must do in order to keep driving. For now, it's our yellow fever certificates (supposedly one vaccine protects you for life) which have run out. We know that when crossing borders, even though irrelevant, this will cause us problems.

David has decided to change the date on his, but I'm the original Miss Prim and Proper and I want to find a hospital and have a booster. Chris, a German man living here on a diet of red wine and fags, was knocked off his motor bike four weeks ago and this morning is cutting the plaster off his leg to reveal a purple seeping puss wound. We insist he comes with us to the hospital.

At the public hospital, the familiar smell of disinfectant is missing and a nose curling pong of fermenting something replaces it. I don't want anything injected into me here so revert to David's plan of changing the date on my yellow fever certificate. We do, however, find a private orthopedic hospital for Chris with a doctor from America who just happens to be here doing a thesis on necrosis which, we're told, is what is happening to Chris's leg. If left untreated, this would lead to the loss of his leg at best, death at worst. Chris is operated on immediately. Not wanting to end up with his hospital bill, knowing we bought him here and he is broke, we leave him there with the German girl he has hooked up with. We never found out who or if they paid the bill, but Chris returned the next day to resume his red wine and fag diet with a dressing rather than a plaster on his leg, broken or not.

It's reggae night here at Wim's Holland House. After two tankards of beer each on empty stomachs, I fall over and David is sick. Hearing these familiar songs reminds me of the night I went to Birmingham on the bus with my friend with the five pounds I had won in a school art competition. I´m not sure if I was fifteen or sixteen, but we went into a pub and ordered a barley wine, the only drink we knew of as her dad drank it. It tasted quite disgusting, but at thirteen pence each (in old money) we bought and drank three. Of course, we were pissed as farts and found ourselves in a reggae club full of Rastafarians. I'm reluctant to share this now, not wanting to be judged as I cannot believe my own stupidity, let alone expose it.

Somehow, my friend and I lost each other and, for some unfathomable reason, I accepted a lift home off a huge Rastafarian man. Coming round from my alcohol-induced stupor, I realised what a dangerous situation I had put myself in. I didn't want him to know where I lived so I pointed at a house, pretending it was mine. He didn't park outside it, but just around the corner, then started kissing me, forcing his tongue down my throat and grabbing my breasts, the smell of cigarettes and body odour making me retch. Terrified, I managed to open the door, get out and run like the clappers, but I could feel him following me in the car, so I knocked on someone's door, asking for my friend. It was late and the owners were pretty taken aback, but it was enough to make him drive off. A few days later at school I found out that my friend Sara (not her real name), unable to find me, had taken the bus home. Both ashamed and shocked by our stupidity, knowing we were lucky not to have been raped or murdered, we never spoke of it or told anyone, until of course now. Just writing about it makes me shudder.

We have been here in Addis Ababa over a week. It's been a very productive time, getting the Egyptian and Sudanese visas, as well as a local SIM card with credit on it. I think I've terminated the bed bugs by putting our clothes and bedding into black bin liners and spraying with a can of insect killer to suffocate them, then washed at the local launderette, adding four sterilising tablets to the final rinse. I more or less did the same with the mattress, only in situ with a plastic tarpaulin over it because it didn't fit into a bin bag or washing machine.

Our next country is Sudan then into Egypt. David tells me there is no road crossing from Sudan into Egypt and we apparently need to get a ferry down the Nile, a ferry that only runs once a week. Wow, how incredibly romantic and exciting! I look forward to this like you would a luxury cruise, blissfully unaware of the nightmare we are about to face.

So far this land of historic famine has delivered a country of cultivation, but years of deforestation allow winds to whip across it, with the occasional lone tree where shepherds sit watching their livestock. It's like looking back in time. Yoked cows plough the plots adjacent to neat wattle and daub houses. Men and women wear a shamma, a long cotton robe, that during the heat of the day they wrap and balance on their head like a tray of injera. Men wear white cotton pants or sheets which they pull up into shorts, their spindly strong legs poking out from the cotton folds. The women wear ankle length once-colourful dresses, sun and earth baked to the colours of sage, green and beige, harmonious with the land.

The road curls and rises before us, over the next hill we have our first sighting of the Nile. The significance of it sends a shiver down my spine. The heavy mist hovering over the river allows only glimpses of it, adding to its mystique. Did you know there is the Blue Nile and the White Nile which become 'The Nile'? This is the Blue Nile, supposedly bright blue at its source, but it's more of an earthy mud colour here but still a spectacular sight. We're following a dirt track to the Blue Nile Falls, Tis Abay, Amharic for 'great smoke', which is inundated with beggars, trinket sellers and supposed guides. Persistent, they stand in front of Lizzybus, blocking our way. It's the dry season anyway, but a hydroelectric plant built in 2003 has reduced the flow of water, resulting in the surrounding area becoming barren, taking away its magnificence.

On the main road there is no question whatsoever that the cow takes priority and avoiding them at all costs is paramount. The cows know this and stand or lie in the middle of the road with no intention of moving. I´m driving when a cow shoots out from between a huddled group of men. We realise it has been thwacked with the stick one of the men is holding, and in that split second before impact, I swerve left as it swerves right, managing to miss it by a hair's breadth. It's a deliberate act for us to maim or kill this prized cow, something we had been warned to watch out for, but had dismissed as gossip.

We arrive at Lalibela, one of Ethiopia's holiest cities and famous for its eleven monolithic churches, carved out of blocks of 'living rock' into the side of a mountain or into the ground. Ten centuries have passed since their construction and what was once dense forest is now barren compacted earth. It's an incredible feeling to be stood on solid ground looking down on complete buildings hewn out of the rock below. Stepping down, we leave our shoes at the entrance with the pile of plastic sandals to join the congregation inside, a congregation of men, women and children swathed in folds of white linen that fill the central nave area. We sit on the floor on the strip of red carpet roughly laid out to the sanctuary and pulpit. An aroma of fermenting damp and incense fills our nostrils, a soothing chanting our ears. Worshippers line up to be blessed by a two foot long sacred gold cross. Hundreds of years' old floor-to-ceiling tapestries hang off nails under florescent strip lighting. Huge columns hewn out of the rock hold the beautifully carved stone roof, the rooms to the side are littered with broken plastic chairs, buckets and old scaffolding.

It's not free to visit; you need to get a ticket from the main office which, like it or lump it, gets you a guide with several other guides tagging along. Despite our lack of religious belief, just being here and seeing these incredible buildings is a very special honour and one that will live within us forever.

My head is a muddle of towns, villages and scenery, I'm weary and worn down by the constant begging. We continue to book cheap rooms for some respite to realise the bed bug bites I thought I was getting in the roof tent are from the mattresses of the rooms we're staying in, despite sleeping in our linen cocoons. I laugh my head off as David stood naked dangles his penis covered in bites in front of me. It's ridiculous as I feel momentarily embarrassed with that side of our relationship seemingly part of the past, and is even more likely to stay that way with a rash covered penis.

Water for showers is usually through a pipe hanging off the wall or brought to us in buckets. On these occasions a bucketful is all I get to scrub face, hands, feet and fanny, but it gives me the pretence of clean. I struggle mostly with my hair, full of sweat and dust, it has the same smell this land has. I envy David with his bald head, and not for the first time consider shaving the whole lot off. The women here are quite beautiful, braiding their hair tightly to their head, or sculpturing it in a sort of mud, making it look almost ceramic. Covering mine in mud is an option, but I can't see how that would work on the pillowcase.

Lizzybus crawls up and over mountain after mountain. In this inhospitable remoteness, if we just as much stop for a pee, people appear. Children become aggressive when we don't stop, throwing sticks and stones at us whilst shouting 'farangi' (white person) and 'birr birr birr' (money). We're in the Tigrai Region of northern Ethiopia where, due to the lack of wood, homes are built of local stone, a beautiful pale bluff colour just like the Cotswold villages in England. The rolling hills are sectioned off by miles of ribboned stone walling, bringing an order to this environment. Framed by imposing mountains, of soft pinks, their paleness salient against blue skies. Even David is overwhelmed by their beauty and likens them to the Valley of the Gods in America when he was on a road trip with another Jane. I´m special - I have a 'Y' in my Jayne. I know David asks himself many times 'Y' he ended up with this Jayne.

In these mountains, we make our way to the scattered remote rock churches on almost inaccessible rubble paths. When it's impossible to drive any further, we park Lizzybus and on foot, climb up winding stone-built stairways. Sitting on the steps are what seem like bundles of rags but are people begging. It's distressing and I just don't see, other than us, who they are begging from. At the church door, the priest demands money, a lot of money, for us to enter. It's an unreasonable amount and we're sceptical the money will help the church, its congregation or the bundle-of-rags people sitting along the stairway. We try to bargain when he starts hitting us with his stick, chasing us away. Back at Lizzybus, a group of children has gathered demanding money for having kept watch over her. We laugh at them and refuse to pay. Driving away, they cling onto the Lizzybus roll cage, leaning into the open windows and, pulling at our clothes, continue with their demands. We don't feel threatened by this, just sad, knowing if we gave money to everyone who asks then we would end up begging.

Coffee here is delicious and at only a few birrs we have been treating ourselves to one each day. Sitting now in a café, we watch a figure, bent double and draped in folds of grey-black, moving among the tables. A pair of bony hands protrude from the folds, one grasping a crooked stick, the other held out begging. Watching others and what they give, we follow suit with the same amount. She pushes back the hood from her cape revealing steel grey hair and little button eyes. After inspecting the amount, the coins are thrown back at us.

We arrive in Aksum, the capital of what was the Aksumite Empire and allegedly home to the Queen of Sheba and the Ark of the Covenant. David is in his element with all the history; I see obelisks reaching to the skies. We visit the three-thousand-year-old remains of a temple, where a wizened old man motions for us to follow him to a ramshackle room through a tiny door. He is the keeper of the museum. It's obvious he also lives here as there is a bed, a pile of clothes and a wash bowl. Next to his bed are shelves, nailed together and groaning under ornate tarnished silver crowns and centuries old artefacts. On the desk are piles of books, brittle and dusty. He rips them open to reveal pages of minutely detailed paintings and ancient script. We're both wanting not to see or be a part of the abuse or any further destruction of these sacred documents. We feel unworthy whilst moved by the significance and simplicity of this moment.

After two weeks of bucket washing and cold-water showers, we up the budget and book an en-suite room with hot water. Washing my hair with shampoo in hot water is glorious whilst alarming on seeing brown scummy water disappear down the drain for several washes before it´s clear. Not having had internet for over a week, I'm crushed at not finding any here, whilst a little consoled to have managed to get credit for our local SIM-card. I use all of it just to hear my sister's voice for a few minutes.

Today we visit the ancient site of obelisks and stele (carved stone slabs); most have fallen over and lie shattered and broken. I look up at the fully erect one which had been taken as 'booty' by the Italians until its return some sixty-eight years later. I don't know how they got it there in the first place. I think it involved cutting it into pieces, but getting it back meant reinforcing the runway to accommodate the weight of the plane. Because of the practicalities and the cost of returning the obelisk, there was talk of the Italians building a new hospital, or upgrading the roads, or cancelling the national debt instead. I'm a pragmatic person and I can see the real benefits of any of those ideas, but even if I don't understand all the ancient civilisations, I do understand the significance of these ancient artefacts to a people and their land.

We're looking at a solid rock reservoir, the size of a football field; some say it's the Queen of Sheba's bath. The water is the same colour as the buff stone it's cut from, with a sweeping curve of steps down to it. The locals bathe, wash clothes and collect water here. The water is as cloudy as the notion that the Queen of Sheba bathed here, but its importance to the locals is as great as its legend. The barren rock it is carved from has ancient paths and terraces. Beyond these is The Church of Our Lady, Mary of Zion which claims to contain the Ark of the Covenant. I don't know why, but I always thought these places of such significance would be significant places, but you almost stumble across them, which makes them even more enchanting and timeless. We're coming to realise Ethiopia is so much more than a land of famine; a lot has changed since we visited, mostly for the good and preservation of these sacred sites and the areas around them.

CHAPTER 8

FEELING PART OF SOMETHING

Our time in Ethiopia is coming to an end. We're joined at our hotel by Simon and John who we convoyed with, and two Dutch lads Roland and Paul driving their parents' Land Cruiser back to Holland. The Sudan is the next country we are all heading for; with only a two week visa each, it is a stepping stone to Egypt. We make a loose plan to meet on the border of Sudan, at the frontier port town of Wadi Halfa, and together get the weekly sailing down The Nile into Egypt, with our vehicles going on a separate barge which we can share.

Roland and Paul left yesterday. Having loved our convoy with Simon and John so much, we agree to go in convoy again across the breathtaking, sultry whilst shimmering, Simien Mountains. Cutting through the mountains is a highway, still under construction, with the original Italian cobbled road winding through it. You might even think they built the road to drive the obelisk away, but that would be an assumption, and I never assume. For whatever reason it was built, the individually carved and laid stones are beautiful to look at, but hell to drive over, vibrating every nut, bolt and bone in us and Lizzybus, until finally it turns into a dirt road. Every few kilometres, the road is blocked by the construction of the new highway. We wait it out in the heat, at times engulfed by clouds of dust, at all times harassed by beggars.

This snaking switchback road is endless, climbing ever higher and higher. A watermelon size piece of rock tumbles down the steep embankment towards us from where a group of boys are stood above. It bounces off the banks and smashes through Simon and John's rear passenger window. A split second sooner and it would have smashed through the driver's window, seriously injuring if not killing Simon who was driving. Simon believes this was a deliberate act; we like to think it just dislodged, but who knows? This, with the cow incident and constant harassment, is wearing us all down. It colours the mood, tarnishing the experience and love for this land and its people. Later, at our hotel, Simon discovers that the rock smashing through the window had landed on a rucksack containing his laptop which, despite being in a neoprene sleeve, is completely crushed into the shape of a banana.

Today Simon is collecting his new laptop from the local computer shop which has been able to transfer his hard drive information. We will push on alone to Gondar, the last town before the border town of Wadi Halfa. Out on the open plains, I see herdsmen galloping along on horseback in tunics of vivid crimson and yellow velvet, embroidered with golden thread in the most intricate patterns, edged with golden swirling tassels – exotic and stunning.

If I was reading this now, I would want nothing more in my life than to be on this journey, and the fact that we both still are says everything. However, I question if we will ever actually get round the whole world. Being forced to share such a close personal space is pushing me to my limits. This journey is exposing us both to each other, forcing us to see what is right and what is wrong in us. For me, the banter and the ironic sense of humour we share is not enough, leaving a gaping hole in me. I'm never going to presume or try to explain David's feelings, or even want to, but I feel he is oblivious to this need in me. I've heard of the term 'friend-zoned' and wonder if that is what has happened to us. We're so focused on the daily challenge of getting Lizzybus around the world, sex or intimacy is a thing of the past. If I'm honest, it's a huge relief under these conditions, but intimacy is not just the physical act of sex, it's so much more and that's what I'm struggling with.

Talking about it would help, but that was never a thing in the past, and most certainly will not be a thing now. I know David thinks I'm just another part of the kit and as long as I'm working, I don't need any maintenance, in this case, talking things over. But unlike kit, it takes more than gaffer tape, cable ties and regular greasing to hold me together. I feel I am falling apart with need.

We're in Gondar, the former capital of the old empire, and our last but one town in Ethiopia before the Sudan. It's here we need to contact the 'fixer' to arrange the sailing from the Sudan into Egypt. As Roland and Paul arrive, we book adjoining rooms in the basic hotel set around an internal courtyard, reserving two more for Simon and John. I get a text message to say it will be tomorrow before they arrive as Simon's laptop is not ready. I open and read this text message over and over, marvelling at how something so very familiar is so very odd in my life now. With the central courtyard being in shade, it's a perfect space for us all to work on our vehicles before the final push, but David is in the room with an upset stomach. I'm so excited to be here with everyone and a little cross with him for what I feel is him spoiling my special time and refuse to pander to him. We're barely talking, which is embarrassingly noticeable.

Today, feeling a little better, David joins us on the ten-minute walk to Gondar Castle with its seventeenth century royal enclosure. Looking round the ruins of a kingdom that once was, seeing the remains of lions' cages, banqueting rooms and stable block, we're brought right back to the modern day when a wedding party arrives. They make an ear-splitting warbling sound, the women in short shimmering pink low-cut dresses, the men in matching silk suits. As they dance and shimmy past, they motion for us to join them. David, Simon, John, Roland and Paul sit in the shade cringing. I don't need asking twice and tag along in a sort of conga. For some reason, I think back to the time we visited my mother who had been 'missing' for five weeks.

Jenny and I were taken to the local hospital that also had a red brick asylum attached to it, to find our mother prostrate on a bed with a load of pulleys and weights suspended from a frame. Mom, suffering from severe sciatica, apparently needed her spine stretching, so during this time my eldest sister was tasked with looking after us. The worst part was dealing with our hair that, as toddlers, had been golden curls but had coarsened to become afro frizz. It had been washed in shampoo then swilled in olive oil and vinegar to keep it fresh and shiny, then wound tightly into what can only be described as sausages all over our head. As we walked onto the ward and saw Mom, who was slim anyway but had lost so much weight she looked like a skeleton inside some torture chamber, we were momentarily frozen, until hearing my mother calling for us to come and hide down the side of the bed so the nurses wouldn't see our hair.

I feel the pain, and confusion of that moment to this day, but now, dancing around with these people in their finery, my afro frizz hair in semi-dreadlocks hanging from my head, dressed in tatty shorts and David's long sleeved shirt, I couldn't care less. I´m Jayne - with bouffant or afro frizz hair, I´m still Jayne.

Being here in Gondar as tourists amongst friends has been the tonic I needed. The food and coffee is so good and cheap we eat out for breakfast, lunch and dinner. Breakfast is Kinche, a cracked wheat and barley porridge, or large pancakes with eggs or honey; lunch is Kitfo, marinated raw meat, served with salads and delicious injera; and evening meal is Tibs, traditional stewed dishes of meat or vegetables, fried in niter kibbeh, a spiced clarified butter with a berbere spice mix. It's cheap and delicious, as is the local Saint George beer. All this wonderful company and finally getting internet and my precious emails from home - I am so content.

What is even better is David has found a soulmate in Simon. They chat endlessly about worst-case scenarios and what bits have, can, and will break, on our vehicles. For David and Simon, this is much needed therapy as responsibility hangs heavy on their shoulders. What these two men do to keep our vehicles moving is a constant; they are both persistent and thorough. David struggled for a long time to find the focus of this journey and the respect he got from his working life, but finally this journey is giving him this and more. Despite our physical distance, this shared experience is bringing a different closeness, seeing in each other reasons to be proud, not just of each other and Lizzybus, but for not giving up.

When David had his meltdown in South Africa, he was determined to ship Lizzybus back to England and forget this whole stupid idea. I was broken by the fact his choice directly affected my choice and my chance to continue. Had I abandoned ship, David at least could have carried on. I felt a little betrayed by this; the decision to quit should always be a joint one, based on things out of our control, like a complete breakdown of Lizzybus, illness or war, not what we can control like emotions, or not getting from the journey what we thought we would. But it was just David adjusting to it and our new life; now he never wants or sees himself doing anything other than being on this journey with me and in Lizzybus.

The Sudan, where The Blue Nile and The White Nile become 'The Nile', is a country of great conflict and dangerous political unrest, with vast deserts and ancient cemeteries. It borders on the Red Sea, a narrow, elongated stretch of water between Africa and Asia with some of the hottest and saltiest seawater in the world. Connected to the Mediterranean Sea by the Suez Canal, it is one of the world's busiest waterways and, although I don't know it yet, Lizzybus will be making it even busier. We're concerned by the fact it's a 'dry country', not in that it has no rain - although in places that's true - but in the production, selling or consuming of alcohol. Former President Jaafar Nimeiri introduced Islamic law banning it, reportedly throwing bottles of whisky into the Nile. We're freaking out at the loss of our much-needed beer o'clock, realising how important and necessary a cold beer is after a tough day. (New laws introduced in 2020 now allow non-Muslims to drink alcohol).

It's with mixed emotions we leave today, excited to be on the move whilst reluctant to leave this little haven. Roland and Paul set off yesterday; having just completed their veterinary training, they have only a six month window to get their parents' Land Cruiser back to Holland, where it has already been sold, and start their new jobs. Simon and John decide to stay one more day, so we will cross into the Sudan alone. Gondar, being in the mountains, had a cooling breeze. Now were in a furnace with flies that land back on your eyes and lips the second you swat them off. In the heat of the midday sun, par boiling in Lizzybus, we wait for the border staff to have lunch. The actual crossing itself is easy. Already having the visa, we're not searched or asked for anything and once we've paid the fifty dollar 'alien registration fee', we're welcomed into their country.

Pressing on into dusk, we set up camp in this wilderness where the earth, sucked dry of its moisture, has split and cracked into mini crevasses. A man passes wrapped in white cotton, riding a teeny-weeny donkey. With so many bales of something strapped to it, it's only the donkey's tail showing. He just waves at us, no begging, no stone throwing, no nothing, just waves. A herd of bony cattle appears, their keepers in tattered earth-coloured tunics and plastic sandals, their blankets for the cold desert night wrapped on their heads like piped meringue. They hold out hide water bladders which we fill with cold water to be rewarded by gleaming white smiles. We're asked for nothing more and in a haze of dust and flies, they melt back into a setting sun.

We pass the capital city of Khartoum, a place of refuge for the displaced making it a city of conflict and internal violence. We're on a highway of double length lorries and suicidal coaches which honk and wave, not in greeting, but to move us out of the way. Through this barren land of endless road, heat, heat and more heat, I'm nauseous and suffering from blinding headaches. My vision blurring, David takes over all the driving. My legs burn from the engine heat and red blotches appear like my Nan used to get sitting too close to the open fire. If we open the windows, we're sand blasted by a furnace wind; our only option is to open the front vents and wet a towel to drape over my legs which helps for five minutes before it's bone dry again. We'd made loose arrangements to meet Simon, John, Roland and Paul at the port town of Wadi Halfa in ten days' time, but feeling like I am, decide to try and get there for the Wednesday ferry, a week early.

Camped beside what is now 'The Nile', David makes a bowl of noodles. I've not been able to eat for two days suffering from heat exhaustion. I dry retch at the smell of them, but David insists I at least drink the broth and almost instantly, I feel a little better. Despite everything we know and monitoring the amount of water I'm drinking; my body is missing salts and minerals and is shutting down. We have rehydration solutions, but I've never thought to take them.

I think I'm still hallucinating as in the folds of the giant apricot coloured dunes I see pyramids. Who even knew that the Sudan had pyramids, let alone the fact that with over two hundred and fifty of them, they have more than Egypt? The Sudanese Pyramids were built as tombs for the rulers during the Nubian - I'm not sure if it's a period or a civilization? - urgh, that's enough, my headache is coming back. All I know is we are at the Meroë Pyramids, untouched by real tourism as there is no actual road to it, just sand tracks. The years of war between government and rebel groups, and nature, have left many in ruins, making it a hauntingly desolate place.

Walking towards us is a caravan of fully laden camels led by children. Camels were used in transporting materials during the construction of the pyramids over two to three thousand years ago - how different life is now. We're persuaded to ride the camels through the ancient pyramids. I'm a horse rider, but camel riding is something else. It's all about balance and as they are too round to get your legs 'round', you just rest them on the camels' shoulders. The young boy thwacks David's camel and whilst it doesn't exactly gallop off, it lollops with me in pursuit. In the wind, the sarong I'm wearing over my head and shoulders wraps me up like a mummy. I can see nothing, but I can hear David squawking, and almost fall off laughing.

Still weak and fatigued, driving on through the desert I'm boiling alive in Lizzybus; even David is beginning to feel the effects and he is never too hot, too cold, too un-comfy. Finally, like a miracle we make it to the desolate frontier town of Wadi Halfa. I perk up a little thinking about my Nile cruise. We've booked a room in a two storey hotel with a metal bed, central hanging fan, off which is a squat toilet and hanging pipe shower. I shower, wet my sarong to drape over me and lie spread-eagled on the bed which I'd pulled into the middle of the room to be directly under the ceiling fan. I repeat this process until night becomes morning and David has stopped feeding me chunks of pineapple whilst forcing rehydration fluids down me.

I feel reborn, but with the outside temperatures pushing one hundred degrees fahrenheit, almost forty celsius, I refuse to leave this room with its ceiling fan. So David, along with Roland and Paul, meet up with Magdi, the fixer we arranged in Gondor. As Simon and John have decided to stay out in the desert for another week exploring the pyramids, it's just Lizzybus and Brutus that will go on the flatbed pulled by a tug, and us on the passenger ferry with Roland and Paul.

I´ve just realised that yesterday was my birthday. Tonight we're all going out for a belated birthday meal and to celebrate sailing down the Nile into Egypt tomorrow which is filling me with expectant joy. When crossing any no man's land, it always makes a difference, non more so than from Ethiopia, with an aid dependency it's struggling to let go of, to the Sudan which, never having been exposed to so much aid, has been a magical place for us. With the soft inquisitive nature of its people and none of the begging or harassment we found in Ethiopia, we're sad to leave, but it's life-threateningly hot for us.

Today we are off on our 'luxury' Nile cruise. The last few weeks have all focused on this crossing and the fact Lizzybus and Brutus are going separately from us is a big concern. David can't eat his breakfast of omelette and fouls (local beans) for anxiety. When David met our fixer Magdi yesterday, he was dressed in the traditional jellabiya, a sort of full-length cotton tunic with leggings underneath. Today, he is dressed in a crisp white shirt, trousers and polished black leather shoes, holding a briefcase. Seeing these shiny leather shoes is so strange, I just stare at them. In convoy, we drive to the outskirts of the dock, to the concrete jetty and the dilapidated tugboat that will tow the flat bed with Lizzybus and Brutus on it down the Nile. We're told to give our keys to the 'captain', a man who looks as old as the pyramids, in a greasy t-shirt and pantaloons. None of us wants to do this. We want to see our vehicles loaded, but we have no option or else miss our once-a-week sailing. We're so glad we fitted the internal cage in Lizzybus as once the back door is padlocked at least our kit is secure. Roland and Paul's vehicle has no such security. Having reluctantly handed over the keys, we're taken to the main dock, a frenetic mass of disorganised chaos. Like low grade royalty, we're dragged to the front of the not-exactly-queues, but rather rammed-together bodies, to the officials sitting behind opaque perspex windows or randomly placed desks, to hand over the thick wad of papers, every one of which need to be stamped, signed or both.

A few hours later, with our half forest of paperwork authorised and lots of smiles and laughter - the Sudanese are wonderfully friendly people - we are done. We're hoping it includes the ferry ticket, but as it's all in Arabic, we don't have a clue. When we booked the ferry, all the cabins were full, we were told to head for the top deck and set up under the hanging life boats, as it's the only shade aboard. Getting onto the ferry up an open sided gangplank, half blocked by people sitting on mounds of possessions, is a challenge. I grab hold of David's hand. It's not quite the romantic hand-holding I anticipated, but a hand-holding of necessity as I have no intention of getting left behind or worse, ending up in the Nile, slopping around with all the debris and diesel spills. In the pit of all our stomachs is the worry of having left our vehicles and keys, our life, our home, our everything, here in this chaos.

Despite not exactly what I envisioned of a 'cruise down the Nile', I can't hide the thrill when the knackered old engine fires up, vibrating the whole boat, pumping out thick black smoke from its funnel. We're sitting crossed legged on kit mats under the lifeboats, eating the included meal served in polystyrene trays of foul, pasta, flat bread, and a shrivelled orange. Floating down the Nile with the most glorious breeze brushing over us is a magical moment on this journey - if only Lizzybus was with us. As the sun disappears into the desert, the deck fills with chanting kneeling bodies, becoming one billowing sheet of cotton, whilst over the tinny tannoy, the call to prayer is captured by the wind. At three in the morning a torch is shone into our eyes, demanding we complete the onboard immigration. When boarding, we reluctantly handed over our passports which were collected in a cardboard box and now, having crossed into Egypt, we need to complete immigration. Everyone apart from us knew this; at least being the only Europeans on board, they know the passports are ours.

David and Paul go whilst Roland and I stay guarding the kit, having been warned of onboard theft. My bones throb on the thin kit mat laid directly onto the metal deck using my rucksack as a pillow, every half hour I wake in agony needing to roll over. I desperately need to pee so make my way over the sleeping bodies to the lower deck and the two squat toilets. I initially thought they dispersed directly into the Nile, but realise they must be contained in something as whatever it is, it's now full and the disgusting stinking mess is slopping over the top. In flip flops I have no choice other than to balance on the metal rim and pee, hoping the horrid mess misses me. Never in my life did I ever imagine I would yearn for my spade and a bush.

Our two-day, one-night 'luxury' cruise down the Nile is over. We're now in Aswan, Egypt, minus Lizzybus. If I thought Wadi Halfa was frenetic, then this is a whole other level. We become one body of people, cargo and us. I am unceremoniously shoved to end up face down on the laps of squatting women, children and baggage. David grabs my hand, drags me to my feet and pushes me through the narrow doorway where armed guards stop me. Letting only a few through at a time, I'm determined they let us through together so hold on even tighter to David's hand. We have no idea where Roland and Paul are. Once on the other side of the door we're searched, our bag is put through an ancient x-ray machine and, as immigration was completed onboard, we're done. We just need to find Roland and Paul and the new fixer Karmal who is meeting us.

We move along as one mass of people, the skinny spindly legged porters dragging cases behind them with more balanced on their heads, bending under the weight. This for me has been one of the most difficult parts of the journey. The lack of personal space and hygiene has been hard, but they are nothing compared to seeing how people survive and what they do to feed their family. It hurts and gets me every time, these windows into people's lives. We're spat out at the other end where Karmal is waiting, along with Roland and Paul. Once bundled into his car, I'm on David's lap in the back with Roland and Paul squeezed in beside us. Two men sit together on the front seat and two more are on top of the luggage in the open boot - nine of us in your average saloon car. Karmal, although driving, is preoccupied with texting on one phone, whilst talking on another.

With no air con, all the windows are fully open. The noise from honking cars and the choking exhaust fumes are making me nauseous and I can barely breathe. I shut my eyes and imagine I'm still on my 'luxury' Nile cruise with setting sun desert views and cooling breeze. An hour later, we arrive at the four-storey, forgotten-in-time Hathor

Hotel with spectacular views over the Nile. The sweat having suctioned us to each other, we peel ourselves apart. The Nile is filled with moored yachts and double or triple parked cruise ships. Recent suicide and car bombings have made Egypt very unstable and the government are advising tourists not to visit. Holiday complexes and hotels are as abandoned as the temples on Elephant Island on the opposite bank.

Egypt, one of the greatest civilisations the world has ever known, with pyramids and deserts, its capital Cairo, language Arabic. We can't relax or enjoy any of this knowing Lizzybus and Brutus are still in Wadi Halfa. We phone Magdi, our contact there. Despite speaking good English before, he now cannot understand a word, but does manage to convey the fact he can't help us, insisting it's up to Karmal to sort it all out. Karmal can only confirm the vehicles are still on the flat bed in the Sudan, waiting for the engine to be fixed on the tug. We expected to arrive at the same time as Lizzybus so have only the clothes we're wearing and a toothbrush. At least I have my little laptop. Basically, we're tourists without a case full of holiday clothes, suntan lotion or diarrhoea sachets, all fearing the worst and realising that's exactly what has happened, the worst! We're in Egypt and our vehicles, our home, our lives, our everything, are still in the Sudan at the mercy of a man nearly as ancient as the pyramids in a greasy t-shirt being able to fix his engine.

It's been three days, days that always start with a phone call to our fixer Karmal, bringing the same sickening news that our vehicles are still in Egypt, and end with us washing our one set of clothes. In my old life, the old Jayne having to go each day to breakfast wearing the same clothes would have been at least embarrassing, but now, knowing they are clean, I care diddly-squat. I care about Lizzybus, not what I'm wearing. We're all feeling the stress, Roland and Paul with their deadline to get Brutus back to Holland and start their new jobs, and us at what is beginning to feel like the hopelessness of the situation. David and I have even looked at getting the next ferry back to Wadi Halfa, but to re-enter the Sudan would mean a trip to the embassy in Cairo for a new visa, and we have no transport. Today, to relieve this pressure, we're going on an excursion with Roland and Paul to Abu Simbel, Temples of Ramesses II, Hathor and Nefertari, a time when Pharaohs ruled this land.

We are picked up at three in the morning by an already full tour bus, our hotel breakfast in a picnic box, it's not long before we're fast asleep. On waking, we realise we have become a convoy of six buses. It's exciting chatting to everyone, a distraction, but a blanket of worry still hovers over us - that is until we arrive at The Great Temples. Craning our necks to look up, we're dwarfed by the gigantic figures of King Ramesses, his first wife Nefertari Meritmut and their children at their feet, carved out of the most beautiful yellow sandstone. Then everything is forgotten. I'm finding it almost impossible to believe that these two temples were physically moved here to avoid being submerged after the damming of the Nile to create Lake Nasser. I can just about understand how you can carve a whole mountain into temples, but how the hell you then move them is just too much for me to grasp. We sit in the shade overlooking these extraordinary temples, eating our picnic box breakfast. What we have been through to get here and what we still face is beyond belief; this is our reward, and it's breathtaking.

CHAPTER 9

ON THE EDGE OF INSANITY

We get news that Lizzybus and Brutus are here in Aswan, Egypt, a whole week after we arrived, but we will only believe this when we see them. Now back in Karmal's car, heading to the docks, we see wedged between rusted steel boats the flatbed with a dusty and forlorn, but intact, Lizzybus and Brutus on it. I feel every single emotion possible, bringing me to tears. The problem is that whatever propelled this flatbed here is not doing it now. It needs to be pushed and shoved by other boats until close enough to the collapsed broken mess of concrete dock to allow ropes to be thrown to the gathering crowd. The two planks of wood lying on the deck are pushed out and laid on these broken slabs of concrete at an alarming slant. As David and Roland have gone off with Karmal to do the paperwork, it's down to Paul and I to drive quite literally down the plank. I was freaking out at this prospect and knew if David was here, there was no way I would do this. It's made even more terrifying as I not only have to drive down these two planks, but I must do it in reverse. Shouted instructions come from everywhere, I can't understand a single word, but I know they all want me to go faster. Not bloody likely! I´m Miss Daisy for a reason and I inch my way down these alarmingly bendy planks at a snail's pace, reverting to my coping mechanism of closing one eye and squinting through the other when it gets too much, which was pretty much all of it.

Somehow, we get down the plank and over the piles of garbage and broken concrete to the locked and guarded perimeter gates to wait for David and Roland in the full midday sun. The euphoria we had at getting our vehicles off the flatbed is lost in the dust, heat and thirst of the passing hours. When David and Roland finally appear with Karmal, I'm so worried about David, ashen under his African skin and shaking. It's been a tough week for us all. I realise how important it´s been having Roland and Paul with their devil-may-care attitude of youth making us laugh. I thought driving the plank was the short straw, but as Lizzybus and Brutus had to be registered on Egyptian plates, which invalidated our original insurance (of course it did), Karmal, struggling to secure the needed Egyptian insurance, had taken them to several offices, several times. Since our first real border crossing from Morocco into Mauritania when we used a fixer, we made a pact to go it alone. This would have been totally impossible here with the language barrier. The money spent on Karmal our 'fixer' has been worth every single penny.

Karmal's job is done - I don't know who is more relieved, him or us. His advice to us on leaving is to slip the port authority another twenty Egyptian pounds (two dollars) to avoid further hold ups. We didn't offer, they didn't ask. Driving out through these gates into our Egyptian adventure is such a momentous moment. Our ordeal which started with my 'Cruise down the Nile' for now is over on being united once more with Lizzybus. We are complete. Lizzybus looks super cool with her yellow rusted set of Egyptian number plates and, better still, she is legal in this country with Egyptian insurance and the huge pile of paperwork stamped. It's incredibly emotional waving Roland, Paul and Brutus off on their journey back to Holland. We head to what has become our home, the Hathor Hotel, to check Lizzybus over and, at last, change our clothes.

The journey for real is about to start again. Our next country is Jordan, but for now we have Egypt to explore and, most importantly, 'The Seniors' - David's parents - are flying out to Luxor for a week. The thought of having family here is just so exciting - I have butterflies!

Waiting to pick The Seniors up at Luxor airport is a poignant reminder I will never have this as both my parents are dead now. My mind wanders, realising despite being loved, we were never supported, guided or encouraged through life, never given the belief or the chance to achieve what we should. Our parents never stood in the rain at hockey matches, or cheered us on at school sports day. With no family car or money for bus fares, we walked the two miles to school and back each day, even in heavy rain or snow. Jenny was always first up waiting for me. She would prod, poke and scream at me all the way to school as I lagged behind in my Jayne world, so we were always late and always in trouble (I'm sorry Jenny, I really am sorry). Lost and floundering, going into our teenage years we had no focus. My elder sisters, working as nannies in Canada, swanned home every now and then with fancy new clothes and tales of Niagara Falls, water skiing and the like. Positions were found for Jenny and I as nannies, but the government added an extra year to the school leaving age, so we lost the jobs before we could even start them.

I rebelled, playing truant, even stealing from shops - mainly chocolate - not for me but trying to buy the friends I didn't have. On leaving school, with no one saying you could have a career, be something, or do something with your life other than to earn your keep, we got jobs in the local factory. At sixteen, Jenny was pregnant. To my mother's credit, without saying a word to my father, she took us both on the bus to his parents' house. My mother made it clear she would support Jenny in any decision she made and that they had a choice. It's hard to imagine now, but what my mother did was a huge thing. Jenny, afraid and immature, just agreed to a registry office wedding. In such stark contrast to David, whose parents were there for him at every parents' evening, every rugby match, every club he ever wanted to join. He was supported and encouraged, given the belief he could do and be anything. I feel sad and a little cheated for Jenny and I, whilst incredulous that despite everything, it's me here at Luxor airport, in Egypt, waiting to pick The Seniors up, feeling part of something, even if it is part of someone else's something.

It's a very special moment as The Seniors arrive, David is even a little teary, Kay, David's mother, had always wanted to visit Egypt with its lost civilization, but Mr T Senior didn't. However, as his son is here, like being stood every Saturday morning on the touch line of his rugby match, Mr T Senior is stood here now supporting David on his epic journey. One thing David just loves is taking and showing me, in particular, but anyone in general, the wonders of the world. As tourists are still not coming to Egypt, the hotel we book into is as deserted as the streets where rows of horse-drawn carriages wait for non-existent tourists. Each and every day, when we leave the hotel, we face a constant onslaught of demands from them, if not to take a carriage, then at least to give money to buy food for the horses. This for me is tough.

I'm in the land of the giants at Luxor Temple, dwarfed once more by an avenue of sphinxes, creatures with lions' bodies and heads of men, rams or birds stretching as far as the eye can see. It's even more special driving to them with The Seniors in Lizzybus. Next, we visit the Valley of the Kings and Queens in what look like barren limestone hills, but are vast warrens of chambers and treasures, accessed through massive entrances into a labyrinth of tunnels, covered in hand-painted ancient hieroglyphics and symbolic scenes. There's a stillness and a coolness on the way to the ancient tombs, the most famous one belonging to

Tutankhamun, even though its solid gold coffin and death mask are now in the Grand Egyptian Museum just outside Cairo. I'm totally overwhelmed; words have not been invented to do justice or convey the full wonder of this place, this lost civilization.

Simon and John arrive today. Their journey has come to an end and they are here arranging a container to ship Proper Job from Alexandria to Portsmouth, England. Tonight, with them and The Seniors, we take one of the horse-drawn carriages for what we think is our final meal out together. It's a wonderful evening, spent reminiscing over our adventure through Africa, the hours we spent securing visas at embassies, and the cementing of our friendship whilst convoying to the border of Ethiopia on the supposedly impassable Masaba Road. We will miss them greatly.

It's over, we are alone. The Seniors have gone back to England. Roland, Paul and Brutus are halfway to Holland. Proper Job is in its container and Simon and John are on their flight. I feel desperately alone. Each time we face and conquer obstacles, I realise they're only a tiny but significant part of the journey. They make you stronger in that you have more experience, but at the same time chip away at your energy and resolve. I can only liken this feeling to the anticipation of Christmas Day - once the presents are opened and the food is consumed, it's just another day. Not ready to face being back on the road, at twenty dollars a night including breakfast, we stay a few extra days in the hotel, but without our friends and The Seniors, the magic has gone.

We're now back on the road and heading for Cairo following the Nile via the city of El-Minya, known as the 'Bride of Upper Egypt', linking the North and the South. It makes me smile waffling on about history like this, wishing so very much my history teacher Mr Smoulden could hear me now, after bouncing a power ball off his head and him locking Gayle and I (dobbed in by the class for it being Gayle's ball and me the person who launched it) in the stockroom where we lit the fag nicked off Gayle's Dad, which led to Gayle's expulsion and my dinner hours spent writing lines. It was such a childish prank that had such serious consequences, not least missing out on the learning of history that might have been an advantage on this journey. We are now facing constant roadblocks, traffic police, tourist police, and police police. El-Minya is a huge city on the banks of the Nile. From our budget hotel window, we see a mess of unfinished hotels, randomly painted brick houses, and crumbling mud and corrugated steel dwellings. It all comes alive at night with tacky neon signs - this is the new Minya. Today we visit the old, once capital city of Minya, a vast ancient city of rock tombs, pyramids, palaces, and mosques.

After Egypt, our next country is Jordon then into Syria, but civil unrest in Syria is threatening its stability and the British government is warning people not to travel there. If it worsens, we will have to put Lizzybus in a container and ship her from Alexandria in Egypt to Pakistan, avoiding both Jordan and Syria. Here I am again, writing all this stuff as if I know what I'm talking about, which of course I don't as this is all stuff David is telling me. I'm beginning to realise how much I've had to fight to keep the real Jayne hidden.

I tell everyone if I can do this anyone can, and I truly mean it, but you need to want it more than showers, flushing toilets, shoes, handbags, safety, even food. It also helps being stubborn and to never admit defeat, ever. When anyone says to either of us "it's impossible, you can't do it", that seals our fate and we know if we fail, it will be only whilst trying.

We arrive at Cairo, the largest city in the Arab world. The Egyptian revolution of 2011 has forced the resignation of President Hosni Mubarak and power is now in the hands of the Supreme Council of the Armed Forces. Every bit of information we have tells us to avoid Cairo, but what we hear does not fit with what we see and feel, so ignore it and press on. From our sixth-floor room in this budget hotel, what we think is a picture of the Great Pyramids hanging on the wall, is real and the frame is the window. With no actual car park at this hotel, we look down at the frenetic streets of Cairo where Lizzybus is parked, the hotel security guarding her.

It's finally happened - I've run out of enough words to convey what I see. I don't like dates, times, facts, mainly because I can't remember them, but they are needed right now for me to hang my thoughts on. We are in the Cairo Museum, opened well over a century ago. It's like everything in this country, gigantic. It has the most wonderful feel to it, just like being in an old curiosity junk shop and if you spent a year here, you would never see it all, floor after floor, room after room of what seems randomly placed and piled high treasures of a lost civilization. Then suddenly you're in the presence of something, something you feel you shouldn't be, taken from where it was laid to rest, Tutankhamun's death mask, constructed from two sheets of hammered-together gold, weighing 22.5 pounds (10.23 kg). I've said before shivers down your spine are an actual thing, now the hairs on your arm standing up is another. With the Cairo Museum bursting at the seams, the then President laid the foundation stone for the construction of a brand new museum, the Grand Egyptian Museum (GEM). As I write, it's still under construction but very close to completion.

On leaving the Cairo Museum, we see our first evidence of how volatile Egypt is with student demonstrations outside the nearby ousted Mubarak's National Democratic Headquarters. Camera crews and riot police are out in force, recording the unrest to what seems to us little more than the waving of placards and the burning of posters. Knowing how things like this escalate, we head back to our hotel.

Adjacent to Cairo is the Giza Plateau and Giza, with the Great Sphinx and the Great Pyramid of Giza (the largest pyramid in Egypt) - and believe me, they are all ginormous which makes this one gargantuan - temples for the afterlife. I apologise to those who know their stuff, you honestly have my full admiration and envy, but in all of this Memphis is mentioned, reminding me of my mother and her love of Elvis Presley and Memphis being his birthplace, but of course that has nothing to do with this Memphis. This is the ancient pharaonic capital of the Old Kingdom Memphis and from our hotel window we see it spread out before us. Today we drive to Alexandria to visit the El-Alamein War Cemeteries, a poignant reminder of the country's more recent past. The cemeteries commemorate the soldiers, mostly from the Commonwealth, who died in the Western Desert campaigns - lost soldiers, little more than boys, many unidentified having only a plaque with the words 'known only to God'. It brings David to tears, a very solemn experience.

Back to our journey. Over a hundred and fifty years ago, the Suez Canal was completed, separating Africa from Asia and, by connecting the Mediterranean Sea to the Red Sea, created the shortest maritime route from Europe to Asia. Many years later, the construction of a tunnel reconnected Africa to Asia. I mention this as it's significant to our journey: we must cross the Suez Canal to get to Jordan. With the unrest in Syria getting worse, David thinks it's best to stay as long as possible in Egypt before crossing into Jordan and travelling on to Syria, in the hope that it will calm down. We're heading now from Alexandria to the Suez Canal, but for several hours we have barely moved in the gridlocked fume-filled traffic. Tired and irritable, we vote to pay to use the motorway and head back to our hotel in Cairo for the night. Just because you pay to use a 'motorway' means nothing as to the quality of it - at times it's four lanes, at others it's one. Locals have even taken down sections of the Armco crash barriers, allowing them to drive along the dirt track in their efforts to avoid the traffic jams, so we follow.

I ask David, "Whose stupid idea was this?" when the truck in front, full of tomatoes, tipped over blocking the track, the tomatoes become a vibrant soggy carpet of blood red. I´m not frustrated or irritated by this, just sorry that this mans load of tomatoes are lost. We help by winching his vehicle upright, but the tomatoes, already rotten, squished on impact. We press on, driving over this sodden mess. Lizzybus smells of tomato and rotten. It's dark by the time we make it back to Cairo, which is terrifying as headlights or street lighting are not compulsory here. On concrete flyovers, we're level with high-rise apartments to see the inhabitants sitting on sofas watching television and eating dinner, seemingly oblivious to the traffic thundering past a few metres away.

Setting off again for the Suez Canal, we avoid the motorway as it's no better than the local roads. With driving being such a huge part of this journey, the endless hours sat next to each other in the heat and mayhem can be an endurance if you let it. Sometimes we do, but mostly we both enjoy driving Lizzybus to see it as part of the adventure, our window into these countries and the lives of their people. Just when I think I can endure no more, when the pain in my bottom goes down my legs and the callus on my elbow, from resting it out of the window, starts to crack and bleed, I see something to distract me, I even welcome roadblocks as a chance to stretch my legs. Yes, driving needs to be as big a part of the journey as the destination. Like they say, 'It's not the destination, it's the journey', whoever 'they' are.

Sailing up the Suez can take over ten hours, with many more hours, even days, getting on the ferry. Driving under it takes ten minutes, with a few hours queuing. We opt for driving under it. It´s chaos as the four lanes merge into the single lane tunnel. You can't get a fag packet between you and the vehicle in front. I´m driving but as the clutch in Lizzybus is so heavy and killing my knee, I nudge the wreck of a car in front. The driver and passenger both get out, pointing to a very rusty dent in their boot. This is damage apparently caused by Lizzybus. We laugh at them and get back into Lizzybus. By now, several cars have swung around us, blocking us in, but once they realise we're not going to fall for this and that they are losing their place in the queue, they give up.

It's terrifyingly thrilling driving through the tunnel. Surprisingly it has overhead lights; not surprisingly, most of them don't work and the ones that do are coated in thick black soot. People are still driving without headlights, tailgating, accelerating. With the screeching of brakes and broken exhausts that sound like jet engines, the noise is something else. The concrete sides of the tunnel are covered in gouges where vehicles either misjudged or got shunted. I'm regretting it's me in the driving seat, wishing I had insisted David drive. Since my meltdown in Paris and refusal to drive again until we reached Africa, I've agreed to take on the morning shift come what may, and right now it's 'my shift'.

Despite my initial failed attempts at scuba diving, I did eventually fall in love with the underwater world of wonder. This resulted in us taking lots of cheap diving holidays to Sharm el-Sheik in Egypt and I can't believe that is exactly where we are heading now Sharm el-Sheik. It's here we will wait it out whilst we see what happens in Syria.

It's so strange being here, even more so in that we drove here via Africa. It's disturbing seeing the places where we used to eat and drink closed or empty due to a terrorist attack, plane bombing, shark attack, the Egyptian Revolution, and the recession throughout Europe. Along the main highway, soldiers are posted every kilometre as former President Mubarak is in the hospital here with a suspected heart attack. I smile at myself writing this, like I think I'm in the middle of some war zone, but the reality is, we are. With The Arab Spring wave of anti-government protests, uprisings and armed rebellions spreading across much of the Arab world, the world David and I are driving alone through. I imagine the headlines: couple from England with an idea to drive a Land Rover around the world have been kidnapped, murdered, blown up or the likes.

I can assure you, nothing in any of the thoughts I might have had about this journey involved getting mixed up in anything, least of all such conflict. Stuff like this just played in the background on the BBC news whilst I ironed David's shirts for work. Not for one single minute did I ever imagine myself in the middle of it. Yes, I disliked my job, the rain, the routine, but I still made the most of my life and quite liked being alive. If someone had suggested I drive around the world in a Land Rover with David whilst conflict raged about us, I know absolutely I would never ever have agreed, and I am in total disbelief that that's where I am.

We book a month at the same all-inclusive hotel we used to stay in for our diving holidays at less than thirty dollars a day. It's a safe haven to recharge our batteries and assess the situation, to decide if we really can or want to continue with this journey, or to accept it's just too dangerous. Is it time to admit defeat, to ship Lizzybus back from Alexandria, to re-think our plans, our goals, our dreams? Is it time to go home? I know if we did, we would never set off again. Needing somewhere to live in England, we would lose the rental income and have to go back to work. Would we be sucked back into our life that was, telling ourselves that we'd had our 'little' adventure, that it's time to put all that 'nonsense' behind us and get on with normal life? But of course, our life now is our normal.

So, we wait it out in our second floor en-suite room with its balcony overlooking the pool framed by vibrant red bougainvillea. The tiny gecko behind the mirror; will be my friend, a reminder of the one in the cross member of Lizzybus, living off our ant infestation.

CHAPTER 10

ARMED REBELLIONS AND CIVIL WARS

Six weeks have passed here in our all-inclusive air-conditioned room in Egypt. David turned fifty and for his birthday the Seniors paid for a diving course, so David spent his days out on the boats to qualify as a Dive Master. We are both a little heavier on our all-inclusive diet and have an all-over tan, rather than just a t-shirt tan. David, suffering with toothache from all the diving, has had his first filling. It's been good having the pressure taken off us, to be able to forget about all this driving around the world and Arab Spring stuff, but we're getting restless. There's also been the added bonus of only spending thirty of our sixty pound a day budget, we've been able to put over a thousand pounds back in the pot. Most people here are on their one or two week holiday ask us the same question over and over, 'How long will it take?' The answer lodges in my throat like a fish bone, firstly because we have no real idea - days, weeks, months, years - but mainly because of the distinct possibility it might never happen.

Going into our third year since setting off from a rainy Brum (Birmingham to non-Brummies), it seems like yesterday, whilst a lifetime ago. The civil unrest in Syria is worsening and now referred to as an armed rebellion or civil war. We're not exactly sure what all this will mean for us, but the reports coming out of Syria are that foreigners are being attacked, detained, tortured or killed. Wow, I don't fancy any one of those. Yes, we witnessed riots in Cairo and, for sure, foreigners are more at risk, but there's always been risk. We're missing our life of adventure, adversity and challenge.

I think of the last day of a holiday and the prospect of returning to the rain of England and work. If someone had said to me then "you can stay here forever", I would have thought it was everything I ever wanted. But that's what holidays do, everything about them is not real. You imagine it being everything you ever wanted, but if every day was like this for the rest of your life, you would remember only the sunny days, the green meadows of England, your family, friends and colleagues, rules and language you understood. You would miss it - I miss it.

We used to come here on a package holiday for our week's diving, meeting everyone only on arrival and departure day, the rest of the time we were out diving. Now we see the people arrive, dragging humongous suitcases bulging with shoes, clothes and bottle after bottle of potions and lotions, spending all day every day around the pool and bar. On leaving, having bought half of Sharm El-Sheikh's tat and finding they can't fit it into their already overstuffed suitcases, they donate it to us. I have pairs of glittery flip-flops, shorts, t-shirts, hats, dresses, and half a chemist's shop of sunscreen, diarrhoea tablets and hangover remedies, with no use for them whatsoever, or any idea how they will fit in Lizzybus, but I can't bring myself to just throw them away.

In the pit of our stomachs, we don't think getting to Syria will be that bad and sort of know we are going to give it a go. We haven't come this far to give up without a fight, although a fight is the last thing we want, but it does beg the question "why are we so focused on Syria?" It's because we want to get to Pakistan, India and Bangladesh and going through Syria would take us into Turkey (avoiding Israel, Saudi Arabia and Iraq) then on to Iran and Pakistan.

Jordan, Syria, Turkey, Iran, Arab Springs, Gulf of Aqaba, armed rebellions, civil wars - what could possibly go wrong?

I feel incredibly emotional being waved off by the hotel staff and the latest group of guests, feeling we might be on our way to the gallows. Leaving the safety of this little haven heading into a known of the unknown, is full of both dread and joy. Following the coast, Israel would have been our next country, but having an Israeli stamp in your passport means you absolutely will be refused entry into Syria and that's why we're going via Jordan.

Heading now for Port Nuweiba, I'm looking forward to the two-hour Aqaba ferry crossing over to Jordan. Driving alone once more through this stunning desert wilderness, I´m overwhelmed with a feeling of being home. Camping on the shores of the Red Sea, in the distance we see Jordan and Saudi Arabia. The sea is a shimmering aqua blue and mill pond smooth. We snorkel over a seabed carpeted in swaying grass with coral pinnacles full of clown fish (think Nemo), puffer fish, lionfish and eels. A huge eagle ray casts a shadow over us as it swims past, on looking up we see a turtle flapping by. It's paradise and I intend to hold it in my memory for as long as I possibly can.

The scene we find at Nuweiba Port is as frenetic and disorganised as when we arrived at the port of Aswan, only twice its size. It's a sprawling jumbled mess of buildings, overloaded trucks and vehicles, mostly broken down and abandoned. Getting past them is the first task, but we know to follow the taxi drivers. With it being a dock, I thought it would have cranes and forklift trucks, but from what I can see the cargo here is loaded and unloaded manually by an army of skinny men with metal cages, the sort you find full of guests' suitcases in the hotel lobby. It's hard thing to watch the daily struggle of these men pulling and pushing those cages in the blistering heat with such tiny wheels over broken concrete. With no fixer, it's down to us and this is where David comes into his own - with Lizzybus still on Egyptian plates, immigration and the Carnet de Passage to complete.

Just at the point of collapse physically and mentally, disappointed they won't let us keep the Egyptian number plates, we sit amongst the chaos eating a boiled egg with a sprinkling of the salt I'm now fully aware I need after my fainting incidents in Africa. The queue begins to move and we're more than triumphant on making it onto the ferry. Most importantly, unlike our Nile crossing, Lizzybus is on the ferry with us! Just wow! It's like we've been transported to another planet. This ferry has clean flushing toilets, soap and a hand dryer, leatherette recliner seats, air-conditioning and even a little café, where we spend the last of our Egyptian money on drinks and crisps. Our passports along with the Carnet de Passage, like our Nile crossing from the Sudan into Egypt, are handed in on boarding as immigration needs to be done, which confuses me as I thought we had done all that in Nuweiba, but I can't be bothered to question it.

Arriving at Aqaba, Jordan, it's just like when crossing any no man's land albeit by sea - the difference is so noticeable. It's organised and clean, vehicles are directed into lanes with painted white lines and put through a vehicle x-ray machine. There are no money changers, no cashpoints, no beggars or sellers of anything. Having spent the last of our Egyptian pounds on board, and with dollars or euros not accepted, we have no way to pay the import fee or to get local insurance. Never mind armed rebellion and civil wars, this is our war. It's pitch black, all the other vehicles have long gone, and they are refusing to let us through or help. We're literally on the edge of insanity with all hope gone when from the shadows a man appears offering to change enough dollars at a made-up exchange rate to pay the fee. We couldn't care less what rate - we're so incredibly grateful to him.

It's all too much for me and I just sob with tiredness and hunger. We think all the offices are closed and that we're going to be stuck here all night, but the man who changed our dollars must have been from Immigration as he opens a side door into a little office where two other men are sitting. They stamp what needs stamping we pay what needs paying, and even get local insurance. Finally, driving out of the gates and into our first night here in Jordan. Emotionally and physically drained, there is no sense of relief - we're too numb for any sense of anything.

Jordan, a country of deserts, mountains, and one of the new seven wonders of the world - the sandstone city of Petra. Despite being in a region with a history of conflict, Jordan is known as the 'quiet house in a noisy neighbourhood'. With the road taking us deep into the desert, thirty minutes later, exhausted, we pull over to camp and crawl into the roof tent, letting our life as we know it settle back around us. It feels comforting, but neither of us can shake this sinking feeling of it being the calm before the storm. And how right we were, but not for the reasons we thought.

We're heading now towards the Syrian Embassy in Amman, the capital, for visas we're not even sure are being issued with the conflict worsening and countries closing their borders. We're in up-beat mode, driving through the desert on immaculate tarmac roads, eating our breakfast apple, when the silence is shattered by an almighty bang and the sound of grinding metal followed by a lack of power.

Lizzybus is broken!

I know it's bad when David slings his half-eaten apple into the desert cursing 'pile of shit Land Rover'. We have no local SIM-card, no local money, and no other vehicle has passed us all morning. Mechanic David, who constantly reminds me he is not a 'mechanic', crawls underneath. I put out warning triangles despite there being no other vehicles - it makes me feel like I'm doing something. I´m still not up to speed with all the stuff that gets Lizzybus to where she needs to get, but transfer box and it driving the axles and wheels is mentioned. David removes the long chunk of metal prop shaft, throwing it into the back of Lizzybus before locking the diffs, so we can at least move forward. I apologise right now to David for my reporting of this, to the mechanics amongst you who know better, and to those of you who couldn't care less.

Breakdowns on this journey are a constant and just like border crossings, they are all learning curves, but at the same time they destroy the confidence in our, or should I say David's, mechanical ability, but worse in Lizzybus. If the temporary fix doesn't work, we really are in shit street. I think I´m a little traumatised with everything we're going through, the almighty bang shattering my already fragile nerves. Neither David nor I could ever admit our true worries to each other, but I know David is also on the edge. Setting off once more at a snail's pace, Lizzybus struggles against the gale force wind. Above its howling, we hear another metallic related noise, more of a clatter than a bang. I see in the wing mirror a melon size piece of metal bouncing away down the carriageway. It picks up speed as I run after it, panting with the effort, until I catch up and knock it over with my foot. Picking it up, it's red hot and burns my hands so I roll it back. David, caring diddly squat about my blistered hands, tells me to 'throw it in the back with the other pile of shit crap'.

Apparently, it's the transmission break drum. All I know is it affects the already useless handbrake, and there are possibly more bits of Lizzybus inside her than attached. I think about all the organs that can be taken out of our bodies that we can live without - spleen, kidney, gallbladder, stomach, lung, reproductive organs, appendix, even half a brain. Loosing half a brain might be a problem for David and I as I´m convinced we only have half a brain between us or surely, we would never be in this situation? That is, on a highway somewhere in Jordan, heading for Amman, with no phone, no local money and half of Lizzybus slung in the back.

Pressing on in silence I´m full of self-pity with my blistered oily hands unaware it's about to get worse but find out when we hear a whining noise. From past experience, we know this is a bearing. Suddenly, on this road of nothingness, three little huts appear, the middle one is a garage. David, overwhelmed and in panic mode, focused only on fixing the bearing, pulls up outside the garage, helped himself to their bottle jack and started changing the inner and outer bearings from his spares. I feel nauseous and weak and collapse in the dirt and shade of the huts. Watching is all I can do. A little group of men surround David, passing him hammers and water, putting down pieces of cardboard for him to sit on and using other bits to shade him from the midday sun. This kindness from strangers soothes me. An hour later, the repairs finished, we cannot offer them anything as we don't even have local money. But they don't ask, they just wave us off with a plastic bag of homemade lemonade and a warm deliciously mouthwatering flatbread. This injection of sugar feels like a drug coursing through my veins and the aroma from the bread reminds me of a Sunday morning at home with my mother baking. Prop shafts, transfer boxes, bearings, visas, civil wars, are all lost in that first delicious mouthful.

It's been another long, long day. We crawl into Amman as dusk falls. Like many major cities, it's gridlocked and confusing. We book a room at a local hostel where they assure us Lizzybus will be quite safe parked on the street. The room is little more than a broom cupboard, with a single hanging light bulb and yellowed blistered gloss painted walls. The tiled en-suite has a protruding pipe for a shower - with no shower head - and a squat toilet. We're both so exhausted, we're beyond caring about our intensive care patient Lizzybus, visas for Syria, or wars. We just need some sleep.

It seems to me that David and I take it in turns to be positive or negative. Today I wake up feeling positive whilst David sinks into a pit of despair, unable even to eat the included boiled egg, cheese triangle and flatbread breakfast served on a plastic tablecloth in the litter strewn communal main room. I know from experience David is able to endure anything, but when his mistress Lizzybus is sick, it's like an actual betrayal tantamount to being cheated on. I want to scream and shout, 'What the hell did you expect when taking an old Land Rover and driving it around the world?' But I don't. I eat both boiled eggs and smoke a cigarette.

Lizzybus can be driven, just, but for now we prioritise getting the visa applications in for Syria over getting her looked at. We take a taxi to the Embassy and once there, we get bad news: under no circumstances whatsoever can a visa for Syria be issued anywhere other than in our home country! I don't swear, but right now one word is going over and over in my head - we're f**ked. David loses the plot and comes up with some crazy idea to drive to the border and ask there. Nothing I say is going to dissuade him. We take the taxi back to the hostel, climb into a crippled Lizzybus and set off for the border. I'm in disbelief and seething inside at this madness. Firstly, we're in a broken Lizzybus and secondly there's no way they'll let us take a nice little stroll across no man's land to the Syrian border to ask the question "Will you issue us with a visa please?". But he is a man at the end of his tether and beyond reasoning with.

As the nominated driver in cities, I´m driving Lizzybus now with no drum thing, prop shaft or handbrake, on roads going here, there and everywhere. I feel, not for the first time, a physical aggression towards David as he shouts directions at me. I could quite happily not just slap him across the face, but punch him in it; in fact, I think that would feel bloody amazing right now.

Amman is built from beautiful sandstone rock with a maze of steep narrow streets. Without a handbrake in a sickly Lizzybus, it's terrifying and not long before we're lost as the geriatric Garmin loses satellites more than it finds them. Navigator David throws the basic map onto the dashboard, swearing, as finally he accepts how futile and flawed this mission is.

Out of everything we've been through, this is our lowest point. My aggression towards David turns to hurting for him, knowing this could be the end of the road for us. Yes, we're both exhausted from the lack of sleep, food and living on our nerves, but it's the hopelessness that destroys us. Sat in silence looking out of the Lizzybus window partially blocked by the spare wheel at what was our world, we realise we do have one last throw of the dice, one last thread of hope. We could send our passports back to England via courier.

Reading this now, I think both David and I had lost all reasoning, it's hard to imagine the pressure we were both under. To even think of being in a country, especially one in the Middle East, without passports is incredulous to me now. When people become so focused on the end goal, they lose all sight of the potential consequences.

The oh-so familiar yellow sign with the bright red DHL letters convinces us that as a German based company entrusted to send precious documents all over the world, all will be fine. The very helpful and efficient man behind the desk gave us even more confidence by printing copies of our documents for ourselves, even phoning a local Land Rover garage for Lizzybus. We walked out like two naughty kids, feeling we had got one over on them, whoever they are. We'll see who can't get a visa! Then the reality of our situation sinks in. We are here in Amman, Jordan, with no passports, no visa for our next country, unable to go back to Egypt the country we've just left, in a crippled Lizzybus, in the middle of what is now officially 'The Arab Spring' with anti-government protests and armed rebellions happening across all the countries making up the Arab World, the countries we're intending to drive through alone in our Lizzybus. I´ve said over and over, and never more so than right now, how the hell is it me here in the middle of all this?

Back at our hostel, our room has been changed to an equally cell-like one, but one where the water no longer floods the already mouldy carpet every time you have a shower but drains away. David's mood has lifted slightly as we have some sort of plan in place, albeit a potentially flawed one, but what has really helped is having a contact for his mistress and that's where we're heading. One street in we realise the map is back at the hostel. As I´m driving I drop David off at the door and make a U-turn ready for when he comes out. I get swept up in all the traffic in the one-way system until I'm totally lost. Pulling over I go into a complete meltdown and sit crying - I don't even know the name of the hostel. The only thing I do know is that the DHL office is just around the corner from the hostel and the man there told us that if we write 'DHL Office Downtown Amman' as the return address, it will get back to us.

I go into a shop and ask the English-speaking owner if he could please get me a taxi I can follow to 'DHL Office Downtown Amman' where I know I can find my way back to the hostel, to David and to the money to pay for it. Following the taxi, I forget all about Lizzybus being sick with one aim in life now, to stick to him like glue. I even drive through red lights when my fuddled brain starts sending alarm signals that we are leaving the city and heading out into the desert. I´m terrified, but a sort of self-preservation kicks in and at the next set of traffic lights, when I see him go straight ahead, I turn off with a horrid screech. The screeching is not tyres on tarmac but gears and locked diffs. I hate doing this to Lizzybus but feel it's her life or mine. Now in a blind panic I know I need to head back towards the city. I´m not sure what's upsetting me most right now, being lost or the thought David will finally lose the plot when he finds me and Lizzybus gone.

I know how fear and panic completely takes over any logical decision-making, but I suddenly have a light bulb moment. I realise that if I look at 'recently found' on the geriatric sat-nav, which I now love more than life because for once it picks up a signal, I will at least know the name of the hostel. This has the same effect as throwing a life jacket to a drowning man and it settles me enough to allow me to think. Somehow, two hours after making a U-turn, I find my way back. We're both devastated by this; wars, visas, passports are nothing compared to being without each other. Even the hostel manager was worried, he makes us both the blackest sweetest coffee to calm our nerves. We drink it in our silent trauma.

Setting off once more, we find Lizzybus has a flat tyre. I shudder. Had this of happened whilst I was 'lost', it would have been a very different story. Having had to deal with many punctures on this journey, it takes only minutes for us to change the tyre, but not wanting to inflict any more trauma on Lizzybus, we take a taxi to the Land Rover garage only to find it shut.

As the sun sets on the streets of Amman, every inch of pavement fills with plastic chairs, boxes, benches, anything that can be sat on. Ramadan, the ninth month of the Islamic lunar calendar is a time of fasting, reflection and prayer, broken each evening at sunset. Although not Muslim, we're welcomed to join the breaking of the fast with the locals and their families. It's magical and exactly what we need after such a traumatic day. Within minutes of the sun setting, everyone eats. Tables groan with flatbreads, falafel, salads, mansaf lamb cooked in a fermented yogurt sauce, and whole fish. It's food for sharing - my favourite way of eating - and totally delicious.

Today, after dropping Lizzybus off at the Land Rover garage, we kill time walking the streets of Amman as we're not allowed into the workshop, but being Ramadan the cafes, bars and restaurants are closed. David can't settle - he hates anyone working on Lizzybus without him being there. Whilst getting Lizzybus ready for this journey, earning the money to fund it meant we had no time to work on her, so we'd made the decision to get some work done at a 'specialist overland preparation company' in England. It was a disaster. Overcharged with shoddy work, David vowed never to let her be worked on again without him being present. He lasts thirty minutes before we're back at the garage, persuading them to let him supervise. I smile and sit watching him from the little reception area. A new heavy duty half shaft, drive flanges, break disc, stub axel, and lots of other things from David's spares and their parts department are changed or fitted. I see some of the worry etched across David's face lifting as he stands a little straighter.

Lizzybus then has a full service with oil changes and greasing, including nipples and bearings. The next stop is to get the two punctured tyres repaired and a replacement battery. I've not really gone on about the battery issue, but ever since David fitted the battery monitor thing with its flashing lights and irritating bleeping, it has indicated that one of the two batteries was not charging. What an incredibly wonderful day. Even though we have an empty wallet, we got the punctures fixed, a new battery and, most importantly, Lizzybus is mechanically sound. This is better than a spa day and the only sort of shopping I like - that of spare Lizzybus parts. Back out on the streets of Amman once more, we join the locals and their families breaking the fast.

Come on, we're in Jordan, one of the most peaceful countries in the Arab world. With our passports on the way to the Syrian Embassy in England and at least three weeks before we get them back, confidence in Lizzybus restored, we're going off to explore. In the middle of this country and its neighbour Israel is a sea, not any old sea but The Dead Sea, the lowest point on earth. It's a hypersaline (salty) sea and stunningly beautiful with the salt giving it a crystallised shoreline, tricking the mind into believing it's ice. We wade in to just above our knees when this natural phenomenon lifts us off our feet so we float around on our backs like otters. Looking back, we see Lizzybus framed by mountains against a gorgeous blue sky; we titter and float, float and titter, swirling each other round like bobbing corks. The water splashing into our eyes stings like acid, we laugh at each other's pain.

Back at Lizzybus, we use all our forty litres of water trying to wash the salt off us, but to no avail. We leave a salt crust outline on the seats and our faces have their own salt mask which cracks each time we laugh, sprinkling us in salt. This area has a little bit of tourism due to the Dead Sea, with a small collection of resorts and hotels. There's also a beautiful campsite with showers, pool and stunning views which we book into for a few days.

It would be fair to say that I'm beginning to understand David's passion for rocks and their formation, even becoming mildly interested in the earth and its shifting tectonic plates, but I'm not fascinated. Today we're in Wadi Rum, or Valley of the Moon, driving along barely distinguishable tracks of deep sand through sweeping valleys of cherry blossom coloured sandstone formed from wind and desert sand. It is a hauntingly beautiful place, but several hours in David wants to keep going to where even more spectacular rock forms await us, but I've had

David and Lizzybus at Wadi Rum, Jordan

enough. Although some faith in Lizzybus has been restored, it's still a fragile one; if we get stuck here we're done for. I refuse to go any further. In my old life I was full of confidence in my abilities, but here I've taken a back seat as far as routes and decisions are concerned for very good reasons. My sense of direction and the world around me is not my strength, unlike David who is quite amazing. It's not just our focus that's changed, but how it is changing us. I am focused on the end goal of driving around the world; David is focused on just driving and it never finishing.

We camp at the base of a peach and ochre-coloured hillock where wind and time has created a magnificent sweeping archway. As I'm writing this, I can see camels in the distance. Above me, David is stood in the archway with a rising moon and a setting sun. I understand why it's referred to as the Valley of the Moon because I no longer feel I'm on earth. We might have different objectives and strengths, but right now, in this moment, we are united, humbled and inspired by the sheer magnitude and might of nature.

The next day, David is unwilling to let go of the need to explore and we head further into Wadi Rum, pushing Lizzybus to her limit in the deepening sand. Discovering a split pipe to the compressor, we know if we let the tyre pressures down for sand driving, we have no way of pumping them back up. Learning to drive in sand was a 'lesson' we had in Mauritania on agreeing to go in a four-vehicle convoy with Canadian Richard and his ex-military German friends following the Iron Ore railway. It was at the beginning of this journey and a three-day ordeal that nearly broke us and Lizzybus, but once it was over, we realised how amazing it was. We learned a lot - no I lie, we learned everything about sand driving from them and they remain good friends. So, knowing how important tyre pressures are, we retreat, much to David's disappointment and my relief.

Bush camping for another night takes us back to a cup of water each for cleaning teeth and washing pits and bits and wiping dirty plates over with a cloth. I'm sometimes astonished by how basic our life has become. The focus is on water, food and shelter - okay, beer and diesel is on that list too. I think we're becoming feral as this feels right and the prospect of being back in the parallel universe feels wrong, not wanting to be consumed by it. With no internet or phone coverage, relying on yourself is liberating and I forgot long ago to be scared, most of the time. I understand why people disappear to a desert island, or remote forests and distant lands. I don't miss for one single minute shoes, clothes, handbags, but I do miss conversation, laughter and the camaraderie of people. I´m so conflicted as many times I feel desperately alone and lonely, whilst at others I'm filled with a sense of belonging.

In a remote mountain basin surrounded by desert is the sandstone city of Petra or Rose City, named for its stunning rose-coloured rock. Over two thousand years ago, Petra was the capital of the Arab Nabataeans' trading empire, a rock landmass torn apart by tectonic plates (see David, some of your teaching has sunk in). It truly is a vast city on a grand scale, made possible by the Nabataeans' irrigation systems. Voted in 2007 as one of the New Seven Wonders of the World, it is visited by hundreds of thousands of people every year.

The main access to the city is through a narrow gorge, the Siq, which leads directly to the Al-Khazneh, or Treasury, an imposing elaborately carved façade, possibly built as a royal mausoleum. You can pass through the Siq on a donkey, on a camel, or on foot; we walk. The city is dotted with palaces, temples, tombs, storerooms and stables, carved into the sandstone cliffs as far as the eye can see, or your legs can walk, or donkey or camel can carry you. It's still not known why this city was ever abandoned, which just adds to its mystique.

Next to Petra is Little Petra, Siq al-Barid, 'the cold canyon', which became a place to stay for visiting traders or passing Bedouin nomads, and tonight, Jayne David and Lizzybus. Alone in the roof tent, looking out over the remains of this ancient civilization, I imagine the world as it was then, amongst the cave dwellers.

We are driving now along the King's Highway heading back to Amman, a 3,000-year-old trade route through the spine of Jordan. The same road used by the Israelites looking for the Promised Land, Nabataean nomads, Romans, Christian Crusaders, and Muslims on pilgrimages to Mecca.

We feel if not quite reborn, certainly rejuvenated after the most wonderful few weeks. This land, this country and its people are welcoming, but we can no longer ignore our situation and our future which depends on getting visas for Syria. Based on past experiences, we worry that our applications could be turned down by something as simple as not having a paper clip on them. At the hostel that initially felt like a prison cell, the relaxed friendly atmosphere and portly, inky black-haired, fag-puffing manager make it bearable. Still, we're beginning to lose hope of ever continuing this journey, and start looking at alternatives to get us and Lizzybus back to England.

It's a real low point, made worse for me as I have an ear infection. A mixture of blood and puss seeps onto the towel I've laid over the pillow, my teeth and eyes ache, my head feels like it will explode. I'm so full of self-pity the idea of going home is most appealing. I tell myself I'm satisfied and content with what I have already seen and experienced and that I don't want or need to do anymore. Having got through the supposedly toughest leg, that of west coast Africa, if we'd had anything to prove - which we didn't - we have proved it, and now have a genuine reason to give up.

It's an idea I like a lot more than I should, but then I remember my daughter and son-in-law are flying out to Turkey (the next country after Syria) and the thought of not being there with them is unthinkable.

CHAPTER 11

ANARCHY ON THE STREETS OF LONDON

Today, in our hands we are not only holding our passports, but passports that have a Syrian visa in them. It's a momentous victory but we know it's only one battle in what has become our war. We see on the tiny hostel television reports of heavy rioting and looting. It's not Syria or in fact any of the Arab world, it's London, following the death of Mark Duggan, shot by police from Operation Trident, an anti-crime unit. We see scenes of looting and arson across the whole of England. People are losing their lives trying to protect their businesses and homes. It's sickening and quite unbelievable.

Syria, despite being the supposed friendliest, most hospitable rogue state on earth, is reportedly falling ever deeper into conflict. It's almost impossible to get any real information since the blocking of social media and news reporting. Today we head for the Syrian border. It's kind of like visiting the dentist. You know you have to, but you would much rather not. Having been stamped out of Jordan, we are now driving across the tarmac of no man's land to the Syrian border. If we are refused entry, we are stuffed.

What we find is a fully computerised system into which our passport information is fed. The passports are then page by page scrutinised by the four men in immigration. We are questioned in detail as to our route here, and where we intend to go in their country. Having established we never went into Israel, we feel an admiration from them for us and our journey. With no more than a cursory search of Lizzybus, we are officially stamped into Syria. Immigration and police gather around us for the flag sticking on ceremony, our hands are shaken, we are on our way, we did it.

Syria is one of the oldest civilizations in the world. The Arab Spring uprising is becoming a civil war, a war displacing millions of people which continues to this day. We focus now having got into Syria on getting through it. I see Syria as the bridge taking us to:

Turkey, Iran, Pakistan, India and Bangladesh.

Only when reaching Bangladesh will we decide on our route going forward, dependent on visas and conflicts.

It's unsettling at first, with all the roadblocks manned by police or military, but extraordinary in that they just wave us through. We're heading for Homs via the capital Damascus. When filling up with diesel the locals advise us to avoid Damascus as people have been killed in the recent riots there. With the sun sinking below our sun visor forcing us to squint we pull over at a truck stop. Asking the owner who speaks good English if we can camp there overnight, although apologetic, he says it's too dangerous. It's been a long hard day; tired and irritable we don't feel safe bush camping. In the distance we see the Krak des Chevaliers Crusader fort, "the finest castle in the world" according to Lawrence of Arabia.

In the grounds of this castle is a makeshift camp where we find a group of refugees fleeing the city. They invite us to camp with them. Seeing the direct effect of conflict on people and their families is hard, we become part of their struggles. It's still early when David and I, exhausted from the trauma and the relief of the day, go to bed. An hour later, needing a pee, I make my way to the squat toilet. On my way back the women, sitting separately from the men, invite me to sit and eat with them. None of them speaks English but that doesn't matter. They feed me the most delicious flat bread, chicken, lentils, and a salad of chopped onion and herbs. An hour later I climb back into the roof tent waking David to tell him all about my adventure. He is so exhausted he ignores me and rolls over. I don't care, I´m full to the brim of delicious food and can see "the finest castle in the world" bathed in hauntingly beautiful moonlight.

Despite knowing we should press on; we visit this imposing medieval castle, rebuilt after an earthquake. The rebuilt outer wall looks like curtains drawn protectively around it. It's one of five Crusader castles guarding what was known as the Homs Gap. As an English person used to the odd castle or two, it's most impressive and moving. I can feel all its history and trauma through its walls. Another moving now, this time moving on. On the main highway, when stopping to check our map, we are blocked in by a police car to the front and two motor bikes at the rear.

Unsure of what it's all about, we just point to the border on our map, they indicate for us to follow them. Now in the middle of this cavalcade, with sirens and flashing blue lights, the traffic parts, we even drive through red traffic lights. Several kilometres later they pull over, pointing out the road ahead saying it will take us directly to the border. We give them two cans of ice-cold coke; they ask if we have any whisky. We don't, but would never admit to it if we had.

We've done it, we have crossed war-torn Syria alone in our Lizzybus and have made it to the Turkish border alive. This might seem overdramatic, but against all the advice, the weeks holed up in Egypt and Amman, sending passports back to England for the visas we never thought we would get, in a temperamental Lizzybus, we really did it!

Firstly, who knew Syria was such a small country? Not me, and secondly, just how friendly the people would be? We have loved Syria and feel cheated we couldn't have explored it more. Having achieved something so significant, the achievement is only a personal one to us. It's only the end of that ordeal and the beginning of the next. I find this the hardest. There is no glass of champagne or hordes of journalists to document this achievement. We are just as dirty, just as tired, I´m just as needy for conversation or a little romance. We still live in a square box. No matter how we smell, how intimate we are, the reward was from its people. Despite them seeing the country they love being destroyed, they welcomed us with kindness and generosity.

Turkey, the heart of the Ottoman Empire with nineteen world heritage sites, historical cities, a sparkling coastline, and stunning landscapes. A supposedly safe country with friendly people. It's known for the kebab, but surprisingly is one of the biggest exporters of cherries.

Let's get on with getting on with this journey. Having made it to Turkey, the focus is on Fethiye, to meet Adele and James, almost one thousand kilometres away. Driving on tarmac roads with no roadblocks, we make good progress. The sinking sun reminds us we need to get off it before being swallowed up in darkness. We see an unfenced lemon grove beside an open concrete irrigation system. A good place to camp. A lot of the choices we make on this journey are made on gut instinct. An hour later with the tent erect and a vegetable stew hissing away in the pressure cooker, we crack open a beer. For the first time in a long time, we feel relaxed and worry free. that was until we heard, before seeing a motorbike.

It parks a little away from us, the man on it looked over at us then drove off. We're not quite sure what to do. Having another beer seems like a good idea. Ten minutes later he is back, with two more motorbikes and four men. Have we been too complacent? Are we about, at best, to be moved on, at worst robbed? It's one of those hovering moments. Taking another swig of beer, we realise they are smiling at us. With barely a word in common, we are now sat crossed-legged on the carpet laid out on a raised wooden platform. Onto this a cotton chequered cloth is put and covered with olives, fresh bread, meat and cheese.

I ponder, with Google Translate now, how different this might have been. Here's the thing, humans can communicate through gestures, smiles and laughter. It's hysterical as David has a full-on conversation with them. No one has a clue what each is saying. It doesn't matter. Before leaving, a man drinks from the irrigation pipe, giving us a thumbs up as a gesture we can use it.

It's morning. David in just his boxers is washing in the irrigation water. The lone man who first arrived on his Honda is back. He has a bagful of fresh bread, salted sunflower seeds, lemons, pomegranates, figs, and a pop bottle full of pickled olives.

Turkey, we love you already.

Pressing on, we pass mile after mile of skyscraper hotels on triple lane highways. The cost of fuel is the highest in any country so far, using all our daily budget just to fill up, we're thankful to find places to bush camp. Tonight, it's behind the walls of a graveyard. David is removing the grille and other stuff from the front end of Lizzybus to get at the jammed bonnet catch so he can check the oil. I'm irritated beyond belief. This little job means everything is spread everywhere and covered in oil and grease. With little to no water to wash tools or us, I want to scream. I leave him to it and go off for a walk amongst the dead, venting my frustrations on silent ears.

On flat open roads free of traffic with distant slumbering mountains, we pull over for a pee. Starting Lizzybus back up, she clicks but nothing more. The relay plug that allows the engine to turn has rotted and corroded (one thing David does not have in his spares). This tiny square inch lump of plastic immobilizes us and nearly tips us over the edge. We need to bump start her but we're alone and it's impossible for us to push her. An old tractor appears, the driver looking as old as his tractor let us attach to him for a tow, Lizzybus starts immediately. He trundles off to tend his lemon trees without a care in the world.

Having suffered from intermittent starting issues with Lizzybus for a while, this is different, this is permanent, it brings a whole other level of worry. I don't think either of us has ever stalled Lizzybus, but it's a real possibility now especially as we're facing a lot more traffic.

We arrive a day later than planned for our rendezvous with Adele and James to find them soaking up the sun and sipping cocktails around the pool in their all-inclusive hotel. As I hug my daughter, I'm aware of her clean intoxicating smell and my engine oil and earth one. It's not the comfort I thought it would be. Sat drinking beer around the pool I feel uncomfortable in my sun-bleached shirt and shorts, oil-filled nails and afro frizz hair. I'm relieved we're not staying at this hotel, but in my old boss Gavin´s villa twenty kilometres away.

It takes a few days, but eventually I´m able to relax and enjoy this, with the bonus of it being the four of us we can push start Lizzybus. We store our kit and go off exploring the ancient sites. I end the week as clean and aromatic as my daughter since the gift set of perfumed shower gel and body lotion, and access to washing machine and showers. All too soon they have gone, but I am not sad because they are being replaced tomorrow by my twin sister Jenny and Richard. As much as I am looking forward to seeing Jenny, I´m most excited about the new relay plug she is bringing. To smell not of oil and earth but of fresh is great, but the prospect of being able to start Lizzybus with the key, not by anyone and everyone pushing her, is next level exciting.

How different it is standing at Dalaman airport waving goodbye to Jenny and Richard from the day they arrived just two short weeks ago, when I stood with my home-made banner, crying, hugging and clinging to each other. Which is what we continued to do on and off for the whole two weeks - the two weeks spent getting pummelled at the Turkish baths, floating in rubber rings down icy cold canyon waters, slithering in volcanic mud, barbecuing on the beach to a setting sun, drinking bitter Turkish coffee, pomegranate juice and beer.

It's over, they have gone, we stand here alone.

You would imagine these pockets of old life would recharge our batteries. They do but at the same time it's like a bubble bursting to reveal our reality, derailing us. Having once been naive to the magnitude of what we were trying to do, I'm now fully aware of it.

The countries we're heading to from Turkey, Iran, Pakistan, India and Bangladesh - are all countries that seem intent on making getting into them very complicated. It's like déjà vu as the only way we can get visas for Pakistan and India is from the embassies in our own country.

Having emailed and spoken to them, we are assured that, on receipt of our passports and completed application, visas can and will be issued.

The decision is made for Jenny to take our passports back to England and to send them recorded delivery to the relevant embassy. So, just like in Jordan, we are once again without passports.

Despite Gavin letting us stay for as long as we need, our mood, like the weather changes to grey. When eventually the sun comes out, on checking the roof tent we find it sodden and mouldy. David starts sealing it where he thinks the rain might be penetrating. I know a wet patch is not necessarily where rain enters so I want all the joints sealed. David says it would look crap. I don't care what it looks like, I want a dry tent. With a tube of yacht all weather sealant, I reseal it - all. David is incandescent as, apparently, I have 'ruined the roof tent.'

This is a perfect example of how overwhelmed we are both feeling, by focusing like this on stupid insignificant stuff and ignoring the elephant in the room of passports and visas. We are incredibly grateful to have this apartment, but also feel imprisoned by it, once more in limbo. Exploring Turkey is out of the question as it's compulsory for all tourist to carry passports. Being in Lizzybus it is obvious we are tourists. We don't argue, scream or shout, just throw the occasional corrosive word at each other.

When you only have each other, when your fate is out of your hands, it's hard to give each other the support you need. I can't cope with David's 'What ifs'. I´m past the stage of just wanting to gaffer tape his mouth shut, I want to surgically remove his voice box. As it's not until we know the outcome that we can make an informed decision, why talk about it?

It's been five tension-filled boring weeks from when both embassies promised on receipt of our passports, application and supporting documentation they would issue us visas. But it was never going to be that simple, was it? On receiving them they then changed their minds, deciding we needed to be there in person. No wonder we are on the very edge of insanity, but they didn't take into account our secret weapon, retired policeman Mr T Senior. Who took the train to London armed with the printed off emails we had been sent to plead our case. It's a classic example of being real, not just languishing in the in-tray of someone's to-do list.

After many hours in the Indian and Pakistani embassies, they did agree to issuing them. That wasn't quite the end of it, as despite Mr T Senior having his own passport, police badge and proof of address, they insisted on posting our passports back to the address on the application. Which was Mr T Senior's address, delaying it a few more days, before being able to courier them out to us.

Today, here in Lemon Apartments, Turkey, in our hands we hold our passports. In these passports is not one, but two magnificent visas, one for Pakistan and one for India. We are on the move.

We're heading for Trabzon and the Iranian embassy here in Turkey, as it comes before Pakistan and India. Having applied online for a visa, generating a number, all we need to do is pay and collect it. Twenty kilometres in, the traffic is at a standstill due to a burning car. We just pull over to the shade of pine trees and eat our picnic lunch, content knowing that we have the Indian and Pakistan visas and it's only a matter of collecting and paying for our Iranian one.

We reach Pamukkale - Cotton Castle in Turkish. It's an area of high land with pearly white layered rock formations and the ancient Greek city of Hierapolis. In a campsite opposite, the setting sun bouncing off Pamukkale creates a spectacular kaleidoscope of colours. It's bitterly cold, not having any internal space to get out of the wind, and the sleet is becoming worse. I sit wrapped in a blanket under the star-filled sky writing when a Canadian couple arrives, with their ten-year-old home-schooled daughter and grumpy Jack Russell. They are teachers who, having given up their jobs, sold their home and bought a campervan with the intention to travel until the money ran out. And I've been told what David and I did was crazy?

Today, barefoot we climb the porcelain white travertine terraces of Pamukkale. This phenomenon creates thermal plunge pools and babbling streams along its way, we sit in some, paddle in others, until reaching the ruins of the ancient Greek city of Hierapolis. Hierapolis is abandoned, but it also feels neglected, overlooked for Pamukkale, very few people explore it, only adding to its charm. Looking out, we just about make out Lizzybus in the campsite below.

Back on the road, a light snowfall dusts the pine forest which glistens in the watery sun. As dusk wraps around us, we pull over into a gravel pit, in the hope it might offer some protection. It just causes a tunnel effect making it quite impossible to put the roof tent up. Not for the first time we park Lizzybus sideways to use her as a windbreak and pitch the pup tent. The ground is so hard we can't get the tent pegs in so just pile rocks over them. I wish more than life right now we could be inside Lizzybus, out of this bitterly cold biting wind. I know it's cold when I agree to zipping the sleeping bags together. David is always a good source of body heat.

We wake to a sleeting drizzle turning the chalky limestone into a thick cloggy clay. It sticks to everything, especially our shoes. We put them into plastic bags and drive on in socks. We're in the magical land of fairies. It's only chimneys and oval doors carved into the rock that gives you any clue as to the underground homes here. I'm not a bee but if I were, I would see exactly what they see when returning to my beehive - a land of honeycomb.

Driving on, the electrics blow, taking out the lights, wiper blades, indicators and heater. The heater in Lizzybus is piss poor at the best of times, but not having any heater is the next level. David changes the fuses; they immediately blow. We hear a hissing howling noise coming from the water pump (changed in Namibia), but drive on, wrapped in blankets, with no lights, windscreen wipers, indicators, or heater.

At the next town we find a small garage. On lifting the bonnet, the leg of the braai (the metal barbeque made for us in South Africa sitting over the spare wheel) catches the windscreen cracking it. On opening the back door, the key snaps off in the lock. The mechanic tries his best, but with the language it's impossible. We make the most of the log burner and being inside his garage. David decides the water pump is on its way out but working and replaces the blown fuses. I gaffer tape the cracked windscreen and we head off. It's only ten minutes before the fuses blow, the gaffer tape peels off, and the water pump whistles even louder.

Driving at night is bad, but driving at night without electrics is suicidal, with sleet that spat at us all day now snow. This whole area is magical, but we can't see it through this blanket of worry. We camp amongst what look like giant termite nests but are abandoned homes. With neither of us brave enough to strip off or wash anything, we just put another layer of clothes on and make a fire. The heat is lost to the wind, but the flickering flames are comforting. David is nursing his broken heart from the betrayal by his mistress. We sit in silence, reluctant to leave the dying embers of the fire.

My one and only grandson, Ben, is one today, but it's only the water pump, fractured windscreen and electrics I can think about. I am mesmerised by this fairy landscape and it's this that comes to our rescue. On seeing hot air balloons floating overhead, we remember yesterday in town we had seen six Land Rovers, the vehicles used to transport the hot air balloons and the tourists. No one knows more than us that being Land Rovers, they will all need parts and servicing, we intend to find out exactly where they get this done.

Their office walls are covered in stunning pictures of the landscape and hot air balloons. They tell us about a local man for running repairs one street away, or Umt Oto, a specialist in Land Rover maintenance and overland preparation, thirty kilometres away. We know our crippled Lizzybus needs more than a local man, she needs a specialist, I see this as a visit to the doctor or the hospital. We are taking Lizzybus to the hospital, for specialist care.

Two hours later in the semi-darkness that drizzle brings, we find, in the industrial area of a busy town, Umt Oto Garage, specialist in Land Rovers. It's literally like arriving at the accident and emergency department of a hospital. A team of mechanics come out of this hanger-sized garage and gather around Lizzybus. They speak little English, but it doesn't matter because the one thing they say over and over is, "No problem".

The cracked windscreen, the faulty electrics, the broken lock, the knackered water pump are all - no problem. I'm instantly in love with the tiny little eighty-year-old owner. With his red face and even redder woolly hat, he looks like one of the little gnomes who, in my imagination, live in the abandoned termite nest houses. This place has two levels, the top level being a treasure trove of every conceivable Land Rover part you, or more precisely we, could ever dream of. I'm so choked I want to cry but hold it together.

Lizzybus is taken for immediate surgery. The team of mechanics are watched over by my little gnome in his white tunic. We are given bitter Turkish coffee and invited to have lunch with them - delicious homemade pasta, fried potato cakes, yogurt, and incredibly sweet pastries. As if this was not enough, in their cosy warm office, they let me use their phone to call my grandson Ben. When I hear him say "da da", it's all too much. I'm full, I'm warm, Lizzybus is getting a complete overhaul and I'm speaking to my son and grandson. Sobs I have no control over come from deep inside me.

I apologise here once more, for people who don't know and don't want to know what I'm on about, but I know there are some who do. We have new o-rings, brake light cover, driver's door handle (eliminating the need to climb in through the passenger door), water pump, reversing light, fan belt, glow plug, bushes, bearings, back padlock, new windscreen and a big box of spares. Burnt out wires have been stripped and replaced, along with fuses. We grit our teeth waiting for the bill, three hundred dollars, including all the spares, new windscreen, a delicious lunch, and more than anything some much needed support and admiration for what we are trying to do.

It's late now, we were hoping to spend the night in the garage but decide not to push our luck. Driving out into the sleet-filled night and gridlocked traffic is made almost bearable by having lights, indicators and windscreen wipers. We really need and should book a hotel, but with the cost of fuel and repairs, we're very aware of the budget. Just outside of town, we pull over into a lay-by, I sit in the passenger seat wrapped in blankets; David braves the cold to put up the roof tent, his hands sticking to the iced metal. David makes up a packet soup and we have it with the stale bread, the hot liquid slithering down my throat is comforting. I wrap my hands around the mug, watching whisps of steam make patterns on the new windscreen.

It dropped to minus ten last night, the ice formed on the inside of the roof tent fell on us like snow every time the wind blew. This morning, the water pump is frozen and the bottle of water in the passenger foot well is a solid lump of ice. Finding myself not dead from hypothermia is a joy, but not joyous enough to stop me being very grumpy whilst cleaning my teeth using chunks of ice to swill my mouth. David, having melted some ice has a pot of coffee on; the aroma is a pleasant distraction from my mild piss smell. Back on the road with working gauges, a windscreen we can see through and no rogue engine noises (other than the rattle of a 1998 Lizzybus), the rising sun having thawed us out, the mood is upbeat. We treat ourselves to breakfast at the local service station. The bread is warm and comes with a dish of scrambled egg and salami and is quite delicious. The best is the heated toilets with soap and hot water. I sort of strip wash, without stripping, I'm now as warm as the bread hot out of the oven.

We have two mountain passes to get over before we reach the city of Trabzon to pick up our Iranian visas. Fundamentally, as mountains are natural elevations on the earth's surface, you would imagine them all the same. In fact, they are all very different due to their rock formations. This thought worries me as it's almost like some of David's fascination with rock is infecting me. Here in the foothills, the rock is of iron-infused green, changing to moody purples in the crevasses. Laid sideways it looks like shards of shattered glass. We're now in deep snow, the road following the mountain contour is on the very edge. Ahead of us, a broken-down jack-knifed lorry blocks both lanes. On one side is a mountain, on the other a sheer drop to a gushing river. We chip away the ice to make a Lizzybus-wide track, filling it with gravel dug from under the snow. Inching our way around it, we manage to miss both the truck and the rock face, or falling into the flowing river below, to me by inches, to David by several feet. But men have always had a problem with estimating length.

This little setback takes away the last of any daylight. Descending cloud makes an eerie soup of fog we can only see a metre ahead in. We know to our left is vertical rock, to our right is a raging river, and ahead a switchback ice-filled road. Then right there, as if someone had made it especially for us, we see a small clearing edged with huge boulders just enough to camp on. After another mug of soup, this time without bread, we put a bottle of water into the roof tent to stop it from freezing overnight. It was a cold night but thanks to the not exactly cloud cover, but being in the clouds, not that cold, the water is not frozen and the water pump still works. Although the rising sun has no real warmth in it, it's cheering. Looking around, we realise we are next to the local graveyard. Neither of us wants to be buried in a coffin in the ground, but if we were to be, this one clinging to the side of a mountain with a flowing river doesn't seem half bad.

We have fallen in love with Turkey, driving through towns and villages, we are greeted with smiles, thumbs up and honking. Finally arriving at Trabzon, a built-up bustling city with a salty sea breeze, I realise we have made it to the Black Sea. The Black Sea is a marginal sea, which sort of means enclosed, with the Bosporus Strait connecting it to the Mediterranean Sea. The Ural Mountains and the Caspian Sea are a natural divide to the continents of Europe and Asia. As we are heading from Turkey into Iran, it's thrilling that not only is it another country, but it is also another continent, our third continent on this journey.

It's time to find the Iranian embassy, with no maps of the area or anything on our sat nav, it's down to David and good old-fashioned navigation. Some things are too much even for him, we pay a taxi driver to let us follow him. It's a good job we did; in this sprawling city, we would have been driving around all day especially as the embassy is tucked away down a back street.

We're confident having applied online and armed with our code, it's only going to be a matter of supplying the documents and paying for the visa. Of course, that's in an ideal world, the world we now inhabit is nothing like ideal. Lengthy discussions take place as our documents are pondered over. Firstly, I will need a new passport photo with my head covered, and the fee cannot be paid here but at a nominated bank. The bank that is closed for the 'bank' holiday. The same bank that, when open, only accepts euros (we had travelled with a wad of euros to discover it was only the mighty dollar everyone wanted so swapped them for dollars), and only accepts them between three and four pm.

Armed with our euros changed from dollars with the street tout, we stand in the queue at the bank thirty minutes before the counter opens. Before we make it to the counter, a sign is put out announcing it closed. Having waited all weekend, I lose the plot and demand to see the manager who agrees to reopen it and accept our payment.

In a strange way it was a good, if not frustrating, four days. In our budget hotel room, there's hot water and an even hotter radiator, a bed with crisp white cotton sheets, soft fluffy pillows, and that distinctive smell of ironing. The same glorious smell is now coming off the two bags of laundry I dropped at reception. It's not just language, friends and family I miss, but fresh laundered linen. Not using a tank of diesel per day, we treat ourselves to a lunch of cheap local food where the taxi drivers hang out. Although today we have our passports back and another page covered with the Iranian visa, I want to stay just one more night in this domestic bliss.

CHAPTER 12

WHO NEEDS FUEL ANYWAY?

Iran (Persia), one of the world's oldest civilizations, has seen much internal and external conflict during its six thousand years' history. Ruled by Islamic Law, women should cover their head in public spaces and be accompanied. We're more worried about crossing into Iran than we were into Syria, mainly about getting fuel. At seven times bigger than the United Kingdom, we do not want to be stranded in Iran with no fuel. Pushing on to the border through driving sleet, the darkness that never lifted is now inky black. Lizzybus struggles against the gale force wind which pushes the sleet in through the rusted gaps in her doors. With woolly hats on and wrapped in our customary blankets, we regret bitterly not having fitted the diesel heater which is sitting in Mr T Senior's garage.

Knowing we won't reach the border tonight; we book a room in a cheap rundown hotel. The room has a sink, a metal framed bed with a multicolored woollen blanket, and a concrete floor. We're just grateful to be in the warmth and out of the biting wind.

This morning I´m freezing as the heating is off. Being so close to the border we feel a real change here, with the distinct lack of visible women. I refuse to use the communal showers or toilet and pee in the sink, using David's mouthwash to clean it. Now I´m laughing at David; back from the communal showers, he is shivering as the water was cold. As there are no cash machines and the American dollar is not accepted in Iran, we use the street money changers. It always makes me feel like some international money launderer. David tries to haggle, but we get a poor exchange rate, less than half - they know we are at their mercy - to end up with six million Rial (three hundred dollars), half a carrier bag of notes. I´ve always wondered what it would be like to be a millionaire - now we are one six times over.

We meet a Belgian family with three young children who've just driven through Iran from Pakistan. They confirm what we had heard that the people of Iran are incredibly friendly and welcoming. What is interesting is that their four-hundred-dollar fuel card apparently does not pay for fuel, it just gave them a fuel allowance. With supposedly half of their allowance left on the card, they give it to us on the understanding we pass it on if we don't use all of it.

We reach the border of Iran. Getting stamped out of Turkey is easy and we're sad to be leaving, getting into Iran is a lot different. In this poorly lit building, the few women I see are in full burkas, now wearing a headscarf, I pull it down over my face. It's impossible to tell who is official and who is not, but an intimidating man in a black trench coat and dark glasses saying nothing takes our Carnet de Passage and passports. David follows him into an office, shutting the door behind them, I am left standing outside.

A while later, the same man holding our passports came out heading for the exit door. Forgetting my lowly position as a woman, I follow him asking for the return of our passports. It's all quite odd as, without really looking at me he hands them over, on checking the passports, I see they had been stamped. With the door to the room David went into slightly ajar, I call him, he came out with the stamped Carnet de Passage.

Unsure of exactly what's going on, we get back in Lizzybus and drive off. We're stopped at the perimeter gate by armed security guards who take David off to a hut. I'm conflicted knowing women are not heard here, but I'm worried about David. After an hour I go to see what is going on. There is one more stamp needed, but unless we buy a diesel permit it cannot be given. We have the donated one, but not wanting to reveal this, it's stalemate. In my lowly position as a woman ignored, as respectfully as I can, I say how incredible we have been told their country is, how much we are looking forward to being here, and that this is not what we expected. I can see David wants to shut me up, and he's right as I feel an irritation from them for being spoken to like this by a woman. We both know this is a scam because the amount demanded keeps changing.

There is a point in every negotiation, however wrong or right you are, you need to accept defeat. We smile and agree to pay one hundred euros, but as we only have dollars, it's one hundred and seventy. This is not for a fuel card, just for the stamp on the sheet of paper they keep wafting in front of us. David shakes their hands, I lower my head standing behind him, we leave with a bitter taste in our mouths. Driving sleet and grey skies prematurely darkens the day. Having spent so long getting across the border and with the two hours' time difference, the insurance office is closed. Not wanting to drive on without insurance, we book a local hotel. Instead of feeling elated at making it to our thirty-seventh country and third continent, we feel worn down with dread for what lies ahead. I realise we didn't even have the flag sticking on ceremony.

It's Friday, a day of prayer not work for Muslims, meaning the insurance office is still closed. With only a two-week visa for Iran, we drive on without it. Arriving here with empty fuel tanks due to the high cost of fuel in Turkey, we fill both the tanks, to find there is only a forty litre allowance left on the donated fuel card.

I hate wearing this stupid headscarf. Unlike most Muslim women, I haven't had a lifetime of learning how to wrap it effortlessly around my head, I end up with it tied tightly under my chin to keep it from slipping off. It's astonishing how this affects me - it crushes my spirit and unsettles me, negotiations from now on will be down to David.

Sleet, hail, rain and gridlock traffic follow us over the next few days. Trying to leave a safe distance between us and the vehicle in front, giant lorries cut in and around us, spraying us in a muddy chalky film. We regret not replacing the wiper blades in Turkey. Now cracked and split from the African sun, they just smear the windscreen whilst making a teeth-jarring screech. Can this day get any worse? Yes!

Instead of being constantly overtaken and cut up, we speed up to match the flow of the traffic, only to be pulled over for speeding. They are taken aback that a woman is driving. Now I like my headscarf as I can pull it down over my face and stand behind David because all I can think about is not having insurance. They advise David to keep an eye on me and my speed and to enjoy Iran. Without asking to see our documents, no fine, no demand for money - just to enjoy Iran. Driving on through the grey drizzle, our spirits are lifted and our faith somewhat restored, thinking that what we were told about Iran might be true.

It's beginning to feel like a conspiracy; a tyre explodes and a blown fuse takes out the fuel, temperature gauge and indicators. I console myself that at least we have lights and a heater. We can't risk pulling off the highway as the verges are a thick gloopy bog, so we set about changing it whilst lorries and cars thunder past, inches from us. The warning triangles soon blow down in their bow wave and our hi-vis vests are sprayed in a filthy mixture of oil and water. I think how tough it must be for our guardian angel to keep us alive right now.

Driving on, David tells me about Iran, its ancient civilizations and extraordinary landscapes. Despite only having a two-week visa with a temperamental Lizzybus, he is determined to show me it, starting with the biggest brick-built dome in the world, the Dome of Soltaniyeh and Mausoleum. It's exquisite with turquoise blue faience tiles covering the dome and eight minarets dominating the skyline. Undergoing renovation, it's covered in scaffolding; on the roof we see men shoveling snow. It's when the sun finally comes out, we see the real beauty. The dome, iced in snow, is not just blue, but all shades of blue against the sky. You think nothing could be more beautiful until you go inside where it's breathtaking, the hand painted tile and plaster walls a vision of blues, whites and golds, topped by the gravity-defying ceiling of this octagonal building. We make it to the city of Esfahan and Iman Square, a vast courtyard area surrounded by three intricately blue-tiled mosques and an imposing palace.

Despite the lack of beer, having to wear this horrid headscarf, the experience of crossing the border, punctures and blown fuses, we are amazed by Iran and begin to feel the kindness of its people. We're in the remote mountainous region of Persepolis, the once capital of the Persian empire, with the Gate of all Nations. The gigantic carved bulls on either side, like this city, lie in ruins, destroyed by Alexander the Great whose armies conquered most of the known world of his day. We're surrounded by groups of students, girls and boys, welcoming us to their country and asking to have pictures taken with us.

We couldn't get a guidebook for Iran, David had managed to download part of one as a PDF, but it's ten years out of date. We're struggling to find a place to stay, every time we stop to look for street signs, vehicles pull alongside asking if they can help. From our experience on the west coast of Africa, any information costs money and we were not always taken to safe places, so we smile and say we're fine. Now hopelessly lost, with night settling around us, we ask for help at a fire station. One of the firemen on his way home tells us to follow him. The hotels he tries are all full, so he takes us to a Muslim prayer school for girls. As it's the weekend, the dormitories are empty and the woman caretaker says we can stay the night. She fires up an old creaking gas boiler, and not long before we have toasty warm radiators and gloriously hot showers.

Before leaving, our fireman tells us about a pizza shop on the corner and it being safe to leave Lizzybus whilst we walk to it. In the pizza shop, we're surrounded by a group of girl students who tell us how good life was under Mohammad Reza Pahlavi, the Shah, with his White Revolution which focused on modernising Iran, redistributing its wealth, and education for all. I could barely speak. What if there were secret police listening and I was drawn into this sort of conversation, a foreigner in an Islamic republic? I'm pretty sure free speech would be frowned upon, even if it was not my speech.

The girls tell me how they rebel by allowing wisps of hair to fall from their hijab (a scarf that covers the head, neck and shoulders), and wearing green in support of the White Revolution. We remember the little piece of green ribbon we found tied to the Lizzybus wing mirror at Persepolis, making us feel part of their rebellion. We admire these girls for their spirit and perfect English. When we try to pay for our pizza, the owner says it's a gift to honoured friends.

A rising sun heats the road ahead creating an eerie low-lying mist and a lake reflects the surrounding snow-capped mountains. In the distance, factories belch out black smoke so thick it obscures the sky. On reaching what we thought were snow-capped mountains, we realise it's white marble. Lorry after lorry hurtle past us, loaded with these dismantled mountains, I think of my sister awaiting the marble worktop to complete her kitchen and imagine one slab of it finding its way to her.

We can no longer ignore the fact we have run out of allowance on our fuel card, at the fuel station, we explain our situation to the man serving the fuel. He asks the lorry driver, also filling up, to let us use his card. There is a dual pricing system for fuel here: tourists (non-residents of Iran) pay more than locals. By using his card, he pays the local rate and we pay him the tourist rate. With fuel being cheap here and not much more than the resident's rate, it's what we do for the rest of our time in Iran with no problems.

Trundling along in Lizzybus, we can't help noticing the high police presence; there are full-size dummy police cars, speed cameras and radar on all main roads. The few times we are pulled over, it's just for a chat, they are interested only in us and our journey. Even though we now have insurance, they never ask for it or check our documents. To say we are falling in love with Iran is a lie, as we are 'in' love with it and sad we only have two weeks. We book two nights at a half-decent hotel, to dry out the roof tent and wash the kit. With the mattress stood against the radiator in our room, and the sleeping bags, sheets and pillowcases dumped at reception to be washed, we go off to explore the desert of Kaluts (Kalouts).

It's not a desert of sand dunes, but an area sculpted by water and wind – yardangs. They look like the sandcastles we built as children on the beach, slowly being washed away by the incoming tide. A huge billboard announces it to be the hottest place on earth, getting back into Lizzybus and turning the key, she clicks and then nothing. David replaces the spare relay plug which makes no difference whatsoever. A tour bus arrives and the people on it offer to push us, she starts on the first rotation of the wheels. We're utterly broken and sick to death of this constantly happening, agreeing that if offered a one-way ticket home, we would take it. The battle is incessant, the worry constant, taking with it all the joy and wonder, replacing it with dread and at times loathing.

Not for the first time I ask myself, how this is living the dream?

Back at our hotel, Lizzybus starts on the key. Reception tells us where a Land Rover garage is; we find it shut, tomorrow being Friday know it will still be shut. However, we have great company at dinner: a German couple in their late seventies driving to Amman, and a young couple, driving from London to Australia. The Australians blew their engine when they 'forgot' to put oil in it. If we had done something like this, it might be easier to accept, but having done everything and more to keep Lizzybus happy, it's hard. I realise we are both now taking this personally.

This morning Lizzybus starts first time. We press on into the second week of our two-week Iranian visa. We visit the vast rambling city of Bam which suffered a devastating earthquake in 2003, killing a third of its population. With the Arg-e Bam Citadel at its centre, it´s the biggest adobe city in the world. Extensively re-built by Cultural Heritage, it's vast, smooth and sculptural in its form, harmonious with its surroundings. We have no interest; all we can think about is if Lizzybus will start.

I cannot believe it, with two days left on our visa we will make it to the Pakistan border today, just under one hundred kilometres away. Driving along adjacent to the Black Mountains bordering Afghanistan, we find the road ahead armed and barricaded. Osama Bin Laden, the leader of the Islamic militant group Al Qaeda, responsible for the nine-eleven attacks, has been shot in Pakistan by the Americans. The reprisals include hostage taking, specifically Westerners, along this road, were told its too dangerous to continue. We ponder over being in Iran with an expired visa and a Lizzybus that sometimes starts and sometimes doesn't or making a run for it with the possibility of being kidnapped.

The soldiers at the barricade are talking about arranging an armed escort for us to the border. Now on the other side of the barrier alone, the guards have gone off to discuss this, we think. An hour later, looking at the road ahead, we know it won't be long before these imposing mountains swallow the day, leaving us in darkness. We begin to question if they really are sorting out an escort, or if we misheard them, deciding it's the No Choice, but Chance time.

It's time to take a chance, relying on the fact no one knows we are here and they won't have time to organise our kidnapping. We are going to make a break for it. Writing this now, I think we must have had sun stroke, what the hell were we thinking? Not least being in a Lizzybus that sometimes started and sometimes didn't, heading off alone on this broken rock road bordering Afghanistan.

The mountains are stunningly beautiful, they call to us like the sirens of the sea. I wonder if terrorists are worse than bandits, or bandits are worse than terrorists. Would it be better to be kidnapped by terrorists, or robbed by bandits? I decide it's a question I absolutely don't want to know the answer too. On the road ahead, we see a pickup truck with six men armed with AK47s in the back, flagging us down. We have a split second to decide whether to try and make it back to the safety of the barricade or make a run for it. We make a run for it.

I'd like to point out once more that my name is Jayne, born into a family of four, to a factory worker father and housewife mother living on a council estate in Birmingham. I had never been on a plane until I was thirty, with no idea whatsoever about the world or what was in it. Who is in this Land Rover, that sometimes starts and sometimes doesn't, with David, facing a truck load of armed men who might be Islamic militants waiting to kidnap tourists, specifically two tourists in a green Land Rover.

David accelerates past; I look in the wing mirror to see them following us. Lizzybus lurches and bangs, scraping on the rocks, we're going to break her if we don't stop. As it turns out, we don't have a choice; they easily catch up with us and cut us off. I feel like I'm having an outer body experience. I think of the pact we made of raising one eyebrow as a covert signal we could use for flight, not fight. Ignoring the fact David never managed to do it, but something I spent many nights perfecting in the mirror. I hadn't added into the equation guns, kidnapping and impenetrable mountains I only ever imagined it as a lone man, his only weapon a pocketknife.

They are Iranian police and military who are indignant that we headed off alone and demand we hand over our passports and follow them. I don't care how furious with us they are, I´m just ecstatic they are not part of any Al-Queda terrorist group wanting to kidnap, behead or mutilate us. The road deteriorates further into boulders which we rock crawl over, I want to get out and 'spot' but that's not an option right now. It becomes more and more remote, every hour or so we wait it out for replacement escorts, they appear from nowhere. Each handover takes ages as the scrappy bits of paper or dog-eared journals are filled out. It does, however, give us a sense of security and of being looked after.

I´ve moved on from it being a nightmare scenario to what is now an adventure. I'm not exactly sure how David is feeling as, as I´ve said many times, this is a shared journey, but our personal journeys thought it are very different. I´m sure after all this he'll be saying "it was fine". Along with the security of having an armed escort, there is also the fact that there are enough of them to push Lizzybus if she doesn't start.

The moonless sky has plunged us into a pitch-black night, we're taken to a room with two beds, a squat toilet and a pipe jutting out of the wall. They ask rather than order us to please not leave it. Since they still have our passports and we have no idea where we are, we have no intention of going anywhere. We get a tap on the door, on opening it were given two polystyrene trays full of fried chicken and salad, a flat bread and a can of pop. We've forgotten how hungry we are and sit on the metal framed bed eating the most delicious food ever, as if at the finest restaurant. Not having been asked for any money, we feel like their guests, but without their presence.

We get another knock on the door at six am, with the only window in the room having a metal shutter on it, it's so dark we didn't even know it was morning. We brought only our toiletry bag into this room and although there is no hot water, there is water. We have a shower and brush our teeth which feels so good, even having to put the same clothes back on. Off the back of Lizzybus, we make two pots of coffee, one for us and one for our escorts.

It feels like a lifetime away since David said we might make it to the Pakistan border, but it was only yesterday, we still have another forty kilometres. Despite the early start, it's now late afternoon and the border is still nowhere in sight. We spend most of our time waiting for escorts, until where told there is no vehicle available, we're introduced to a man. He is not in uniform, but in traditional dress, armed with an AK47 who will travel with us in Lizzybus. He sits on the front seat; I am squeezed in amongst the kit in the back. I'm wondering just how effective this single man will be in an ambush and, more importantly, how much further the Pakistan border is.

He speaks very little English, but we manage to tell him we need fuel, so he takes us to a one pump fuel station. They refuse to sell us any, but after an animated discussion, it's agreed to let us have enough to get us to the border. Whilst this discussion is going on, I buy two dustbin lid-sized flat breads off a woman. Back on the road, I share them along with our boiled eggs. Looking out of the window at the stunning mountains, eating warm bread and boiled eggs sprinkled with salt, driving through Iran into Pakistan under armed escort feels so normal. I don't ask myself how the hell I got here, I´m just here.

We made it, we are at the Pakistan border, and just like when leaving Turkey, we are sad to leave this wonderful country of Iran. Our escort apologetically asks for some money for his bus fare back to his village, it's the first money we've been asked for. We give him all the Iranian money we have left, a huge wad of notes, but it has very little value. He rewards us with a yellow-toothed grin before dissolving back into his life, having touched ours forever.

Leaving Iran was a lot simpler than getting into it. Once our documents are stamped, everyone comes out to wave us goodbye, wishing us not just good luck on our journey, but to stay safe. It makes us feel very special, although I can't help thinking they know something we don't.

Pakistan, at over three times bigger than the United Kingdom, has vast deserts, ice-capped mountains, rivers, and plummeting waterfalls. It's also home to the rich fertile lands of the Punjab, the Khyber Pass (linking Pakistan to Afghanistan), the Himalayas, and the Karakoram Highway, an old silk road to China. As once part of the British Empire, English is widely spoken.

I'm still wearing my headscarf and for now intend to continue wearing it. Immediately it feels different, edgy and slightly lawless. We're taken by police straight to the head of the very long sort of queue for immigration. It's what we're getting used to, and what I want to continue for the rest of my life. At this point, neither of us is aware that Olivier David Och and Daniela Widmer, a Swiss couple in a campervan driving alone along this very route, had been kidnapped at gunpoint by the Pakistani Taliban and held hostage for eight months before turning up at a military checkpoint. Had David known this, he would never have told me anyway, as I deal with things better in my Jayne world of ignorance. I operate on a need-to-know basis, and I certainly did not need to know this. But even if we had known, we are here now, and have no choice. Of course, a choice for me would be choosing the red dress or the yellow dress, meat or fish, not to be kidnapped or stranded in a country with no visa. But there you go, shit happens as my friend Gayle says, "Deal with it".

On the surface, Pakistan seems a lot poorer and unloved than Iran, with piles of garbage festering along the roads, and houses little more than shacks. The pong of urine catches my throat. It feels beaten by its years of conflict, which continues. The trucks belching out black acrid smoke are brightly painted and adorned with bunting, tassels and bells, overloaded with people, goods and livestock.

We're warned again how dangerous this stretch of road is, connecting Turkey, Iran and Pakistan. We know why, as any vehicle on it can be seen for miles from the vantage point of the surrounding mountains, the Hindu Kush part of the Himalayan range. I love words that feel nice to say, they give your mouth a hug. Hindu Kush does that for me, but you should never be beguiled by the feeling of words in your mouth. Hindu Kush can mean 'Hindu killer', or the one's I prefer 'sparkling snows of India' or 'mountains of India'. Nothing bad could happen in the sparkling snow mountains of India, surely not.

Having crossed into Pakistan at Taftan, we apparently need to get to the relative safety of Quetta in the province of Balochistan, over seven hundred and twenty kilometres away. I'm always loath to give distances as our routes are forever changing, but sometimes I think it's necessary to give perspective. It took two days to do the one hundred kilometers to the border in Iran. At that rate, it will be a week to get to Quetta. As for this little 'road trip', it is also necessary for us to be under armed escort.

It starts.

We set off following a pickup truck with two soldiers and two policemen. It's already getting dark. The road is of broken rock, with the occasional boulders falling from the surrounding mountains, which are cleared by our escorts. We realise being kidnapped is the least of our worries; taking out the Lizzybus sump, despite David having fitted a heavy-duty guard, is a distinct possibility. We ask to stop for the night.

We're taken to the compound of a local police station. It's the first time in weeks we'll sleep in the roof tent. The compound has a razor wire topped wall around it, with metal gates that are left wide open; people walk in and out of it freely. We have a steady stream of visitors – any one of them could be local terrorists checking us out and passing on information about us driving along what apparently is the only road out of here tomorrow. By head torch, I make my way over to the corrugated metal sheets housing the squat toilets. They are alive with revolting cockroaches and caked in excrement. It's just too much; I pee behind Lizzybus, police compound or not.

A cart arrives pulled by a tiny donkey, driven by two boys who look no more than ten years old. They fill the compound's water butts from

Taftan, Bolochistan Region, Pakistan

two oil drums on their cart, a stark reminder of the child labour here. We ask them to fill our two jerry cans, giving them a few rupees and our last two boiled eggs, sprinkled with salt and pepper.

After all the grotty, windowless, dimly-lit rooms we've been staying in, it´s so good to be in our roof tent, seeing the star-studded night sky and woken by a rising sun. The same soldiers and police from yesterday are waiting for us in their pickup at the gate. As we head out of town, all vehicles, bikes, donkeys, camels, and humans blocking the road have a gun pointed at them. Just like west coast Africa, having the loudest horn and honking it all day is a must. Our ears ring from the decibels, our eyes sting and we choke from the pollution.

I feel a real unease here, stay dressed in trousers, long sleeved shirt, with my headscarf pulled down over my face. Dusk has already settled as we wait once more for the next escort. I'm standing at the back of Lizzybus, David is speaking to some people at the front. I become aware of a group of men forming a circle around me; they grope my bottom and breasts. I feel incredibly vulnerable. Pushing them away, I manage to get back into Lizzybus and lock the door. I get a tap on the window but refuse to open it, until realising it's the police, I crack it open an inch. I know they know what has happened, but at this point David has no idea. Although David and I are not married, I tell the policeman my 'husband' David is a very jealous man and will be insulted by this behaviour. David, still not quite sure what has happened, is given a bunch of bananas - to give to me. Yes, a bunch of bananas.

I´m really shaken by how vulnerable I am as a woman and how quickly things can become serious. But I just couldn't help laughing at the ridiculousness of this, which was the best reaction as it defused the situation. I vow from now on that, unless it's daylight and I can stand right next to David, I will not get out of Lizzybus again until this 'road trip' is over.

Pakistan is everything I thought it would be, with its under-maintained infrastructure, open sewers, and buildings holding each other up mainly by the mangled mess of electric wiring strung between them. There's also opulence in the grandiose houses and buildings that sit behind gated elaborate entrances. It feels like a country of either rich or poor, with nothing in between. The days and the handovers merge with each other; we wait more than we drive along this never-ending road.

Today is special as we're joined by Daan and Luuk, two Dutch men on Triumph Tigers. The bikes are fully overland kitted out, making them as wide as they are high. It was not exactly a dream of David´s, more a desire, to do this trip on motorbikes. He had a Triumph Speed Triple when we first met, then an Aprilia Mille RSV 1000, loud and very fast. I sat on it once, but the noise when he started it up rattled my fillings. David reminded me how soulless I was, before changing it to a single seat, which I was more than happy with. Despite me encouraging David to go out on it, or away with friends, he was happiest cleaning, admiring, and putting an even louder and shinier exhaust on it. Apparently, being Italian, Aprilias are temperamental and don't like the rain, which we have a lot of in England.

The bike, like all our possessions, had to sold to fund this journey. David who never manages to say anything more to me than 'you look pretty' and only when prompted. On the advertisement for the sale of the bike, he wrote the most fanciful outpouring of slush I have ever heard, to the point I felt they needed to get a room. I just wish he could find some of those words for me now, who knows what they might bring. Of course, all that really matters on this journey, is being able to trust each other, not how many times a week we do, or in our case don't, make out, but it is beginning to hurt.

We're in a proper convoy now: our escorts up front, Daan and Luuk on their motorbikes in the middle, and Lizzybus bringing up the rear. In the open back of the pickup the four men in traditional shalwar kameez (a knee length tunic with loose fitting pants) are all armed. It's like a scene from Lawrence of Arabia, but with trucks not camels. Their billowing cotton tunics captured by the wind wrap around their AK47s. As we all need fuel, the petrol station is cleared so we can fill up. It's like most of this journey, as if I'm watching it from afar, not present in the moment, and quite bizarre. After another long day of handovers, we're taken to a rundown hotel. We're a little surprised when we're asked if we want to buy a beer. You bet we do! We have been so focused on ending the day alive, we've forgotten all about beer o'clock.

The next morning no one arrives. We ask reception if they can contact the police, but they say they have no authority to call or speak to them. Daan and Luuk are on a tight schedule and need to push on. We know we have almost reached Quetta, so unanimously decide to head off alone in our own convoy of three. It's the strangest feeling, of devilment at having escaped and of fear we are no longer protected.

It's not long before we know it's not working; without our escorts we face gridlocked traffic. The bikes can weave around it, but we get stuck. Then David and I get sick with deli-belly, constantly having to stop, we agree to go on alone. The next few days are a blur, driving and sleeping. We're both so sick and weak we book cheap rooms along the way, but only where Lizzybus is safe.

Without realising it, we have cut right across Pakistan, through Quetta and into the Punjab, we are now in the city of Lahore, on the border with India. Colonial rule is evident everywhere in the incredibly grand and ornate buildings. Lahore has wide open boulevards and is a recognised city of literature and film. I feel a small change here, enough to ditch the dreaded headscarf, but keep my head covered with my baseball cap.

We're utterly exhausted when we book a cheap room, sleeping on and off for forty-eight hours. Emerging very weak, but feel we are finally over the worst of it, squinting in the sunlight. We have lost so much weight, hip bones are a real thing, whilst breasts are a thing of the past. Well, mine are, not that they were ever really something, but if they had been, they would now be a thing of the past.

It's eerily quiet. We're told it's because today is the public holiday of Ashura, a world Islamic holiday and something to do with the Prophet Musa, the parting of the sea, and the beginning of the Battle of Karbala, I think? But history just fuddles my brain.

I loved art at school. At eleven I drew a strip cartoon of a Midsummer Night's Dream by William Shakespeare. To this day, I cannot understand how I knew anything about Shakespeare. I won a regional award for the 'simplicity' of my drawings, and thirty pounds worth of book tokens. All I wanted was a set of felt tip pens. They had just come out and had the most exotic translucent colours, and way beyond my pocket money. I was devastated when told I could only spend the tokens on books. I chose, or more accurately were chosen for me, a flip board sized world atlas and a children's illustrated Bible. Covering the centre two pages of this Bible was a picture of a man parting the sea with people walking through it behind him, and fish poking out of the parted water.

Was this atlas and Bible meant to be and did they seal the fate of my eleven-year-old self?

Men and women dressed in black parade through the streets slapping their chests and chanting. During this year's event, thirty people are killed in Iraq and sixty-three in Afghanistan from suicide bombers. I much prefer my memory of fish poking out of a parted sea in my children's Bible.

Turning into the main street, we get swept up in a huge procession before reaching a barricade where men and women are separated and searched. For the women a screen is set up, where I am given a full body search, the women ask what I can give them. I say nothing. There is a high military and police presence, television crews, and a long line of ambulances that look like they've come from the local museum, they're so rusty and battered. I want to leave but the whole area is cordoned off. People are gathered around a central area where men, stripped to the waist, start flagellating themselves with wooden poles with chains and razor-sharp metal claws on the ends. They rip chunks of flesh from their backs until blood drips down onto their stark white cotton pants, turning them a sickening crimson red.

I feel a bile rising in my throat, but not having eaten for days it's dry retching. A man is telling them when to stop as they go into a frenzied trance. Flying above us is a helicopter causing a downdraught, creating a whirlwind of dust and rubbish. I think of the Wizard of Oz film when the cyclone lifts Dorothy's house up, wishing it would lift me up too.

CHAPTER 13

CONVOYS AND SICKNESS TAKE THEIR TOLL

We're leaving Pakistan, not with the same feeling as when leaving Turkey or Iran, but with relief, despite knowing there is so much more to see, specifically in the mountainous Gilgit region. We're so physically weak and emotionally drained from the convoys, illness, and the Lizzybus starting issues. On the way, we visit the Walled City and Fort at Lahore. The Mughal Emperor Akbar demolished the original mud fort and citadel to rebuild it in burnt brick. It's stunningly beautiful, especially the Picture Wall with its vibrant glazed tiles, mosaics and frescoes, the Palace of Mirrors, the Summer Palace built underground to keep the ladies cool, and the Khilwat Khana royal ladies' ancient spa retreat.

From the ancient to the modern, we head for the shopping mall, a gated area guarded by the military. They were not going to let us in because it's not just a shopping mall, but a residential area full of impressive mansions. Shops here sell every conceivable luxury item at extortionate prices, with mouth-watering displays of food from all over the world. David with his full beard and me with my afro plaits, in sun faded shirts and shorts looking like we both could do with a good meal, are followed around the store. If they only knew what we have been through to shop here, they would salute us not follow us.

We reach the border of Wagah Attari on the Grand Trunk Road, once the only road between Pakistan and India. To book a room so we can stay overnight and watch the spectacle of the closing of the border ceremony. Already a small crowd has gathered on both the Pakistani and Indian sides. We're pulled out of the crowd and placed on the front row seats set aside for VIPs. It feels right, to finally be recognised as the intrepid explorers we are!

It's hysterical as the Indian Border Security Forces (BSF) and Pakistan Rangers, resplendent in full uniform, try to outdo each other in an elaborately coordinated goose-stepping march of rivalry and brotherhood. A jester performs acrobatics whilst encouraging us to scream 'Pakistan' louder than the opposition can scream 'India'. It's uplifting and funny; we're joyous shouting and laughing with everyone.

After all the tough times we've had at borders, this is just the tonic we need.

India: the Golden Temple, twelfth century forts, the Himalayas, lost cities and civilizations, Darjeeling tea, and the iconic Taj Mahal. On gaining independence from the British Empire, it was split into Pakistan, India and Bangladesh, a time of great conflict when millions of people were displaced, some never to be heard of again. Learning history in real life rather than from a book has been good, although at times, it's been a tough lesson.

In Birmingham, we have what is known as the Balti Triangle, an area of mainly Bangladeshi restaurants, which we visited many times. Balti refers to the round flat bottomed metal bowl with handles its served

Attari-Wagah border between India and Pakistan

in, and is still manufactured in Birmingham. With all signs of sickness gone, we can finally start enjoying the food we are familiar with - curry.

In great spirits after such a fun evening, we're driving now through the imposing gates closed in the ceremony last night, to cross no man's land and the border with India, our thirty-ninth country.

India, being one of the most populated countries in the world, is manic - there's just so many people. Having secured the visa from the embassy in London, we relax knowing it's just a case of queuing and patience. With no preferential treatment that's exactly what we do, queue most of the morning. It's with a huge sense of victory we stick the Indian flag on Lizzybus. The aroma of India spices and incense is overwhelmed by urine and acrid smoke belching from factories and cars. Our eyes sting and our noses run with a sooty black snot. Eddie, a six-foot English man we first met in Lahore, is squeezed into the back amongst our kit. We had visions of giving lifts to people along the way, perhaps even charging to help with the budget. It soon became obvious that with no internal space, it just didn't work, still we try to give lifts where and when we can.

We book rooms at a once-palatial building now blistered through decay, with solid dark oak floors, four poster beds, an inglenook fireplace and floor-to-ceiling half-boarded up, but still beautiful, stained-glass windows. It feels very English, not in the council house I grew up in way, but of the stately homes I'd visited.

I feel like I'm in a little family as David, Eddie and I walk through the streets of Amritsar to the Golden Temple, a marble-domed building lined with real gold that seemingly floats on its sacred lake. The minute you enter from the chaotic streets a real sense of calm descends. We're each given an orange bandana to cover our heads and asked to take off our shoes which are stored in open shelving manned by volunteers. Hundreds of pairs of them; I wonder how they are ever going to find ours amongst them all. The most impressive thing is not the seventy thousand daily visitors, or the hundred kilos of gold used in its construction, but the feeding of all these people in the football-sized marble-floored room.

Sitting crossed legged on the floor in rows, with a metal tray on our laps, volunteers walk up and down ladling dahl, vegetable curry, and a delicious coconut rice pudding into each of the tray's sections from stainless steel buckets. The lines of people appear and disappear like a finely rehearsed ballet. Water is sprinkled where the bottoms once sat and mopped ready for the next row of dinners. This simple act of eating together - men, women and children - soothes me. Throughout this journey, I have struggled with those beliefs and practices that ensure the gulf between rich and poor, men and women, is perpetuated. This matters not here. Who or what you are is irrelevant, we all eat together. I am filled not just by the food, but by the unity of it all.

My lasting memory is of the volunteers, sitting chatting around a huge cauldron, shelling peas with all the time in the world. Which is how long it will take them, all the time in the world.

Today, we say goodbye to Eddie as we are heading to Shimla in the foothills of the Himalayas, the summer capital of what was British India, due to its cooler climate. There's a world heritage railway to it that I really want to go on, but we're driving so I can't. I dismiss the ongoing starting issues, focusing on it being the Himalayas and steep enough to bump start her if needed. India is home to over a billion people and we think every one of them is heading to Shimla on this single near vertical road. (A major highway has since been built). Even the kamikaze African truck driver is preferable to the arrogant white four-by-four driver here. They force carts, bicycles, rickshaws, mopeds, auto rickshaws, even pedestrians, off the road, but not our Lizzybus. We hold firm, the odd dent or two doesn't bother us. Hit us if you want, we're not moving.

The journey, promising spectacular mountain views, is obscured by a heavy cloud of pollution and progress is torturous. It takes a few days until we rise above it to arrive at the cobbled streets of Shimla which are lined with trinket tourist shops, Domino Pizza, and coffee houses. Shimla, in the North of India, borders China, and its influence is evident in all the Chinese food restaurants. In our wooden room built on the cliff edge, we eat a Chinese takeaway making it feel like a Saturday night back home. Except, that is, for the troop of monkeys cavorting in the trees outside the window.

I can't shift this foul mood, the drive to Shimla was just that, a drive not to progress the journey. I always thought that having no real time scale other than visa restrictions was the greatest thing ever. The reality is, I need more structure, a purpose, dare I say, an end. We all know David wants to meander like this for the rest of his life.

Descending back into the blanket of smog with the ear-splitting honking of horns and hairpin bends, I'm beginning to loathe it. Our shrivelled stomachs complain bitterly at the amount of Chinese food we crammed into them last night. It's difficult admitting to not enjoying any part of this journey. I know it's a once-in-a-lifetime opportunity and experience. It's made worse by this being in my own head without conversation.

We're heading now to Delhi, or should I say New Delhi, the capital of India, one of the most populated and polluted cities on earth.

Travel weariness, sickness and breakdowns are taking their toll. We drive with open windows in the inferno of heat and humidity. It's so much harder to be wowed by fabulous views obscured by a haze of pollution, to face the constant police checks with a smile, or to embrace the vibrancy and flavours of this country. I´m beginning to resent and judge it. I think I am missing family, friends and the familiar; you could say I'm homesick. It's late December and approaching the festive season, a point in the year for family and friends to enjoy time together.

We reach Agra, home to the iconic Taj Mahal. Unable to get Lizzybus into the car park of our hotel as the roof is too low, we park her on the street by reception. From our second-floor window, we can see the Taj Mahal. 'A teardrop on the cheek of eternity', the Taj Mahal is considered to be one of the most beautiful buildings in the world. Built on the banks of the Yamuna River, it's a memorial from Emperor Shah Jahan to his second wife who died in childbirth. I'm a sucker for a story, and knowing that the devoted Shah Jahan, overthrown by his son, spent his remaining years imprisoned in the red sandstone fort opposite, makes it to me equally impressive.

Before walking to the Taj Mahal today, David removes the dead pigeon from under Lizzybus. The Taj Mahal is everything and more it proclaims to be: intricate whilst substantial, mysterious whilst enchanting, warm whilst ice cold. It took twenty thousand artisans twenty years to build and is everything a real masterpiece should be.

In our room with a view of the Taj Mahal, we rest, read, write, watch DVDs, drink beer, and eat curry for breakfast, dinner and tea. David is using antibiotic eye drops for his eye infection, bought from the pharmacy for a few rupees. Having sat on my only pair of glasses, I replace them for a few more rupees.

It's a week until Christmas. Smart phones, social media and Wi-Fi have still not taken off, it's by email and text message I keep in touch with family. I'm feeling more and more isolated, as hard as I try not to. No one knows what they are capable of and it's only when we're tested do we find out. I don't know what is more incredible, David and I being on this journey, or our determination now we are on it, to make it to the end.

We are in Udaipur with its five lakes and impressive palaces. Not wanting to be unkind, but it seems as if India is sinking with pollution and traffic, like a disintegrating doily. We are sitting on the roof terrace of a four-storey house, sipping gin and tonics with Janne, the artisan mother of two Dutch girls we met in Amritsar, after the note found on Lizzybus inviting us to their home. It overlooks the skyline of hotels; where they say when they first settled here, there was nothing. We talk about India and our gut feeling of not being entirely at ease here. This mildly eccentric lady, having lived here for many years, explains how for her the legacy and rigidity of the caste system (fixed social groups an individual is born into), despite many changes, still exists. It's just the tonic we need; chatting over drinks as the sun sets over the new India, and making sense of our feelings.

We're heading now for Mumbai, using the toll road in our effort to make some progress. At some of the booths, we are waved through with smiles as honoured guests in their country, at others we pay the few rupees. Even though it's a toll road, we see fully laden camels, oxen pulling carts, and tuk-tuks. We're not sure if they are still building it or repairing it. The normal heavy equipment used in the construction of bridges and roads is replaced by women dressed in once-beautiful saris and children in tatty shorts. They supply the cement, chain gang style, one bowl at a time balanced on their heads. Labour is cheaper than machinery.

Mumbai (Bombay) is the largest city in India and made up of seven islands. We access it by a causeway, but the Coastal Road Project should now be completed with a new tunnel. Surrounded on three sides by the Arabian Sea, it became an important naval dock, and is home to what is considered one of Asia's biggest slums Dharavi, the Bollywood Film Studios, Elephanta Island, and the Gateway to India. The Gateway to India caused me lots of confusion. Built to commemorate the royal visit of King George V, it's more a symbolic entrance to India as it's free-standing and not attached to anything.

From here we take a boat trip to Elephanta Island. I never cease to be amazed at how excited I get to be doing anything, in this case a boat trip. We are packed tighter than sardines in a tin and so overloaded there is only a few inches between us and the sea of floating plastic waste and debris. I have a splitting headache from the rattling machine gun engine and am almost asphyxiated by its thick black smoke. But nothing can quell my enthusiasm, I'm just so happy to be out and about with people. A world heritage site of rock caves and temples, named by the Portuguese, it once had a large stone elephant on its shore, but not now. There are flights of stairs leading to the temples and caves. It's alarming how much we puff and pant walking up them, still both so weak. High above the caves, a troop of monkeys bomb us with rocks. They are incredibly accurate in their stone throwing; one man is holding his bleeding head. Of all the scenarios I thought might bring this journey to an end, being taken out by a stone throwing monkey was not one of them.

It's Christmas Day here in our cheap hotel room with plastic boards and metal bars covering the window. We both have stinking colds. I saved for today the top-up my sister put on our phone in England (which I can't do from here) to call home. Hearing their voices is both comforting and distressing. Not wanting family to worry, we say how exciting it is for us to be here in Mumbai, how well we are, no mention of the stinking colds, or of the loneliness I can't seem to shift.

Jenny is cooking Christmas dinner for everyone. She tells me about cooking the turkey last night to make room in the oven today for the pork, roasties, pigs in blankets and sprouts, about the miniature bottle of brandy to set light to the Christmas pudding, and the new board games. I hear Christmas songs blasting out, and laughter; bleeps then silence as the credit runs out. Of course, my sister would have called me back, but it was when you needed credit on your phone to make or receive calls. I hold it for a moment listening to the silence. It's worked its magic, I feel loved and part of their day, ready and able now to embrace mine.

We go out for breakfast. With the majority here being Muslim, Christmas, or the celebrating of it by the few who are Christian, is not evident on the streets. I've brought a bag of chocolate toffees which I hand out to the children. On this journey, we cling to anything that is the remotest bit familiar. A cafe we have only ever visited once becomes our local café and where we order our favourite breakfast of dosa, a thin pancake stuffed with potato, onion and mustard seed. I'm a morning tea drinker; I like the process of pouring hot water over tea in a teapot and leaving it to brew. Tea here is boiled in a saucepan with milk and sugar, making me shudder as it is both bitter and sweet. I'm sort of getting used to it, but David refuses even to try it. He is a black coffee drinker, which comes with a cup of hot water and a tube sachet of Nescafe, so you know you are getting the finest 'Nescafe'.

I've spoken to family, handed out presents of chocolate toffees, and eaten out in our local 'once visited cafe'. Back in our room, I make the most of the glorious hot water and wash my hair, and then wash it again. As we're out of Black Africa, hair types have changed from Afro frizz to beautiful, long silky locks. Unable to find the breast-feeding local women to plait it, I re-plait it myself.

Happy Christmas everyone from Mumbai, India!

It's time to leave Mumbai, but before we do, we take a walk through the streets of its past. We visit the imposing Edwardian building of cathedral proportions, Victoria Terminus (renamed Chhatrapati Shivaji Terminus), designed by the British architectural engineer Frederick Williams Stevens. It's the clock that is most intriguing. Can you imagine all the significant moments in people's lives it has witnessed? It's a significant moment for us too, and now we are part of these ticking moments in time.

We are heading to Goa for New Year, six hundred kilometres away; some call it the party capital of India. With the main highway shut, we face lengthy detours. We're both in our own world of frustration and isolation, from finding all hotels or rooms fully booked. Driving down a dirt track to a sheer drop, seeing a spectacular view of lakes, mountains, and a snaking train, we set up camp. Once the roof tent is up and we're sat eating our bowl of noodles, we're surrounded by people. We are in India after all, one of the most populated countries in the world.

It's morning. The sunken cloud in the valley, burnt off by the rising sun, reveals again the snaking train and milky blue lakes. Finally, we make it to Goa, with its promise of untamed beaches, chilled hideouts, and yoga retreats. A place to reflect, gather thoughts and chill. Baga to be precise, known more for its twenty-four-hour night life, where drugs, liquour and sex are freely available. We find a place with chalet type rooms around a small pool, but it's not available until tomorrow. They allow us to camp in the car park which pleases us no end when given access to the toilet, shower, pool, and Wi-Fi, for free.

On New Year's Eve, we join the mass of intoxicated people, trying to hold each other up or trampling on those with no one to hold them up, on the beach. Music blasts from all the beach bars, clubs and restaurants, but with no Big Ben chiming out midnight, it's around about midnight the fireworks start going off. The sky lights up like one gigantic firework and rockets shoot off in all directions. Fireworks explode as people try to light them and a blanket of smoke obliterates everything. Drunken men squeeze between the women, groping bottoms and breasts. I know mine will be a huge disappointment since the weight loss has reduced them to flaps. I think about how strangers on this journey have groped me more than David.

Holding David's hand, more to make sure I don't fall over, we are united in this moment. The question I ask myself over and over, of how this is happening to me, is one I will never know the answer to, just thankful beyond words it is. New Year's Eve on a beach in Baga, Goa, India, being groped and almost decapitated by exploding fireworks is all perfectly normal to me now.

So here it is, 2012, our third year on the road. My goals, aspirations and New Year resolutions used to be things like getting properly measured for a bra, having my eyes tested and choosing one of the fancy frames on display instead of heading to the pound shop to buy a pair, getting rid of all the junk in the spare room. Now they are to master eating and washing my derriere with one hand, squawking less when driving up or down vertical mountains, and to be less critical of beards and body hair.

We're all on a journey through life. We're finally beginning to realise just what we have already achieved, knowing if we did throw in the towel, there would be a small army of people barricading the port at Dover and shoving us back on the next boat, reminding us of what we said: "We are going to drive Lizzybus around the world". So just like the film, 'Carry on Regardless', despite all the challenges, the logistics and red tape, we intend, for now, to do just that, to 'Carry on Regardless'.

Happy New Year everyone!

CHAPTER 14

WADDLING LIKE A DUCK

Our next country, Bangladesh, is where we need to decide on our route going forward. It has China above it and Myanmar (Burma) beside it. To go through China, we need a pre-agreed itinerary and a guide and, unlike in Iran and Pakistan, this escort is not free. The guide needs to live in Lizzybus with us, or for us to pay for their accommodation. For Myanmar, with its years of internal conflict and Al-Qaeda's interest, getting a visa is almost impossible and our safety would be a real issue.

We are back to our choice or chance option, but the reality is we really have no choice. We're not afraid of a little internal conflict, or the obstacles put in our way, in fact I think we secretly enjoy it. It's the cost of a guide for China and the visa issue of Myanmar that make the decision for us. We will ship Lizzybus from Chittagong in Bangladesh to Penang in Malaysia. All we need to do now is get to Bangladesh, but first we need to get the visa from Kolkata.

I'm going to tell you something now that will become pivotal to us. We have a three-month visa for India, the one we got by sending our passports back to the UK. It's a single-entry visa and, if for any reason whatsoever, we want or need to go back into India, we have to reapply in the UK. This can only be done after thirty days have elapsed.

Pushing on, we begin to feel the real charm of Goa, how its rivers and estuaries thread through this tropical landscape and water buffalo wallowing in mud holes have linen white egrets perched on their backs. We find a beach hut for two dollars a night when Janie and Tom, a couple from Essex, arrive on a scooter. Tom, a lorry driver, and Janie, a social worker, gave up their jobs a year after meeting each other and bought a one-way ticket to Asia. There's such a warmth and familiarity exuding from them, it makes us forget all about what might lie ahead. Janie lost both her sons in tragic accidents; we all find much-needed peace here. There is a simplicity to life in our mango swamp despite the swarm of mosquitoes, with magical evenings full of conversation, card playing, laughter and hugs.

Eventually Janie and Tom find their way back to England, marry, and buy a barge moored on the canal. Not quite the open road, but they can sail away whenever they want.

We have already been in India a month and it's time to press on, albeit with heavy hearts. I hadn't realised what a massive country India was at almost thirteen times bigger than England. Heading now for the border with Bangladesh, over one thousand five hundred kilometres away, I think of nothing other than the fact we are making progress, and that makes me feel good. I've not mentioned tyres or punctures for a while, but it's a cause of great concern. We live in dread of another puncture or exploding tyre and for good reason. Here we are again, with our lives hanging in the balance on the highways of India, changing a tyre.

When courting, an old-fashioned word I know, but I am old-fashioned - some even say Victorian - I remember the piles of magazines in David´s bathroom and bedroom. Not of pornography, but of tyres, David's porn. David, who is never too hot or too cold, whose bum never aches or mosquito bites pulsate, is passionate about tyres and fixates on them. He talks of nothing else; I suppose I should be grateful he is at least talking.

Tonight, down an overgrown track there is a bridge under what we think is a disused railway track. It's just high enough for us to put the roof tent up, perfect for getting out of the evening drizzle. We're woken by an ear-splitting whistle and a vibrating tent. It takes a few moments before our brains work out what is going on - it's a train passing overhead. Fear is an unpleasant emotion caused by the threat of danger, pain or harm, and exactly what I´m feeling right now. It takes a while to calm down, but eventually we drift back off to sleep, only to be woken again by another train. This time, clods of dirt and shrapnel dislodged from the vibrating bridge fall on us.

It's morning. We fumble around, knackered, with one thought - tyres. We've been unable to source the tyres we need here in India; David thinks two truck tyres might do. Along with the tyre issue and the starting issue, we now face the visa issue, as we head for the massive city of Kolkata and the Bangladeshi embassy.

Despite this cloud of worry, we're enjoying driving through these little towns and villages, getting much more of a feel for the real India. We treat ourselves to breakfast at the roadside of wafer-thin batter, filled with curried onions and potatoes, or fluffy steamed buns made from fermented rice and lentil, served with a mint yogurt sauce, all for a few rupees.

Along the way, we visit Hampi (Victory City), one of the largest Hindu empires in India's history. A vast area with hundreds of temples, palaces and fortifications, its complex irrigation system with gardens and pools lies mostly in ruins. For over a week, I have been in agony with my ankles; they look like tree trunks. The pain is so bad I am shuffling, not walking. Sitting under the shade of trees by the river whilst David goes off sightseeing, I´m surrounded, not by people, but monkeys. I can't go anywhere as David won't find me. Remembering Elephanta Island (without any elephants) and how the rock throwing monkeys cut a man's head open, I gather a pile of rocks as ammo against any attack. They sit menacingly in the trees around me squawking, squabbling and barring their teeth. I sit on guard like this for an hour until David returns. On the plus side, I did forget all about my throbbing ankles.

I can no longer drive with the pain in my feet. I wrap them in a wet towel and elevate them on the dash. It's then we have another puncture; with both spares shredded it's a disaster. I´m lightheaded from the pain in my feet and not having eaten and insist we leave Lizzybus and have breakfast to consider our options. I'm totally overwhelmed and sit sobbing. Although it might seem David is the one who worries most over issues like tyres, it affects me in equal measure. I also worry this is going to push David over the edge. Before we left on this journey, David, feeling the pressure of his demanding job and unrelenting hours, was told to change what he was doing or he wouldn't be doing it much longer. David, like Mrs T Senior has historically high blood pressure, I know this is going to be bad.

I look across at David, physically a third of the man he was, but a giant in all other respects, pushed to his limits. I see him shaking and holding his shoulder, when realising that behind him is a tyre garage.

Lizzybus, sitting on her steel rim, is jacked up and the wheel taken away for repair, David is taken away to a place that sells truck tyres, I go to the garage with the punctured tyre. In my past, getting a tyre changed or a puncture repaired involved a rotating electric machine with a foot operated metal arm to break the bead, here it involved tyre levers, hammers, muscles and fire. A fire is built in the wheel to seal the tar-like stuff they use for the puncture. David now back with two new truck tyres, the back tyres are put on the front, the tubed punctured tyre becomes the spare, the two shredded tyres are ditched, and the new truck tyres put on the back. Not ideal as we have only one spare, but more than the no spare we started with.

David assures me, the me who now thinks she is some sort of tyre expert, that as the truck tyres have the same rolling diameter and we have no other option, they will do.

Driving Lizzybus I'm convinced the steering feels tight. I've had enough, I don't care what the cost is, I want brand new tyres, including spares. (it's what we both want but have been unable to find any). With most of the day already gone, we pull up between the rows of lorries parked in a compound. Once the roof tent is up, the men in the truck in front call David over; he returns with a tub of curried something and four hot chapattis. The food is delicious, but it's the act of kindness and generosity that fills us. We feel looked after and safe by people who have so little, their trucks, their homes and livelihoods. They will never really know what a comfort this is to us, but I hope they do.

Not wanting to wait for the reluctant sun to dry out our wet tent, we pack it up and press on. The first thing we both do is check the tyres and find the offside front one is flat - f…..it. David puts a blob of spittle on the valve, it bubbles - a leaking valve. We re-inflate it with our on-board compressor, hoping it holds until we can find a garage as even David's tyre string can't fix a leaking valve.

I'm still unable to drive with the pain in my feet. On checking the faulty valve find it's now holding pressure, so decided to visit the ornate Sun Temple at Modhera, approached by a long boulevard. I tried my very best to walk down it, and a little ashamed hobbling along, holding onto David's arm, seeing all the limbless beggars along its path, but the pain is excruciating.

I remind myself I am brave and have had this confirmed during my volunteer twin research when our pain threshold was tested. For some reason they did this on Jenny and I together, putting a heated electrical disc on our arms, that when it got too hot, we were to press a button. There was no way either of us would be the first to give up, both ending up with mild burns. The lady doing the test was shocked at how tolerant of pain we were. But I won! I make it to the main temple to see the magnificent carved lions, elephants, horses and chariots, but all I can think about is how the hell I'm going to walk back.

Driving now through the brick-making area, with hundreds of conical chimneys belching out even more black smoke set up camp for the night amongst the brick factories. At around midnight, a group of locals tell us we must move. It's pitch black, but we find our way back to the main road and park amongst the rows of trucks on the central reservation. What a night, with vehicles pulling in, out, or thundering past us all night rocking the tent. This, with the pain in my ankles, I ask myself if this nightmare will ever end.

In case you'd forgotten, we're heading for the border of Bangladesh, but first we need to get visas from the consulate in Kolkata. Just outside Kolkata is Fort William, which sits on the banks of the Hooghly River, a tributary of the river Ganges, where the saying 'the Black Hole of Calcutta' came from. As most of the British and Indian employees of the East Indian Company imprisoned in the dungeon here died of asphyxiation. The Fort is vast and looks magnificent, but I can't walk around it.

Approaching Kolkata, we see a skyline of ornate gold and marble colonial buildings sitting beside modern hotels and office blocks, with vast shopping malls, restaurants and cafés. The India we have come to know exists in its back streets, with whole families living in a single room, selling street food, or ferrying people around in auto rickshaws to make a living. Booked into a cheap backpacker on the outskirts of Kolkata, we head off to the local hospital to get my feet looked at. I'm overcome with emotion at the possibility this pain might end. I´m examined and blood tests are taken - just having my feet cupped in the hands of the doctor is so comforting. I´m given a handwritten prescription for anti-inflammatory medication and pain killers. The examination, blood tests and prescriptions cost less than two dollars.

Back at our backpackers, I pull the bed away from the wall to avoid the spores of mould, then shower, and wash our clothes; David returns with a takeaway. We are in Kolkata watching a DVD of 'Gandhi', who led the campaign for India's independence, tucking into a delicious takeaway, clean, and with the pain easing in my feet. We are both fast asleep before the film really begins.

Despite the pain being bearable now, I´m still hobbling, so we take a taxi to the Bangladeshi consulate. The security guard tells us it's Republic Day and all public offices are closed. But of course they are! We explore this city with its vast boulevards, botanical gardens, palaces, religious and public buildings. The white marble Victoria Memorial, commemorating Queen Victoria's Diamond Jubilee, is quite magnificent, but overlooked for the iconic Taj Mahal.

Being a public holiday, the streets are crowded – well, more crowded than I imagine they usually are. We sit on the kerb so I can rest my feet as a procession of military marching bands, carnival floats and beautiful white horses pulling intricately adorned carriages pass by. They are heading for the park, so we follow, momentarily forgetting all about my elephant legs. Like any public holiday in any park anywhere, children cartwheel, gambol, play cricket, as families picnic. Being part of something so familiar is very special. We buy curry wraps and a big ball of candy floss on a stick from one of the many stalls, such a wonderful day. Visas? Who needs a visa anyway?

We're back at the consulate, this time we walk as my feet are feeling a lot better. Having gone by taxi last time, we hadn't realised it was right under a flyover with a ring road around it; crossing this ring road is death defying. We join the snaking line of people queuing to get the two-page application, to be told we need two copies. Copies that can be bought at the hut opposite, involving crossing that road again.

Once filled out, each application needs two photographs, which is not a problem as we have printed sheets of high-quality passport photos. But attaching them to the applications is, as one needs to be glued, and the other one stapled. Fortunately, of the two old men sitting on upturned plastic crates, one has a glue stick, and the other a stapler. I find this humbling how people, not exactly make a living, but survive, with a glue stick and a stapler. It's a service rather than begging, and one we pay a little more for than they ask.

I sit in the dust next to the gluer and stapler businessmen whilst David queues for an hour to hand in the completed forms. With instructions to return in two hours for an interview, we go for a coffee with Mike, a lofty, tattooed, softly spoken English man, who'd stood at the altar, decided it was not what he wanted, left his bride there and went travelling.

I'm always nervous having embassy interviews; my mind goes blank when asked about the places I've been and the places we're going to. It's a relief we are being interviewed together. It all goes well, but we can't collect the visas until Monday, three days' time.

It's like a miracle - the swelling and pain in my feet has almost gone and I can at last walk around this impressive city. In the street, a stool and box is the barbers; a stool, brush and tin of shoe polish is the cobblers; a piece of canvass and oil drum a café. Lizzybus is taking up precious space parked on the street, the manager keeps asking us to move her, but as we cannot leave until Monday, we just keep dodging him.

In the back streets of Kolkata, we see people washing at the standpipes, goats living on garbage, the buildings black with pollution have trees growing in their cracks. Children tug and pull at our clothes begging, barefoot in rags. I sit down amongst them; they're taken aback, becoming timid and shy. I´m rewarded with smiles and laughter sitting together in the dust. Facing all the begging has been hard, deciding long ago never to give to children, as we felt adults were the beneficiaries. Along the way, where we can, we have visited schools and hospitals, donating some of the boxes of pens my daughter in the corporate world gave us, and any medical stuff we had.

We're outside the imposing neo-Gothic High Court, the oldest court in India; just its presence fills you with fear. On the streets leading to the courts, people sit behind benches with manual typewriters, preparing and typing out court documents for a few rupees. Inside this formidable place, a central cascading fountain is framed by arched walkways. Piles of musty, dusty, string-wrapped documents spew out from the rooms. A world heritage site, the design of the High Court was inspired by the cloth hall in Ypres, Belgium. It leaves you in no doubt of its intentions, of its authority and the justice, and at times injustice, dispensed here.

We are in possession of our passports complete with the Bangladeshi visa and should be heading off today, but last night, David, for the second time, had blood in his stools. David is so frustrating in that he tells me about this, and then tells me to forget about it. Sharing is not always caring. I'm having none of it. Having visited the hospital for my feet, I insist he gets checked out before we leave. At the hospital, David gives urine and stool samples, blood is taken and, surprisingly, he's even given an ultrasound scan.

I think by now it's well documented how private I am - well, I was, specifically around bodily functions. It's not something I want to discuss and honestly, I´m more than happy to keep it that way. David is far more open about this, and for now has a valid reason to talk in detail about it. Today we are returning for the results. David's prostate is slightly enlarged, perfectly normal for a fifty-year-old man. It's noted that his stool sample, whilst being offensive (and don't I know it), is normal. Nothing else is picked up in the ultrasound scan or blood tests. The whole lot came to twenty dollars and well worth it as it's one less thing for David to worry about.

That's enough of being sick, we just don't have time for it, we need to push on. Time is ticking away on our Indian visas, we need to get to Bangladesh to arrange the shipping of Lizzybus from Chittagong to Penang for our next continent, Asia. But what we are about to face is something we could never have predicted and will stop us dead in our tracks.

It's great to be able to drive again. Although David is happy to drive all day long, I think he now realises it's good to have a break from it. Three hours later, we reach the border to join the snaking queues of vehicles, people, and their belongings. People are calling us on; still finding it hard to let go of our English need for queuing, we're hesitant. No one minds, they just wave us through, honking their horns, until we're at the front. It's so simple, even stamping the Carnet de Passage is drama-free. Before we know it, we're crossing no man's land to the border with Bangladesh.

CHAPTER 15

IMPOUNDED IN BANGLADESH

Bangladesh, also known as the People's Republic of Bangladesh, is a lot smaller than the UK. Although not quite as densely populated as India, it's still ranked eighth in the world. Muslim is the main religion; the legal system is a mixture of Islamic law and British common law. It has the world's largest mangrove forest, a huge textile industry and, due to its fertile soil, grows many crops. Apparently, Bangladesh people rarely smile as this can be seen as a sign of immaturity. I'm going to look like a child with all my smiling. The national animal is the Royal Bengal Tiger whose roar can be heard up to three kilometres away. It's one of the most disaster-prone areas in the world, due in part to its low-lying deltas formed by the Ganges, Brahmaputra and Meghna rivers.

Immigration goes well, but it's when we hand over the Carnet de Passage everything changes. We are left sitting in the main entrance room for over an hour before being called back in. Facing the unsmiling senior immigration officer and two others, I'm thinking how mature they are trying to look. When setting up the Carnet, you must stipulate all the countries you will travel through. As our route was dependent on many things, David had listed every country he thought we might possibly need to drive through.

The Carnet is handed back to us, declaring under no circumstances can Lizzybus be brought into their country on it. We have a sick feeling, thinking we had missed Bangladesh off the list. Checking the Carnet, we're relieved to see it is on the list and point this out. It makes no difference; the Bangladesh government has overruled this and is no longer accepting Carnets. We're asked to follow them, in Lizzybus, to Benapole customs headquarters where we're presented with photocopies, not in English, of government documents stating Carnets are not valid here and will not be accepted. Their government requires a two-thousand-dollar bond paid in local currency into a specified bank. Another document states Lizzybus has been impounded.

The reality of our situation sinks in. As it's Friday, a Muslim day of prayer, banks are closed, even if we could get the cash out, with the limits on each withdrawal it would take weeks to get the amount needed. With only a single-entry visa for India, we can´t go back, but worse, having been stamped into Bangladesh, the clock is ticking on our visas.

Parked now outside this two-storey administration building with a grassed area, gardens and houses where the staff and their families live, we're given the option to leave Lizzybus and backpack around Bangladesh, then return to India. Of course, that would mean getting another visa which we can only get from the embassy in England. Or pay their two-thousand-dollar bond.

With no intention of going anywhere without Lizzybus, I look up at the building where we're parked with its security guard, and having used it, I know there's a toilet and basic shower inside. I say, "Okay, as we cannot go back into India or take Lizzybus into Bangladesh, we will stay here. We like it here, it's very nice."

They are a little taken aback and puzzled, not quite sure what to do, when Customs Officer Mohammed (Mo) arrives, speaking excellent English. On hearing of our situation, he is most apologetic and vows to do everything he can to help us. He agrees to us camping here until Monday with access to the toilet and shower.

As Pakistan, India and Bangladesh were all part of British India before gaining independence, you can see the British influence in all three countries, but the difference between them is striking. With Bangladesh only recently becoming independent, it doesn't seem to have the money that creates the massive divide we felt in India. In a way we prefer it; living amongst the locals, we feel a real warmth. At seven each morning, the children climb the ladder to poke their heads into the tent shouting, "Good morning ant-ie, uncle". They take us out for street food and invite us into their homes. They open the school so we can talk about and show pictures of our journey on the laptop, we hand out more pens. It's becoming a very special time.

Respect in this community is given according to your level of education and position in life. With David's criminal law background, it makes him a most honoured guest. I can relax as it's no longer compulsory to cover my head and women are more visible. In the evening, I even join the women in track suits, worn over their saris, in a jog around the compound. I used to jog around my local park back home, never thinking for one moment I would be jogging around a park in Bangladesh, with ladies in gym kits over their saris, having been impounded in Lizzybus. But nothing about life surprises me anymore.

We investigate the government bond, with the limits on daily cash withdrawals, no guarantee when, or if, we would ever get our money back we ditch this idea. Neither David nor I are overly concerned with our situation as we have emailed the British Embassy and the AA (who issued the Carnet) and they are now in negotiations with the Bangladeshi government over what they see as a reneging on an international agreement.

Customs Officer Mo has become a firm friend and daily visitor. Today he insists on taking me out on his motor bike. I hate bikes but agree on the proviso it will only be in the compound. Once on the back of his bike, I'm taken straight out of the gates and onto the streets of Benapole. I don't want to, but need to hold onto Mo who tells me how beautiful I am. He takes me to visit a cattle market and a brick making factory. We arrive at an almost derelict building; apparently Mo is meeting friends here and would like to know if I fancy taking a shower.

Take a shower? No, I don't! I realise how vulnerable I am but don't want to upset him being our negotiator. I've no idea where I am or how to get back. I demand to be taken back right now as my husband is a very jealous man and will be most offended.

Back at Customs House, David is waiting. I say nothing and climb into the roof tent, zipping it up behind me, my way of slamming the door. David is confused, knowing something has upset me, but engages in polite conversation with Mo. I'm broken and overwhelmed by what happened, almost thinking I had encouraged it. Despite this little hiccup, we are having a very special unique experience here. It's such a privilege to not only see the life of this community, but to become part of it. I can't imagine a government building in the western world allowing us, not only to park, but to live outside and use the facilities.

Today, we are invited to join in the celebrations for a ten-year-old boy's circumcision. I thought circumcisions were carried out on newborns, but it can be at any age, for religious reasons, hygiene, or even just preference. We are taken on a cart pulled by a donkey; I sit with my legs dangling off the back, lurching this way and that through the honking traffic. I don't even hold on and wave to all the people we now know. We arrive in the manicured grounds of this palatial house, where rows of tables, draped in white linen, are adorned with china, glass and flowers, as the women in beautiful saris cook over huge cauldrons. Dropped off by our donkey and cart beside the gleaming cars with their chauffeurs, I´m not the slightest bit embarrassed, just sad we're not in Lizzybus.

But I do have my limits and reach them when invited inside the house with its marble floors, white leather furniture, and beautifully draped curtains. The ladies are in saris of the finest silk, the men in military outfits adorned with gold epaulettes. In our 'embassy' outfits of white shirts, now African-stained red, and trousers hanging off our hips, my afro frizz hair and David's caveman-grey beard, it's toe-curling. David has never felt any of this in any aspect of his life.

It's something I´ve struggled with ever since visiting my mother in hospital who told me to hide so the nurses wouldn't see my hair. I see the ridiculousness of it now, wanting only to defend my mother. She was a proud woman from a time when holding your head high could only be done if everything about you looked good. Just your petticoat showing below your skirt, or your bra strap hanging down could sabotage this. I understand Mom, and I truly forgive you.

We are introduced to the boy who has just been circumcised. He is sitting on a throne of cushions, resplendent in full traditional dress, his eyes relaying both actual physical pain and relief it's over. Back outside, we're seated with the other guests for a banquet of traditional food and entertained by dancers and drummers. I've mentioned before that David, and I often visited the 'Balti-Triangle', but so far, we're yet to have our food served in a Balti bowl. The food is fresh, fragrant and varied, family recipes handed down through the generations, and totally scrummy delicious. Back at 'camp', I find a posy of flowers on the table from the children.

There is a warmth and generosity here, but the pressure is beginning to show. Being under such intense scrutiny and interest twenty-four hours a day, we begin to flounder, to lose hope. We have endless meetings with Mo and Zaher, who phone, fax and write to the High Commissioner in Dakar on our behalf. We are at the mercy of governments, oblivious to the reality of our situation, just another item on the agenda. But it's very real to us, our future and our journey hangs on their decision. There is also the worry of having been stamped into Bangladesh, we could face visa issues here. For some reason, we only have a thirty-day single entry visa, not the standard three months.

Today I'm at breaking point. I need some space so sit alone under a tree in the grounds. Within minutes, I'm surrounded by people who all want to talk when I just want them to shut up. I feel so bad about this, especially the children who don't understand our situation, so I agree to play cricket with them. A man comes over from the administration building and tells me he's the assistant to Mr Magoob, the High Commissioner, who, returning from his business trip, saw me out of his window and wants to meet me - us.

This is the turning point, the breakthrough we needed.

The charming and eloquent Mr Magoob sits behind a conference-sized desk, dressed in a white cotton tunic with elaborate gold embroidered epaulettes. His beard, which covers most of his chest, is the same rich red henna colour as his halo of frizzy hair. I'm hot and sweaty from playing cricket and my mouth is dry. Offered a drink, I immediately answer, "yes please". A tray is brought with one can of Fanta lemonade and two glasses with a slice of lemon and an ice cube in each. I pour us half each and drink mine in one go, the bubbles shooting up my nose; the cold and the hit of sugar is immediate. I´m embarrassed as it causes me to burp very loudly.

Mr Magoob starts with, "Your vehicle", to which we both nod, and continues with, "is not a vehicle", which confuses us. He declares, "It's a home and homes are exempt!" Of course, we both agree because Lizzybus is our home. Right there, right now, he gets out a rubber stamp and proceeds to stamp and sign the Carnet. Walking around the humongous desk, he shakes both our hands and informs us we are free to go.

We are speechless, momentarily unable to digest what he is saying. It seems the Carnet was being abused by Bangladeshi people with British passports living in England. Bringing vehicles in and selling them, even forfeiting the money for the Carnet, avoids paying import tax, making it a very lucrative business. Many genuine overlanders have been caught up in all this, their vehicles impounded at the docks incurring huge storage fees. The owners, unable to pay these fees, abandon their vehicles, their dreams, and their life.

(As I write, a vehicle permit from the Bangladesh Road Transport Authority BRTA is required).

CHAPTER 16

FREEDOM COMES TO THOSE WAIT

Eight days after arriving at the Customs House, Benapole, the impressive gates are opened one last time for us as we drive out in our official 'home' - Lizzybus. Mr Magoob, resplendent in his dress of office, and half the people of Benapole are lined up ready to cheer. But first, we have the flag sticking on ceremony. The experience we have had here has been unique, a real window into life. We will forever remember the people of Benapole, their kindness and generosity.

We're heading now to the port town of Chittagong, via Dhaka the capital of Bangladesh, over eight hundred kilometres away. It's there we will arrange the shipping to Malaysia. With just over two weeks left on our visa, we aim to get to Chittagong in a week, leaving us a week to make the arrangements. It's a main highway in name only. The blanket of black smog turning day into night spares us the sight of the miles of gridlocked traffic, in part caused by broken down lorries, their carcasses stripped, and the parts used to keep others moving. But also, as Bangladesh lies only ten metres above sea level, with rivers and vast deltas, many of the roads have been washed out making them impassable.

The River Ganges melts into her shore, muted, muddied, and timeless. It's thrilling seeing this river, regarded as sacred by Hindus, her journey having started in the Himalayas. All we must do now is get the ferry across her. In the snaking queue of traffic once more, we are called forward to cheering and waving - even the police stop the traffic for us.

We drive Lizzybus onto the single deck ferry. Vehicles are parked so close you couldn't fit a fag packet between them. We immediately get out of Lizzybus before the next vehicle traps us in. I can't believe how many people choose to stay in their vehicles, as much as we love Lizzybus, if the ferry goes down, she's on her own. On deck they are serving lunch - chicken and curried rice for a few takas. A group of students who had been admiring Lizzybus press two brand new ten-taka notes into our hand for the journey ahead (about the cost of the lunch). We have learned to accept these gestures with the generosity they have been given. All too soon, our ferry 'cruise' across the Ganges is over.

Standing beside Lizzybus, waiting for the next vehicle to move so we can open the door, I look down to see a limbless trunk of a man on a square of wood with wheels. He is smiling up at me; I sit with him. In perfect English, he tells me he has lived on this ferry that crosses the Ganges day and night for as long as he can remember. The vehicles are now on the move and the drivers are honking their horns for us to move Lizzybus. I hug him, and remembering the two ten-taka notes we were given, tuck them under the stump of his arm. I feel a little broken inside by it all.

We arrive in Dhaka. The modern-day city is of glass and chrome, the old of magnificent Victorian buildings and vast gardens from its Mughal Empire and colonial British Indian past. It's a city you could spend days looking around, but we have no such luxury. After a night in our budget hotel room, we're up early, showered, eat the included breakfast, then hit the road. If we thought the traffic was bad before, it's nothing to what we face now. Having only managed three hundred of the eight hundred kilometres in two days, we realise getting to Chittagong in a week might be a little ambitious.

There are no visible lanes or lines of traffic, just traffic. It's at this point we are rear ended and pushed forward into the car in front. We haven't done any damage to this vehicle; we're just resting on its bumper, very different to the car which ran into us. Its front end is caved in, the crumpled bonnet smashing the windscreen and radiator, boiling water and oil pours from it.

David had fitted steel corner protectors and a cross bar to Lizzybus, so the damage to us is nothing. A lot more concerning is just being here; despite being hit from the back, we're in a very precarious situation. I'll just mention insurance here. Whenever we've been able to buy insurance, usually on crossing the border, we get it. So yes, we have insurance, but the reality is, it's mainly to get through the police check points. Claiming on it would be a very different matter. David checks that no one in the car is injured, I get the man in front to pull forward. With no one dead, and just enough space to pull out, I shout for David to get back in as we force our way back into the traffic, for once appreciating its mayhem.

We're driving through one of the world's largest shipbreaking yards, where decommissioned warships, supertankers, or any kind of ocean-going vessels are dismantled. It was once a tourist attraction until its poor safety record and working conditions came under scrutiny. Many people lost their lives making a subsistence living in these hazardous toxic conditions, dismantling vessels with little more than blowtorches, sledgehammers, and physical force. All along the roadside salvage scrap is sold, anything from engines and wiring to personnel lockers and ships' funnels, even life rings. A slick of green sludge runs beside the road where not a single tree, blade of grass or even weeds survive.

Three days later we make it to the port area of Chittagong. Like all ports, it attracts a lot of migrant workers and as crime is part of life here, we're told not to stay as it verges on lawlessness. For us, 'any port in a storm' is good we need be close to the docks. This is where our journey ends for now, where Lizzybus will be put into a container and shipped to Penang, Malaysia. Once Lizzybus is securely parked, we eat a curried egg takeaway in our hotel room watching a promotional documentary on the television of the Shipbreaking Yard and Cox's Bazar, the world's longest beach. I find it almost impossible to relate it to the reality of what we have just driven through.

Today is Friday, we've forgotten to remember it's the Muslim day of prayer and that all shipping offices are closed, remembering this now, we go off to explore. We take a tuk-tuk to the WWII Memorial Cemetery to honour the forces who died on the Burma front. Looking around this neatly manicured and peaceful cemetery, I wonder how we are not part of the dead after our death-defying tuk-tuk ride here. We walk back to the hotel.

News of our impoundment in Benapole has been broadcast to all shipping agents, Mr Ashen, the Managing Director of our shipping company, comes personally to meet us at our hotel. Although Mr Magoob declared Lizzybus a home, we realise trying to persuade others of this fact will not be without issues. Mr Ashen assures us from now on we will be treated as honorary guests in his country and all formalities will be dealt with as a priority. True to his word, over the next few days, we are dragged around many offices by his second-in-command, getting the one stamp needed on each sheet of the alarming number of sheets in our file.

Finally, today we will get the one last stamp, that of the Chief Commissioner. The importance of this stamp is not lost on us, knowing

Lizzybus is officially unofficially illegal here. Dressed in our 'embassy outfits', we go with the clerk to a shabby four-storey building, each floor has a security guard who needs to get authorisation before we can proceed to the next floor. On the top floor, shabby becomes chic with marble floors and whitewashed walls. Beside the dark wood door, with its shiny brass plaque, are two occupied chairs. We stand at the end of the queue of people, all loaded down with files. The security guard asks the occupants of the chairs to stand up and calls us forward to sit on them. Having overcome my English need for queuing, I'm still uncomfortable about this.

The Chief Commissioner, sitting behind another enormous desk, barely looks up. The clerk indicates for us to sit in the chairs opposite, placing our folder of documents in front of him. We don't say a word as each sheet is scrutinised and questions are asked of the clerk in Bengali. Never more so than right now, I think of all the people on our journey who have held our future in their hands. I feel this scrutiny is more about ceremony appropriate to the Commissioner's status. Finally, stamping and signing the documents, he slides the file over to us. David and I walk around the desk; I want to hug him, but feel it's more appropriate to offer my hand. The Commissioner looks up, smiles, shakes our hand and in perfect English, wishes us good luck.

There is no time to relax or celebrate with only six days left on our visa. We face the mammoth task of getting Lizzybus into a container and us onto flights to Asia.

Today, I am driving Lizzybus to the docks following the tuk-tuk with David and MD Mr Ashen. I had thought driving Lizzybus, rather than going in the tuk-tuk, would be the least terrifying. How wrong was I? My knuckles are white gripping the steering wheel, bile rises in my throat at the thought of losing them in all this chaos. With almost every vehicle being a tuk-tuk, trying to follow theirs is almost impossible, not soon enough did we reach the armed gates and entrance to the docks. Once inside, I think I've gone deaf and blind; the silence is complete, and snow-white painted lines dazzle on the smooth black tarmac.

A cursory glance is given to the paperwork before we're taken to the container that will 'contain' Lizzybus for her sailing across the Indian Ocean. Despite removing the top box and deflating the tyres, Lizzybus still won't fit. With two port workers, Mr Ashen and David hanging off her, to a resounding cheer she is in. We collapse in fits of laughter and exhaustion. In the semi-darkness we lash Lizzybus down with the ratchet straps and wooden blocks we brought with us. I kiss her, tell her to behave, promising to rescue her soon. The clunk of the lock-rod and metal bar securing the doors sounds so final, like the door on a prison cell. The plastic seal with its unique serial number is secured and recorded on the paperwork, not to be removed until she arrives and opened in front of us. We feel intense relief, along with a sense of bereavement, as to what this inanimate chunk of metal means to us.

We both want, and need, a moment, telling Mr Ashen we will walk back to the hotel. He is adamant it's far too dangerous to be on the streets after dark. It's interesting how others view danger. We're squeezed into this tuk-tuk without wiper blades, the evening drizzle making fuzzy blobs on the scratched opaque plastic windscreen, with no street lighting, in gridlocked traffic. Now this is dangerous.

Although Lizzybus is in her container, we can´t leave without the bill of lading, issued only when she is loaded, the proof that, if the ship goes down, she was on it. Today we have it. Lizzybus has been loaded and due to set sail in two days, so we book flights for three days' time. Although it's the last day of our visa, if for any reason the ship does not sail, we will still be here. We'd rather face visa issues than be on another continent.

Finally, with nothing more we can do, despite the warning from Mr Ashen about the dangers of walking the streets at night, we are out on them. We feel at home here; it's alive with smells, sounds and energy. We sit eating delicious street food of deep-fried dumplings, with both sweet and savoury fillings. A man is playing a flute and another a drum. I dance and skip around them, oblivious to the onlookers and the rain. I've always found it poetic that you never know the person you pass, their struggles, their achievements, their life. No one around us knows how very special this evening is, bringing this chapter to a close.

We're skinny now, our clothes the colour of earth hang off us and our skin is dark and leathery. My hair is matted, David´s head has become almost bald. This journey has pushed us to beyond anything we could have imagined. There is no limit to what you can endure, to what you can conquer and most importantly, to what you can absolutely embrace.

Having received confirmation that Lizzybus has set sail, we can get the flights booked for tomorrow free of worry. I want to shout and scream, "We did it, we actually did it!" From being impounded in

Benapole, rear ended in Dhaka, to navigating the Delta and crossing the Ganges, David and I did it.

With just a small rucksack each, our change of clothes and toothbrushes in mine, the folder full of our documents in David's, we are ready for our next adventure. On this tiny plane the included in-flight refreshment is a plastic cup of orange squash and half a cheese sandwich wrapped in a serviette.

We're not actually heading directly for Malaysia, but are on an internal flight back to Dhaka for a connecting flight to Malaysia. Looking out of the window below us, I see the meandering rivers, deltas and sea. It's beautiful, belying the reality and chaos we faced down there. Aboard our flight to Kuala Lumpur, Malaysia, everything changes starting with the size and quality of the aircraft, and the in-flight refreshments which are served in sealed packets with individual tins of soft drinks.

Kuala Lumpur airport is a hub taking you to the delights of Asia. I feel a buzz here with the expectation of the exotic holiday to come. For us, it's just another part in what seems like our never-ending story. From here we must get to the port of Penang, hundreds of kilometres away and rescue Lizzybus. This airport is something else, gleaming chrome and glass with miles of automated walkways and high-end duty-free shops. Normally when crossing that strip of no man's land, the change is always striking. Skipping two whole countries, the change is quite astonishing. Air we can breathe, smooth tarmac roads, towering skyscrapers, working traffic lights, and litter-free streets. It's as if we have been transported, not just to another country, but to another planet.

We get an overnight coach to Penang three hundred kilometres away, a distance that in Africa would take us days, but on this luxury coach with reclining seats, we're no sooner asleep than we arrive. That's because we are not in Penang; we're at the train station in Kuala Lumpa. The two things guaranteed to make me irritable and miserable are being tired and hungry. I've now added a third - finding out that the coach only takes us to the train station, and now we must get a train. In any other circumstances, I would have been excited to have a train ride, but I´m knackered. I´m slightly pacified on finding this 'new planet' has trains with reclining seats; it also serves the most delicious bowl of noodles. My eyelids involuntarily close and I'm fast asleep.

David is quite amazing; always watching over me, he finds the trains, the buses, the routes, from scribbled notes and local maps. After my nap and snack, I´m ready to get going with the next adventure. Arriving at Penang train station, we now need to get a ferry to the island of Penang, the tip of this peninsula.

Two flights, a coach, a train, a ferry and a taxi, two days later, in the same clothes we set off in, we arrive at our pre-booked hotel on the Island of Penang. I'm no longer giving a single thought to Lizzybus, only to beer, food, shower and sleep.

Welcome to Malaysia, its capital Kuala Lumpur, with muddy estuaries, coral-reefed and sandy-shored islands, dense jungles, mountains, and vast cities. Nutmeg, cloves, pepper, rubber, tin, and timber were once its main exports, now it's electronics and electrical machinery. A former British colony, traffic drives on the left-hand side and English is widely spoken. At around a third larger than the United Kingdom, it's the forty-first country and the third continent on our journey. This will only be acknowledged when we are reunited with Lizzybus with the flag sticking on ceremony.

We are on the world heritage island of George Town where the cataract of pollution covering our eyes has been removed. A few days have passed since arriving here, and as they only allow two people on a motorbike here, I have been left in the hotel room. David is being ferried on the back of a motorbike around various offices with the 'fixer', sorting out the paperwork needed to get Lizzybus back, who is still in her container on a ship in the Indian Ocean.

Why is everything so complicated? Before we can do anything else, we need an International Circulation Permit (ICP), something our fixer said can easily be arranged, but something he now can't. A bit like the change in government policy with the Carnet in Bangladesh, this is a change by the Malay Transport Authority, in that it can now only be issued at its headquarters in Kuala Lumpur, where we arrived four days ago.

You´ve got to be kidding me. I'm so fed up. Not only have we paid this agent to sort this out, but we could have got it before leaving Kuala Lumpur. It makes not one iota scrap of difference; it's not like you can sue or get your money back. It's down to us to sort this mess out. We have no choice other than to go back to Kuala Lumpur.

I could have stayed in the hotel room as it's paid for, but we know from experience how important it is to stay together. We're now on an overnight coach heading back to Kuala Lumpur. On the plus side, it is a direct coach; on the minus, it arrives at five in the morning. We get a taxi to the immaculate sprawl of red brick government buildings with their beautifully manicured gardens at six a.m. Obviously it´s closed, but the security guard lets us into the main building, allowing us to wait outside the third-floor office. Here we find soft leather sofas which within minutes I´m curled up asleep on.

Two hours later the staff arrive to find us both fast asleep. They are apologetic about our plight, immediately issuing us the free International Circulation Permit. Free, if we had not had the cost of overnight coaches, taxi fares, and two nights for a hotel room we couldn't use. We're invited to use the subsidised canteen for a delicious breakfast of egg something, steamed something, and fresh coffee. We're also given a polystyrene container full of chicken and rice, all complimentary. On our overnight coach with reclining leather seats, we feel a warmth from the generosity and kindness we were given. We might like you Malaysia.

Yesterday we had confirmation that the ship had docked; today we're collecting Lizzybus. We're standing here now with Raja our fixer (who didn't really fix) in front of the very same container that only a few short weeks ago, but feels like a lifetime, we stuffed Lizzybus into. A simple signature is all that is required of us, the seal is checked against the paperwork, the doors are cranked open, and there she is. I'm overcome with emotion, relief, and a little guilt at having locked her up. Thinking about it, tucked up in her container, she's had the easy bit compared to what we've just gone through.

Lizzybus fires up on the first turn of the key, coughing out the familiar puff of smoke. With David and two dock workers hanging off the back, I reverse her out into the glorious sunlight of her new country and continent. The first thing we do is have the flag sticking on ceremony with the dock workers and fixer. To re-inflate the tyres and simply drive out of the unmanned exit gates into the next chapter of this incredible journey.

CHAPTER 17

THE DESIRE AND NEED TO EXPLORE

We now have two choices, to head from Malaysia directly to Singapore for the next shipping to Australia, or head north and take Lizzybus into:

Thailand - Vietnam – Cambodia - Malaysia (again) – Singapore

This journey has never been about ticking any boxes, but about getting Lizzybus around the world whilst seeing as much of it as we possibly could. Neither of us wants to ignore these countries, even though effectively it means we will be driving backwards, not forwards. David is relieved, he thought he would be facing far more opposition from me.

A priority before we head off is new tyres, as I´ve become a bit of a tyre expert now, both David and I are a little disappointed that we can't get our preferred BF Goodrich mud terrains. Still it's astounding to me that you can drive into a garage with floor to ceiling shelving, loaded with every tyre you could ever want, and those they don't have, like the Lizzybus tyres, or they can offer a good alternative. Not only that, but they fit, balance and track the tyres here whilst you watch from an air-conditioned office, drinking coffee. Within a few hours, we have six brand new Goodyear all terrain tyres, not what we wanted but better than what we had, specifically the two Indian truck tyres.

For two days, David lies prostrate under Lizzybus or is bent over her engine replacing missing bolts and worn bearings, oiling and greasing nipples and door hinges, adjusting steering, and doing other stuff I don't care to remember. This maintenance of Lizzybus does not guarantee trouble-free driving, but it certainly ups the odds.

Our 'fame' is spreading. Mr Kia from the local paper interviews us at our hotel before we go for a photo shoot at what was the old fish market with a picturesque collapsed wall full of graffiti. A man living under canvas has made this his personal car park and wants us to pay him to film here. Sweat pours off us whilst putting up the rooftop tent side awning, table and chairs. Ignoring the car park attendant's demands for money, we ask him to become part of our photo shoot.

He sits in one of the chairs watching as we spread out the map, as aromatic as the stagnant canal beside us. His weathered face is like leather under his shredded straw hat, smiling now, he reveals one yellow stained tooth. He is in disbelief as the cameraman explains where we have driven from, pointing with his wizened finger to places he has never been to or will ever go. The simplicity of these moments fills me with warmth. On leaving, we pay him, not for letting us use 'his car park', but for being an extra in our film.

The song "Hit the road Jack and don't you come back no more" plays on loop in my head; we are ready, it's time to move on.

We have a problem - David's passport has only two blank pages left. It can be renewed in Australia, but even if we go straight there from Malaysia, we still have Singapore to pass through which will use at least one, possibly two pages with visa exit and entry stamps. Most countries insist you have one clear page in your passport so you can be stamped back out. We have another option of applying online and having the passport posted back, if we can provide a secure address. This means not having to send the old passport back, but on receipt of the new one, we are duty bound to cut the corner off the old one. David can still travel using his old passport until the new one arrives. The decision is made; an online application has been filled out and a day later we are at the Thai border.

Thailand, capital Bangkok, known for its sandy beaches, tropical islands, museums, remote hill tribes, palaces and Buddhist Temples, also has the unenviable tag as a sex tourism destination. Prostitution itself is not illegal, but many of the activities attached to it are – whatever that means. A blind eye can be turned to the husband visiting a prostitute as it's seen only as empty sex. I wonder if perhaps David might fancy some empty sex.

This to me makes it nothing more than a bodily function, no more than eating, peeing, or pooing. Where's the romance, the wooing, and let's not forget about sexually transmitted diseases. Don't judge me, I won't judge you; I know I´m a Victorian drama queen. I´m so happy for all the sexually liberated people out there, but happy in my pickiness with who I do or don't copulate with.

Normally after being holed up somewhere, getting back on the road fills us with trepidation as to what lies ahead, but it´s just thrilling to be on the move again. Crossing no man's land, we see picturesque stilted wooden houses with tiny songbirds in cages hanging on verandas. Scooters and motorbikes once more have whole families aboard, the helmets hanging idly from handlebars, not on people's heads. It's the monsoon season and Lizzybus is leaking like a sieve, pools of water form in the footwells; we remove the carpet to let the water find its own way out.

David's passport will take at least three weeks, he signs up for a dive instructor's course on Ko Tao, a late birthday present from the Seniors. As the course includes accommodation for us both, we'll save money. It also gives us a secure address for the return of David's passport. We store Lizzybus at the backpackers in the coastal town of Kumasi and take the five-hour ferry to Ko Tao.

When we arrived in Thailand, we were told Lizzybus only needed to be registered on the local 'Simplified Customs Form' not the Carnet de Passage. David, looking through our paperwork now, realises the form is only valid for four weeks. If Lizzybus is not out of the country by that date, we could face a twenty-five thousand dollar fine. With David's passport now being delivered to the dive centre, we have no choice other than to go. I feel sabotaged. Just when I think we can relax and do something other than worry, this happens.

I swallow the recurring lump of bile rising in my throat thinking of the worst-case scenario, like the passport application being rejected and us being stranded on this island, with Lizzybus on the mainland and the possibility of a huge fine. I'm asking myself if getting around the world in your own vehicle is the way to go. At times, it seems like we lurch from one situation to another with her, because in some ways we do. But this is nothing to the freedom, the places that are made accessible to us, and the choices she gives us. Faced once more with a situation out of our control, with nothing we can do about it, we ignore it for now.

The days find their own rhythm. David brings me a morning coffee, checks to see if his passport has arrived, then goes off for classroom, pool, or boat stuff. I walk, swim, sleep and write. From wanting space, I begin to feel lonely, so go diving in the afternoons; the need for a 'buddy' to dive means I get teamed up with a buddy-less person.

With time to reflect, I re-read my journals from August 2009, over two and a half years ago. Leaving that morning in the pouring rain, as if I was just popping to the shops for bread and milk, I remember looking over at David and thinking how I had placed my future firmly in his hands. Having never got an answer from David as to how he felt, I ask him again. He admits to having been terrified - of the responsibility of me and Lizzybus. I love this vulnerable side of him and put my arms around him.

We both know that when pushed to our limits, physically and mentally, our words can be caustic and destructive. I´m a real believer in talking about stuff, how things make you feel, but this only works if you not just listen, but hear. What we are going through is way beyond anything life has taught us. We need to be united and, most of all, we need to be friends. I've found this lack of conversation far more painful than the lack of intimacy. It's not about accepting change; it's about having changed!

We have no idea who the prime minister is, what song tops the charts, how much a loaf of bread costs. All our focus is on visas, crossing borders, food, shelter, water and, right now, David's passport. As travel companions there is no one other than each other we would rather travel with. Although if Omar Sharif, Richard Burton or Laurence of Arabia were to be re-incarnated any time soon, David, who is David?

I have accepted we both have equally important roles in all this, me in keeping David from completely imploding, David in sorting out the logistics, and both of us for making it happen. We make another pact. David will try to talk more about feelings and less about worst-case scenarios. I will try to talk less about feelings and let him talk more about worst-case scenarios. In this moment we come together; it's not exactly a night of raw passion, but of a much-needed closeness. Let's just see how long it lasts.

David not only has in his possession a new passport, but is now a fully qualified dive instructor, I'm bursting with pride in him. We celebrate by diving together, as David is now qualified to guide me. When underwater, with a great big regulator in your gob, everything is done with hand signals. My favourite and most valuable one, although not exactly recognised, is the one finger. I use this whenever David signals for me to ascend due to low air. From someone who could not even bear water on their face in the shower, I'm now like a baby seal. I want nothing more than to stay submerged in this magical underwater world, air or no air.

Tonight, there is a big party for all those completing not just instructor courses, but all dive courses, but with only five days to get Lizzybus out of Thailand and into Cambodia to avoid the possibility of a huge fine, we can't go. Instead, we take the five-hour ferry and taxi back to the backpackers to collect Lizzybus. It's always emotional being re-united with Lizzybus, like an old friend or a loved pet, we miss her. We have four days to do the nine hundred kilometres to the Cambodian border; another mission. Having had such a wonderful time on Ko Tao, David with a new passport and passing his instructors course, intimacy and communication restored, all's good in the Lizzybus camp.

This newfound harmony is tested immediately when next morning we find the exit blocked from the backpackers by a broken-down car, which we simply tow off. Getting back into Lizzybus; she won't start, this ongoing starting issue, or more precisely, not starting really tests us. Some men from a cement factory opposite come over and offer to push start us. Although a little hurt by his unfaithful mistress, David surprisingly takes this on the chin.

Through a day surrounded by palm oil plantations, debilitating heat and humidity, the traffic builds as we near Bangkok. With dusk settling around us we pull over at a service station to fill up. We park up amongst the rows of trucks, knowing we'll be safe. There's a hut with a standpipe and toilet. David holds the door shut and fully clothed, I wash with my bar of soap. We always feel safe and looked after in these places, the truckers many times offering us food.

Bangkok is a vast metropolis with a spider's web of flyovers and fly-unders. Driving over an elevated section, we get a three-hundred-and-sixty-degree panoramic view of its skyline and halo of smog. We have no time to stop and explore this sprawl; it's hard enough navigating through it. A few hours later, we're in an expanse of barren paddy fields awaiting the rains. We have been warned that Thai police have a reputation for targeting tourists to, let's just say, boost their poor salaries. It's not been our experience; on facing several police roadblocks, we are waved through them.

We arrive at the border with a day remaining on the Simplified Customs Form and follow the diverted traffic to a building where everyone is given application forms. I become suspicious when they offer to fill the forms out for us. Since when do border staff fill out your forms? Never! Unless there is something in it for them, in this case twenty dollars per person. David checks the man's security pass which states Tour Operator. It's an unofficial, official scam between the border staff and them. We make it quite clear we will collect and fill out our own forms at the real border and leave.

Handing over our completed forms, we hold our breath when they get to the Simplified Customs Form. Without even checking the date, the man just stamps it. It wouldn't have mattered how long we stayed, but of course we didn't know that.

Cambodia, capital Phnom Penh - low plains, high mountains, the Mekong River, Tonlé Sap Lake, and what is considered to be the largest religious structure in the world Angkor Wat. We are just outside the monsoon season with everything crossed it's not early this year.

The border of Cambodia is set up to make money in any way it can. One way is when someone is trying to use a new passport and the exit stamp from Thailand is in the old one. Another way can be when the photograph needed for the application is not the right size, like the American couple beside us. What they don't seem to grasp is whatever we might think, however unfair we feel this is, it's best to just agree, apologise, and ask how we can make this right. The Americans are indignant, saying how corrupt border staff are, the scams they have faced, how this would never happen in the States. At this point, they are taken off into a private room for an interview.

We, however, are apologising profusely, offering David's old, supposedly invalid passport which we had not cut the corner off. They are happy with this suggestion, but even though we ask if they could put the stamp on one of the half-used pages, they refuse. They put it right in the middle of the last two free pages. After the issue with the Simplified Customs Form, we insist, well beg, to have the Carnet de Passage stamped. They ponder this, passing it around each other until one man grudgingly stamps it. There is no "welcome to our country", no shaking of the offered hand, or acknowledgment of our gushing thank you. They just seem irritated to not have got any money out of us. The Americans are still being interviewed.

Hello Cambodia. After the flag sticking on ceremony, we book into a six dollar a night room and go out for dinner at the café opposite. With no menu, we point at the bowl of food being eating on the table next to us. It looks like a boiled egg, chicken and rice. I'm splitting my sides laughing waiting for David to bite into his boiled egg. It tastes like the smell of the gasses emitted from the worst fart you could ever imagine. A fermented egg, over pig's entrails with liquid rice. David and I will eat almost anything but this tests us, not just in the eating of it, but in not retching whilst doing it. With all eyes on us, we don't want to offend.

I'm beginning to really enjoy this little adventure, considering going backwards usually makes me most grumpy. It's such a beautiful country. We're heading for Siem Reap and the temples of Angkor Wat (City of Temples). The main temple is pictured on the Cambodian flag. We're in a now familiar landscape of corrugated metal, wood, or concrete houses set into jungle. Our biggest issue is avoiding the low hanging electricity wires strung from lopsided wooden poles, rooftops and trees. Thirteen years ago, David and I did a three-week backpacking trip to Cambodia and Vietnam. Three of those days were spent at Angkor Wat, clinging to the back of motor bikes. I was in awe of what I was seeing and never ever in my wildest dreams did I imagine I/we would not only be back one day, but that we would drive here via Africa in Lizzybus.

We call in at the Cambodia Self Help De-mining Charity, with a small Museum set up by Aki Ra, a surviving boy soldier from the Khmer Rouge era, when Pol Pot reset the country to year zero, forcing everyone to work on the land. The educated, non-ethnic, or people with political views were tortured, put to death, or just died through disease and starvation. It's estimated over a million or more people lost their lives during this period in what is now known as the Killing Fields. Its legacy has been the many unexploded land mines causing death and destruction. Behind this Museum is an orphanage for the children who have not just lost mothers and fathers, but limbs due to stepping on land mines.

When holed up in Egypt waiting for news on Syria, I was given bags and bags of unwanted holiday stuff. Pairs of crystal encrusted flips flops, sequined hats, and glittery T-shirts, along with bottles of sunscreen, diarrhoea treatments, re-hydration packs and pain killers. I didn't really have the space for them, nor the heart to throw them away, so stored them on the roof of Lizzybus. This is the perfect place to donate them because the children here are all the same, with missing parents and missing limbs, it's normal to them. In the matter-of-fact way of children, they share flip flops depending on which leg they have left. The oversized sequined T-shirts hanging where arms used to be, are tied on with glittering belts by the children who still have arms. Adult

Angkor Wat, Cambodia

sun hats flop down over ears so all you see is a huge grin. Although some of the boys love a footie T-shirt and the girls a bit of glitter, most don't care.

The children sit cross-legged in a circle around us; the ones who don't have a leg to cross are propped up between the ones who do. It doesn't matter that the children don't understand our words, they see and are transfixed by our maps and pictures. Looking out over this sea of little faces, I wonder how much more this journey could be if we were able to speak the language. I´d love to be able to chat to these children, to hear their stories. Still, it's been a very special magical moment on this journey.

I have such a mix of emotions, from profound sadness to untold admiration for the staff and the children here, their resilience and acceptance of what has happened, their kindness to each other, their laughter.

Being here again at Angkor Wat is both a pinch-me and a revelation moment. My overriding memory of our three days here was of the heat, humidity and scale of it; each temple significant and unique, but all merging into one – I was told this was Temple Fatigue. This time, getting Lizzybus to Angkor Wat is our achievement and the best part of this day was visiting the orphanage.

Keeping Lizzybus going is a constant battle. Most frustrating is the starting issue, which is a huge worry especially when camping in remote areas alone. The rainy season is upon us. With the humidity and constant downpours, our bed linen is becoming mouldy and damp. I have a boil on the back of my neck which is so painful I can only lie my side. David continues with his greasing regime, leaving a greasy residue on everything, this with body odour pushes me to my limit. I would at this stage let David give his thoughts, but all thoughts right now are best kept to ourselves. Which just about sums up our day. Thoughtless.

The huge boil on my neck burst last night, it's such a relief, but the dried green puss mixed with blood on my pillow is making me nauseous. I realise there is an advantage to the rainy season, as the bowl I left out last night is full of warm water. I dissolve a sterilising tablet in it and soak both mine and David's pillowcase. Worried my open boil will become infected in these conditions, David cleans it out with neat alcohol. It stings like hell but is most satisfying, then he covers it with a sterilised dressing. This, along with clean pillowcases hanging in the back of Lizzybus, means every so often I get a waft of clean, which pleases me no end.

In Phnom Penh, having been warned about petty crime specifically from vehicles, we book a room with secure parking. It's one of the places we visited whilst backpacking and has changed enormously. The unlit streets, mud roads, and near derelict buildings are gone; now there is street lighting, tarmac, high class restaurants and bars – it's a city on the mend.

Today we visit S-21 (Security Prison 21), a former secondary school used as a prison by the Khmer Rouge. Of the estimated twenty thousand people imprisoned here, only twelve were known to have survived. It's made real to me how similar in layout it is to my infant school. But the classrooms don't have desks and a blackboard, they have torture devices and chains; the windows don't have panes of glass, but metal grilles and barbed wire. You don't look out to a playground, but to gallows where people were hanged.

The Khmer Rouge required the prison staff to make a detailed dossier of all the prisoners which included a passport-size photograph. The dossiers were lost or destroyed, but some of the black and white photos were found and are displayed on boards in the classrooms. The prisoners are looking into the camera, their eyes vacant and confused. I see the terror and hopelessness they felt. It's incredibly distressing and I ask myself why we are visiting. I think to ignore this is to deny it. Usually, I can see some good in most things, but today I don't.

For many years, the Royal Palace of Cambodia was the official residency of the King of Cambodia and looks like all the Buddhist temples we see here, but on a whole other scale. The Royal Palace is made up of many buildings, halls, and pavilions, with each successive king adding more. Entrance is denied to anyone with uncovered shoulders, skirts or shorts above the knee. We're given a sarong to cover up - even the men - which amuses me no end.

The white elephant seen as sacred is often gifted to a king and depicted everywhere in huge life-size stone statues or frescoes. For elephants to be classified as white, they don't necessarily have to be albino or white, just pale in colour, especially their eyes, toenails, hair, tails and genitals. In the main courtyard is an actual live example of a white elephant. If you stand in front of him, he pats you on the head with his trunk, both a blessing and an indication for you to put money into the urn beside him. I'd much rather see the sculptured-in-stone elephants than this chained up head-patting one, even though he is quite magnificent.

It's Easter Sunday, our third since setting off on this journey. I think about where we were on this day as the years pass - Ghana, Ethiopia, and now here in Cambodia. I no longer feel the same homesickness I had, or the raw longing to be with my family. I'm comforted by Lizzybus, David, this adventure, this life - although a chocolate egg would not be sniffed at, that's for sure.

Heading now for Laos, the furthest north before turning back, we decide to keep driving in that direction until we see something we want to look at, or until we have had enough for the day. The first hour is back along the still under construction, main in name only, highway. Any home in the way is bulldozed; not all of it, just the bit in the way, leaving half houses. In the exposed rooms, the beds are still made, the once sat at tables and chairs are empty. The curtains flutter in the breeze with old pots and pans scattered amongst the rubble.

Along the road, children are cooking in steel drums, with people sat on wooden stools eating, so stop for breakfast. We get deep fried bread spread with margarine and sprinkled with sugar, David loves it as he has a sweet tooth and craves sugar. We pay a lot more than they ask for, giving the children a McDonalds toy each, the ones given away free with a Happy Meal. Not that I have ever had a Happy Meal, but a bagful of them was given to me by people whose children were made 'Happy' on a regular basis.

In this humidity, showering has become a priority, so we book basic rooms rather than bushcamp. As night falls, the rooms come alive with flying and scuttling things. I sleep in my cotton cocoon pulled tight over my head, almost asphyxiating myself, which is preferable to what I can only hear and not see.

We take the scenic route adjacent to the river where bleached latticework wooden homes are balanced on stilts to avoid getting washed away in this marshy swamp. In the shaded area underneath, naked children play with the latest puppy or kitten. On the bridge ahead, the crane that had been replacing the rotten wooden planks has broken-down; we head back to the main road. The monsoon season is kicking in, the dirt roads have become rivers of mud, littered with bogged down and overloaded trucks. Driving Lizzybus with her new mud-terrain tyres, low ratio and locked diffs, she is our formidable warrior.

We follow a sign to Boeng Yeak Lom to find a perfect circular crystal-clear crater lake bordered by virgin rainforest. Wooden platforms projecting into the lake are full of locals picnicking and swimming. I join the children diving and jumping off the skeletal remains of half-submerged trees. The families share their food with us, hard-boiled quail's eggs dipped in salt.

Beautiful Laos, our forty-fourth country on our third continent, with cascading waterfalls and rivers, is known for its relaxed vibe. The main religion here is Buddhism and based on Buddha's teachings. I hadn't realised Buddha was an actual person, Siddhartha Gautama to be precise, an Indian prince who chose to live a simple life having meditated for forty-nine days under the Bodhi tree. I see similarities in how we are living and relate to his belief of all things being equal.

David is beginning to panic when they again refuse to stamp his new passport. At last they agree to squeeze the stamp onto the corner of a half-used page. Crossing the border, we didn't want to switch Lizzybus off, but immigration insisted. We are now being unceremoniously pushed across the border by a group of British backpackers, at least we had an audience for the flag sticking on ceremony. (To all you mechanics screaming at us to get this fixed, believe me, we have tried, by changing everything remotely linked to starting. But, as it's an intermittent fault, you think it's fixed until it happens again.)

On the outskirts of town, I'm pulled over for speeding. David is laughing as I am sat at the desk with two police officers. On the desk is a huge, dog-eared ledger, in which they point out the names and the fines handed out to previous offenders. I don't mind paying, but noticing the fines paid by other speeding motorists are less than half of what I'm being asked for, I call David over. For some reason, they mistake him as a comrade, an officer of the law and shaking his hand, wish us a safe journey.

I've not written my journal for a few days; despite agreeing to heading north, I can't shake the feeling we are travelling for travelling's sake and losing sight of our real goal. It's almost as if David had lied to me about driving around the world, when all he wants to do is drive. I know I'm being the traitor as we were united in wanting to see and do everything we could. But you don't realise the full implications of this, the pressure you are under, especially with this starting issue. It's like letting the genie out of the bottle - once these thoughts are out, I can't get them back in.

I ask David, "If you never went back to England, what would you miss?" "Nothing."

I ask, "If you finished travelling, what would you miss?"

"Everything."

It's not in any way that family are not important to David, or that he doesn't love England. It's just that this life for him is so powerful.

But then 'Simply Beautiful Laos' works her magic; driving along mountain tracks with soaring limestone casts protruding from virgin forest takes my breath away.

We visit caves where a collection of bronze Buddhas had lain undiscovered for years, when a local searching for bats for his dinner came across them. With six others on a wooden pirogue propelled by an ear-splitting two stoke engine, were on the river going through the Tham Kong Loa caves with cathedral high arches, stalactites, stalagmites, and emerald green pools. All trying to plug the holes and scoop out the water of this leaking pirogue, our laughter is lost over the ear-splitting engine noise.

The mighty rivers of Laos have become her downfall, evident in all the colossal hydroelectric plants. The once pristine virgin forest has become a barren landscape of skeletal stumps as far as the eye can see.

It's the five-day Songkran (Water Festival), celebrating the start of the Laos New Year. In every village, town, or collection of huts, locals lie in wait to throw water and coloured powder over you. The music blasting from huge speakers encourages the gyrating of bodies, the consumption of alcohol, getting wet and being covered in a chalky rainbow dust. We buy our very own water gun to get them first. Buckets of water and handfuls of coloured powder are thrown at Lizzybus, until psychedelic and so pretty.

Luang Prabang, a laid-back post-French colonial town on the banks of the Mekong River, is a supposed spectacular drive. It is, but for us, it's also purgatory as the temperature inside Lizzybus reaches over fifty, and the humidity ensure we sweat it out. We visit the Royal Palace, but have no real interest in it.

Having reached Laos it's time to head back. As Vietnam runs parallel to Laos, we could drive back through it, but our International Driving Permits (IDP) are not valid there. The decision is made to head back through Thailand, Malaysia and onto Singapore. It's there we will sort out shipping Lizzybus to Australia. Although effectively going back on ourselves, in Jayne world, we are going forward. What is even more exciting is a part of it will be on a ferry with Lizzybus down the Mekong River.

It's not exactly a ferry, more a barge, the back end of which is big enough to take Lizzybus and a few motorbikes. The front end has a domed roof where we sit with our legs dangling under the small rail running around it. Next to me is a group of Irish backpackers who, having set off a year ago alone, are now travelling together.

Being able to chat about feelings, emotions, the highs and lows of travel is a real tonic. Listening to their struggles in the constant packing and unpacking, carrying everything with them, missing family, and money worries. We don't need to talk about where we have been or how incredible it all is, we all know this. Just being able to say out loud, without judgement, how we sometimes feel is such a release.

One girl shows me the six postcards she has been trying to post to her family and friends back home, her tiny writing completely filling them. She passes them to me to read. Holding them in my hand, a gust of wind snatches them from me. They flutter past the group, hovering just out of reach, before landing in the Mekong like leaves. I'm broken by this; I know how precious they are and the words written on them. There is nothing I can do, either in replacing them or getting them back. It's hard to explain how shattered I am by this and something I will never get over.

CHAPTER 18
ROTTING IN THE JUNGLE

Crossing back into Thailand, immigration still refuses to let David use his new passport or to put the stamp on a half-used page. It's all about thumping out the miles now as we bushcamp our way back. The monsoon season has kicked in, we're facing constant downpours and washed-out roads. The humidity is rotting everything including us. The mattress, bed linen and pillows have mould spores on them, we have trench foot from the water in the foot wells. Despite washing us and our clothes with a bar of soap in the tropical downpours, our bodies have a greasy grimy layer.

Thailand is incredibly clean, even the squat toilets in ramshackle cafés are clean. There's always buckets of water, and sometimes even showers, especially at petrol stations. Whenever we find a shower, fully dressed and armed with our bar of soap, we wash us and our clothes, then stand in the midday sun for a few minutes drying. Getting back into Lizzybus clean, if only for half an hour, is a real treat.

We reach the Siam-Burma Railway, the Death Railway, named as for every sleeper laid, one civilian or prisoner of war forced to work on it lost their life. Built by the Japanese to connect Thailand to Myanmar (Burma), Bridge 277 over the River Kwai (one of two bridges built, the original in wood and this one in steel) was immortalised in the film 'The Bridge on the River Kwai'. I watched it in black and white as a child. Walking out across this bridge, its significance is palpable.

Were now at Hellfire Pass Memorial Museum set up by Australian Prisoner of War J.G. (Tom) Morris and the Australian Government. This section of the railway was cut through solid rock, dug out by emaciated prisoners using stone age tools or bare hands. It became known as Hellfire Pass because the sight of emaciated prisoners labouring by burning torchlight was said to resemble a scene from hell. Walking along this disused railway, we don't walk on the sleepers knowing that each one laid represents one life lost. The museum sensitively chronicles the suffering and ingenuity of the prisoners and enforced workforce, keeping their spirits alive even in their deaths.

I'm beginning to wake with dread for the day ahead, with a flare up of shingles across my buttocks and back, pulsating mosquito bites, and the blister from the seat belt on my once-broken collar bone when thrown from a horse. Some might say, specifically my sister Jen, that I fell off it, but when one's horse disappears into four feet of bog beneath you, it's hard to stay in the saddle.

We pull into a car park with a notice board indicating a scenic walk to cascading waterfalls and caves. There is a dual pricing system here, with tourist rates at least ten times that of locals. The cost of visiting is listed on the board, but the place is deserted. As it's 'beer o'clock', we grab a beer and go off to explore. The cascading water has created individual rock pools which we sit in. It's so soothing on my shingles and mosquito bites. Drinking beer and watching the sun swallowed by the jungle, I have a feeling of being totally alone on this planet.

At the crack of dawn, we pack up and leave, feeling a little victorious; not only have we avoided paying the tourist rate, but any rate whatsoever. Off the shores of Phuket are the Similan Islands which we would love to dive, especially with my now 'Dive Instructor' David. But it's an indulgence we just can't afford.

The acres of palm oil plantations change to picturesque limestone casts, framed by billowing white cloud. We stand on the shore at Krabi, looking out at an ocean of penis-shaped jungle-covered limestone protrusions - it's super comical. Although we're pounding out the miles, we're still trying to break the days up. Today we visit the hot springs where oxidised copper minerals seeping from the earth's crust have formed hot rock pools. We soak in them until our hands and feet are pruney. I'm in hysterics at David limping back to the car park on his tender feet. It's late, the last of the day trippers have left, we spend another night in another car park, wonderfully clean and with the bonus of it being free.

I know it's bad when David, who never smells anything, is complaining about the stink in our tent, a rotting sickly sweet smell, the pillows being the worst offenders. I cover mine with our towel. In this tropical humid environment nothing dries, my mission now is to find a launderette.

Today, back at the Malay border, David hands them his new passport. They stamp it without question. The no man's land has a huge shopping mall with a private golf course behind it, you can park overnight under the corrugated roofed area with toilets and showers. The luxury of a shelter in the constant evening downpours is heaven. A chauffeur driven Bentley pulls up, two men in smart golf attire get out. All I can think about are the sheets I hung out to air, the bright yellow stains on them from the leaking roof-tent looking just like pee stains. Of course, they don't even notice; they are interested only in us and our journey. They leave behind a delicious lingering waft of aftershave.

I'm still struggling with this black cloud hanging over me and fixating on finding my way back to England. I'm adrift, neither connected to this journey nor to the life I had. David, oblivious to this turmoil in me, is consumed by a sometimes-starts-sometimes-doesn't Lizzybus, whether we will be allowed to drive a 1998 Lizzybus in Singapore, and how we are going to get her cleaner than when she rolled off the production line in Solihull, England, to pass AQIS, the Australian Quarantine Service inspection to get into Australia. Oh, and did I mention sorting out the shipping?

It's David who bears the brunt of all this, but it's both of us that makes it happen. I'm the fluff, the good cop. I schmooze, compliment, smile and even, when needed, cry. I'm so fed up with myself, I think I should be strapped into a container and shipped home. That idea is far too appealing.

Then, when we can no longer support ourselves let alone each other, our guardian angel steps in. She delivers us to Alyna and Attack of Black Hawk Workshop (Land Rover Specialist) and Chairman of the Land Rover Owners Club Malaysia. First they find us a budget hotel room close to their garage. Then their team of mechanics work on Lizzybus, fitting a new starter motor, upgrading the alternator, oil seals to the transfer box and doing oil changes to everything that has, or should have, oil in it. This fills us with hope the starting issue will be no more, but only time will tell. As Alyna and Attack not only prepare vehicles for expeditions, but lead their own, this is so much more than just a business, it's a passion. We can store kit here and use their ramp and jet wash to clean Lizzybus for Australia.

Before we start cleaning, we're going to join Alyna and Attack for a club weekend away - it's time for some off-roading fun. As the sun wakes up, we arrive at our rendezvous and are given a walkie-talkie with the call name 'Lizzybus'. In the middle of this six-vehicle convoy, it literally sends an electric shock through me when the walkie-talkie springs into life. "Lizzybus, are you receiving us? Over." David answers. I collapse into hysterics when he finishes with "Roger." You're kidding me, people really say this stuff?

David, once an officer cadet in the Territorial Army, is my little star. It reminds me of when I got it into my head to be a tank driver in the Territorial Army. Having passed the medical and acceptance exam, I stood in the line-up, so proud in my uniform. I realised the drill sergeant was calling my name. He informed us all that it had come to their attention that I was 'too old' to join the Territorials. A tiny bit of the hurt from the huge chunk of what I felt on that day is being healed by this day, in convoy in the jungles of Malaysia in my tank Lizzybus.

But reality is sometimes, no, always, far from your fantasy. It's not long before we sink door deep into thick red mud and need to be winched out. I have this nagging feeling we are being tested as overlanders driving around the world. Until every one of us is stuck, winching and digging each other out, we're part of a team. We set up camp beside a fast-flowing river, surrounded by bamboo forest. A single rope is strung vertically between two trees and draped with a canvass to provide a communal shelter. One end has camp beds and mosquito nets, for those with no rooftop tent, the other tables and chairs. But no ordinary plastic chairs - little hobbit size ones cut out with a chain saw from the fallen trees. They let me use the chain saw to cut my very own little hobbit chair, the offcuts used for the communal fire pit.

I must tell you about Malaysian mealtimes. They occur with the same frequency we would have a cup of tea. On meeting the convoy this morning, we had breakfast, a few hours later a sort of brunch. On our arrival at camp in the late afternoon, we had a bowl of noodle soup. Crickets are roasted on the hot rocks beside the fire pit as snacks - they are surprisingly tasty. We go with Uncle Felix (Bear Grylls in disguise) to collect bamboo canes and banana leaves; he points out all the edible jungle plants and their medicinal uses. Back in camp Uncle Felix wraps banana leaves with coconut-soaked rice, stuffing them into the hollow bamboo canes, which stand vertically like a tepee over the fire. Dessert for later.

I already feel I have had the greatest adventure ever, but there is a whole afternoon of fun waiting for us. Attack's twelve- and fourteen-year-old sons give us a demonstration on winching and rock-crawling. Uncle Felix makes us fern hats, Alyna and the women start cooking the evening meal of skewers of beef, chicken and vegetable, with homemade satay sauce, fried rice and flat bread. The coconut rice stuffed bamboo canes are ready and cut into cylindrical inch long pieces of caramelised yummy sweet deliciousness. Just like the skin of the rice pudding Jen and I fought over when we were little. We have such a sense of belonging, washing in the raging river or under the tumbling waterfall, sleeping in our rooftop tent, foraging for food - exactly the tonic we needed.

So that was yesterday. Now it's time to get out of this jungle, starting with mending the broken bridge. More fallen trees are cut it into sturdy logs to bridge the gap, then we're asked to test it out. I hate the word 'awesome' but struggle to find another more suitable word for what we have just experienced.

We probably should have done some survival and off-road training before we set off. It's crazy to think we didn't, but we were so focused on earning the money to fund the journey and preparing the houses for rental, it was impossible. So, yes, in an ideal world we would have taken all sorts of courses - survival, mechanical and first aid - but we didn't. There were many times we thought it would never happen, that it was just a fanciful dream. With no intention of asking for sponsorship or to be beholden to anyone, this was our dream, our goal, and we would, and somehow did, make it happen.

The real work begins of cleaning Lizzybus. Internally, we strip everything out including the seats and frayed carpets to be re-stitched at a local upholsterer. With Lizzybus up on the ramp, we drop the fuel tank and anything else we can get at before jet washing her. This was the scary bit as it's mainly the rust and the mud holding her together. I feel a little sad; the gecko that was living in the cross member has abandoned ship, as once the mats came out its food supply of ants was jet washed away.

I concentrate on cleaning the equipment, even down to scrubbing the tent pegs and hiking boots, wrapping them in cling film and writing the date on each one. Having found a launderette, I spend most of the day there. The jet washed mattress is drying in the sun, the pillows are replaced with new ones. I sand and re-enamel the rusted Coleman cooker-housing. All food, even the salt and pepper, is given away.

I´m in heaven with all this cleaning, but it's obvious my idea of clean and David's is worlds apart; we start bickering. I distract myself with images of jet washing David and wrapping him in cling film. We know if we don't get this right, we only have ourselves to blame, so for now David recognises my being anal as a good thing.

Fortunately, there is something else for David to concentrate on - shipping and getting Lizzybus into Singapore. Having found a shipping agent in Australia, Graham, we're told that due to age and emission restrictions in Singapore, we won't be able to drive Lizzybus there. If this is the case, we would have to drive back to Penang in Malaysia (where we started) to ship to Australia. I don't normally swear, but I'm increasingly finding a potty mouth. What the f…..?

We have been invited to join one of the Malaysian Land Rover Club charity events at the Thong Sum Old Folks Home and the Selangor Handicapped and Mentally Retarded Children Centre. I wonder how unintentionally uncaring 'mentally retarded' is, but I think it's just how it translates. As we are halfway through the cleaning, we don't really want to be involved in any more mud. When we are assured it's all on tarmac roads, we accept.

In our convoy of eight we arrive at the charity funded Old Folks Home, where industrial-size bottles of washing powder, dried milk, cooking oil and fresh fruit are donated to the kitchen. In the dormitories, metal frame beds are in rows a few feet away from each other. Beside each bed is a single bedside table where residents store their few belongings. A goody bag is given to each person containing a towel, soap, talcum powder, mirror, brush, and a disposable razor for the men. We also have a hot meal for each resident in polystyrene containers. Some residents can sit at the tables, but for the disabled or the ones too weak to get out of bed, we help to feed them. With a frail bony hand in mine, I look into little button eyes that have a whole lifetime behind them. Scooping fried chicken and rice into his open mouth, I momentarily feel uncomfortable, but I know spending time with the residents is as valuable as the donated items, even just holding their hand.

I know this since my elder pediatric nurse sister persuaded me to volunteer at my local children's hospice. Just seeing the broken children was quite shocking. I'm utterly ashamed to say this, but I didn't want to touch anything, or anyone, in case I caught something. It took a few visits before I could move past this and see that underneath their deformed bodies, they were just children. It taught me a lot.

We're off to the Selangor Children's Centre. Again the storeroom is filled with donated essentials, this time the personal goody bags are filled with a soft toy, a book, crayons, and a few sweets. It's bright and cosy with sectioned off rooms for the more disabled children; the able-bodied sit on soft mats on the floor in the communal area or out on the veranda.

David stands behind me as I spoon food into the open mouth of a young girl propped up by bean bags. He leans forward and wipes away the dribbles. I feel incredibly close to him right now, and so proud of him. I know I lost my way on this journey; this has given me a sense of purpose. We're often asked what charity our journey is in aid of. We decided long ago not to tie ourselves to one, but whenever we could, to give of what we had, mainly our time. I'm determined that when we do, or even if we don't, reach our goal, we can revisit these places, or places like them, to help; this gives me focus.

The supposed week long sanitisation of Lizzybus, with our difference of opinions on cleaning and social calendar, has turned into a month. Today, we are guests of honour at the local police commandant's wedding. I am dressed in my only skirt of floral rose print and our Lizzybus T-shirt. Everyone is dressed in stunning silks and satins, adorned with beautiful gold jewelry. The newlyweds are sitting on a podium, framed with fresh flowers. We are asked to sit next to them, for pictures. We look more like the most wanted than honoured guests. I just take a deep breath and smile, whilst reminding myself of the time I peed in the jungle with my audience of women and children, when all heads bent down to see if my bottom was as white as my face. I´ve got this.

Tonight, in the heart of Kuala Lumpur and in the shadow of the iconic Petronus Twin Towers, we have been invited for dinner. The Towers have eighty-eight floors of glass and steel designed to resemble motifs found in Islamic art including the Rub el-Hizb, an eight pointed star, and are connected by the Sky Bridge. Before it was built, generations of Malay families lived here in their traditional wooden homes where they would sit on their verandas, listening to their caged songbirds. Having fought the developers, they not only won, but their homes became a protected area within the city and a bit of a tourist attraction.

We're given a little tour of these houses before going into the home of the president of the resident's association, a meek engaging man who invites us to sign the visitor's ledger on the intricately carved wooden dresser. Sat in his courtyard garden, out of what I thought was an ornate pool, he plucked six of the fish swimming in it. After gutting and wrapping in banana leaves, they are cooked over a charcoal fire. I can't help feeling I'm eating their pet fish. It's like being back in the jungle with Uncle Felix, but in the heart of the city. A very special evening, hearing all about a life that was, and how the changes have affected the life that is, here in this little warp of time.

We have been hearing more and more about AQIS and its ability to seize, destroy, detain, fine at the stroke of a pen, any vehicle, person, or item, on the huge list of items contravening its laws. Most vehicles arrive in Australia in containers. On arrival, they are taken to a holding warehouse, opened and inspected by AQIS. Despite owners asking to be present for this, it is often done without them. On failing the requirements, their vehicles are cleaned and sanitised by a verified cleaning company, leaving the owners with an extortionate bill for storage and cleaning.

The advice is not to take your own vehicle to Australia, but to hire one when you get there. This would never work for us; our journey is about driving around the world in Lizzybus. We come as a threesome or not at all.

It's here, the actual day we leave this room, home to us for six weeks and the tiny black puppy living in the bushes. We are off to Singapore for our rendezvous with the shipping agent. Lizzybus is set to sail in just ten days' time. This is an enormous step into the unknown. We have given serious consideration to ignoring Australia completely and shipping directly to the Americas. The most immediate concern is the restrictions imposed on older vehicles being allowed into Singapore.

So, what qualifies as circumnavigating the world? Countries visited; borders crossed. Technically, circumnavigation is seen as the complete navigation around a land mass like an island, a continent, or even the moon. It's a supposed route that can be completed in either direction. It's well recorded that, for both David and I, it was always about visiting and experiencing as many countries as we possibly could, whilst driving around the world. If we're honest, it was more of a statement, to have an answer to the question, "Where are you going?"

Lizzybus looks and smells new; the only thing letting her down now is us, with me in one pair of David's cotton boxers and long-sleeved paint-splattered shirt, and David in trousers so threadbare, his bits are only held in by his second pair of boxers.

Having said all our goodbyes and thank yous last night, no one is here this morning to wave us off. A good job as David, unable to find his laptop cable, accuses me of throwing it away in my normal gung ho way, proceeding to rummage through everything I had neatly packed. I seethe at his 'gung ho way' comment and find his cable in his laptop bag. To keep the foul words in my head from coming out of my mouth, I lock myself back in the room. One hour, a coffee and two fags later, in complete silence, we set off. This suits me just fine.

Singapore, like Malaysia, requires its own ICP (International Circulation Permit) issued, not at the border - that would be far too simple - but at the AA offices in Singapore. We must leave Lizzybus at the border and cross into Singapore on foot to get it first. Why is everything so complicated?

Singapore is at the very bottom of the south east Asian continent and separated by the Johor Strait, a once British colony captured by the Japanese and then re-captured. It's famous for the iconic Raffles Hotel, where you can sip a Singapore Sling in the Long Bar. What is important to us is it having one of the world's busiest ports; fingers crossed that it is about to get a bit busier. Lizzybus is on her way.

Today, without Lizzybus, we cross the border into Singapore. It hits me what little ants David and I are in this unfolding chain of events. We join the many thousands who commute daily to Singapore, for work, study, to visit, or for us an ICP permit, on the bus over the causeway bridge. On reaching Singapore, our passports are stamped with no fuss and we are issued with entry cards for any further visits.

It's a whole other border experience, being whisked along on miles of moving walkways, past spectacular cascading water features and magnificent topiary trees, back to the waiting bus. Of course, it's only simple if all we had to do was cross the border. For us, it's a lot more complicated; we need to find the AA offices and get the ICP.

We're still at a point in this journey where smart phones, wifi and apps are not a thing, but maps, cash and confusion are. With only a basic map and getting on and off the wrong and right buses, it's almost midday before finally we, or should I say David, finds the offices of the AA. I see this as our secret mission, something we don't exactly enjoy, but challenges us. We see the real Singapore as a local, the hundreds of high-rise apartment blocks, with communal areas and parks. Clean, safe, no graffiti, local cafes, restaurants and street food - we love it.

At the AA offices, we meet the manager Rose who is so impressed with us and our journey she makes it her mission to do everything possible to help us. Lizzybus is too old to get insurance and will not be allowed into Singapore. It's crushing news, a huge blow having booked and paid for Lizzybus to sail in six days' time.

Our world crumbles down around us. I look across at David who begins to shake and hold his shoulder, a sure sign he is stressed. These constant battles and responsibilities are taking their toll. I put my hand over his to stop it shaking; it's clammy and cold. But Rose won't give up. She sends us off for lunch, whilst continuing to look at our options.

The smartly dressed office workers pouring out onto the streets of Singapore are oblivious to our unfolding nightmare as we join them for a bowl of rice noodles and milk tea, a confusing mix of tea with a swirl of coffee. I don't like it, but drink both mine and David's. David can't stand tea anyway, but tea mixed with coffee is apparently the devil's concoction.

We arrive back at the AA offices with heavy hearts. Rose hands us the ICP she has issued and a stamped Carnet, along with the wonderful news that an insurance company is willing to insure us for six days. There's also the option of putting Lizzybus on a trailer to the docks for the same cost. We ponder letting someone else drive Lizzybus on a truck across the border to the port - how simple this would be. But to us it would feel like cheating; we want to drive Lizzybus here, to park her outside the iconic Raffles Hotel whilst sipping on a Gin Sling in the Long Bar. Nothing less will, or was ever going to do, whatever the cost.

In unison we say, "The Lizzybus insurance please."

Armed with the ICP and insurance certificate, we're joyful, believing the worst is behind us and that it should be plain sailing from here on in. The stinking colds we just can't seem to shift are much more bearable. In fact, all this drama has been a great distraction, especially for David who, of course, has man flu.

We set off for the second time to Singapore, this time with Lizzybus, full of trepidation and expectation. Rose recommended using the Tuas Bridge crossing because it's quiet. She was not kidding; it's deserted and feels just like a huge underground car park. Whilst sitting inside your vehicle, you hand over your documents, with no physical searches of your vehicle. The registration is electronically captured, and the entry cards issued to us yesterday are scanned. The efficiency is mind blowing. It's all going well, too well when we are asked for our Vehicle Travel Permit.

In this city, vehicle registration readers monitor your movement to levy charges, on a pre-pay or charging system, a sort of road tax. The staff in the booth can't issue one; they suggest we leave Lizzybus and find somewhere, or someone, who can. It's a maze of lifts, floors and concrete, before we reach street level. Two hours later, we have in our possession a Vehicle Travel Permit, with a ten dollar top up on it. All we need to do now is get back to Lizzybus. Thank goodness for David - I have been known to lose my car in the local multi-storey car park.

Now we have the flag sticking on ceremony.

CHAPTER 19

A GIN SLING IN SINGAPORE

Singapore, our last country on the continent of Asia, is not much bigger than some capital cities. It has strict laws on littering, spitting, vandalism and public urination, and the selling or importing of chewing gum. Heavy fines and Corrective Work Orders are imposed on those who don't adhere to this, making it the cleanest city we have ever seen. It's common practice in Singapore to reserve a table at a hawker centre (food court) by placing a packet of tissues on the table. I love this idea and am determined to get me a packet of tissues to do that very thing.

Driving Lizzybus through Singapore feels like being in a film of a futuristic city, the architecturally designed mass of ultra-modern buildings a far cry from its colonial past. The roads of this metropolis are full of cascading waterfalls, topiary trees, and hedges as architecturally designed and precise as the buildings. We arrive at our pre-booked pink-painted box of a hotel nestled amongst coffee houses and cafes too early to check in, so we sit drinking iced coffee on the street corner with the locals.

Prostitution here has none of the sleaze associated with it in England. On the other side of the road the ladies of the night become ladies of the day. They stand in shiny PVC hot pants, boob tubes, body hugging cat suits or chic chiffon dresses. Most of them clomp around in huge platform shoes; as beautiful as Singaporean women are, height is not part of their DNA.

I wake with a huge sense of both accomplishment and dread as to what lies ahead. With one day spare before meeting our shipping agent, we are taking Lizzybus to Raffles, named after Sir Thomas Stamford Raffles, who was born on a ship off the coast of Jamaica and educated at Mansion House Academy, London. At the age of fourteen, he became a clerk at the British East India Company, going on to become Lieutenant Governor of Java and the founder of modern Singapore. It's totally fascinating to me how people become who they are.

The colonial-style luxurious Raffles Hotel is extensively restored and extended, but clings to its traditions. From the crunching gravel driveway, you're greeted by the Sikh doorman, dressed in a Gieves & Hawkes military uniform with white gloves and gold belt buckle. Parking Lizzybus outside Raffles, we're asked to move her; we ignore them. We might not be royalty or famous, but we drove here, on our own in Lizzybus, and that makes us special, if only to us.

We are making the most of the Lizzybus insurance by driving around Singapore, but what we didn't consider was that the Vehicle Travel Permit needs topping up. Having tried and failed, we think, sod it. Where are they going to send the fines anyway? The Pink Square Hotel, Ladies of the Day Corner, Singapore? Good luck with that one!

Today, it's with mixed emotions we are driving Lizzybus to the docks for her voyage on the high seas, the penultimate step, before the final one of getting on our flight. It's a relief when we see John, our Singapore shipping agent, as he has our port passes. I'd expected a real hustle and bustle here, but like all of Singapore it's incredibly clean, tidy and organised. There are wide laid out tarmac lanes and neatly stacked containers, six high, with mega-automated lifting structures. In the centre of all this is a tarmac parking area, the size of a football pitch, which is where we will leave Lizzybus. This is a roll-on roll-off ferry, meaning she will be driven on, not by us but a port worker. We wanted to travel with Lizzybus, but it's a cargo only vessel.

Lizzybus looks abandoned parked amongst all the other vehicles, the only clues as to her journey are the forty-five stuck on flags representing each country we've driven through. We take one last look at Lizzybus, who sparkles in the midday sun from the six weeks of cleaning, hoping we have done enough for her to pass the dreaded AQUIS inspection, know we did our best. The driver's door is left unlocked with the key in the ignition. It won't be us driving Lizzybus onto the ferry, but a random man doing his job, which hurts a little, with it being such a huge step in our journey.

It's difficult to say how we feel leaving Lizzybus and driving away in John's white van. Relief is right up there along with a sense of abandoning her. Lizzybus will take six days to sail to Australia; we'll take six hours to fly, but we cannot leave until we have the bill of lading, issued once she's been loaded.

Grahame, our shipping agent in Fremantle, has advised that cargo, which Lizzybus is, is dealt with on a first come first served basis. If our original documents are the last to be received by the port authorities, we'll be at the back of the queue. We need to get to Australia as soon as possible to submit the bill of lading. Once more, we're full of anxiety - the relief of getting Lizzybus dockside is just temporary.

With the news Lizzybus has been loaded, we make our way to the shipping agent's office to collect the bill of lading. Although loaded, she has yet to set sail, still we commit and book flights for two days' time, on the chance or choice option. The chance of not being able to take the flight due to delays in setting sail, and the no choice of needing to deliver the bill of lading.

It's time for some distraction. We buy a two-dollar tourist pass with unlimited bus and train travel to explore Singapore.

We visit the Changi Chapel and Museum, which honours the lives of the prisoners detained in Changi Prison after the fall of Singapore during World War II, before being sent to almost certain death in the construction of the Burma Railway. The Botanical Gardens famous for its orchid house, where the re-creation of habitats produces rare specimens of orchids, which sometimes dazzle and sometimes underwhelm. It's here in this aromatic paradise we get a text message to say that Lizzybus has set sail. Tomorrow we will be on our flight ready for the next chapter in this incredible journey.

We have one last breakfast of roti and fried egg noodles, watching the Ladies of the Day. They wave at us - or are they calling David? - I´m not sure. Despite my encouraging him to go over and see, he is having none of it. On the very efficient bus and train system, with only a small rucksack each, forty minutes later, we're at the airport. The plane is almost empty, we take a whole row of seats each, like on all these significant moments, we are not able or wanting to talk.

As the sun disappears over the arc of the horizon, we fly not just over ocean but also land, heading for Perth, near the bottom of Australia, a flight of over five hours. Crikey, if it takes this long to fly over one little edge of it, how long is it going to take to drive a Lizzybus around it? Lost in our own thoughts, my mind plays the last three years over like a kaleidoscope. How naive and innocent we were to the perils, trials and tribulations we were about to face, but something greater than us had infected us; we had no choice.

It's been two years, ten months, forty-five countries (including UK) and three continents since setting off on that rainy day from Birmingham, UK. But that has no real meaning because it's not the end, it's just an answer to the constant question of where we have been and where we are going. A question we quite like, because we can answer it; the one not so easily answered is, have we changed?

In practical terms, of course we have. We are proficient at driving off-road, navigating border crossings, living in a box with the bare minimum, but real change is imperceptible. You can knowingly change your ways or habits, like in stopping smoking or losing weight, or being less critical of others. A change within you, your reactions to circumstances and situations, is a change you don't realise has happened. By comparing these situations to similar situations from the beginning of our journey, then we see how we have changed.

So yes, we have changed in every way possible. We are still two people who, for reasons we have never really figured out, found ourselves on this extraordinary journey. After we set off to drive around the world, six weeks later, we'd only made it through France to Spain. Standing on the shore of the Mediterranean, looking out at the daunting silhouette of Africa, the realisation hit us that this was no dream, this was our reality. I can hear how it called to us as clear in my head now as it did then. Whatever driving force was pushing us on, we had no say in it, we were just tasked with making it happen.

This comforts me; knowing it is our destiny, it makes me feel purposeful. We are the most unlikely pair who, by some unfathomable reason, seem to be muddling through all this. And hey, it might as well be us.

I look out of the window at the vast ocean below, knowing Lizzybus is down there somewhere. I promise her we are on our way.

CHAPTER 20

G'DAY AUSTRALIA

Australia, at thirty-two times bigger than the United Kingdom, is the oldest, flattest and driest inhabited continent in the world. With ancient lands of emerald rainforests and fragrant eucalyptus mountains, at its heart lie deserts, to the north-east tropical rainforests, to the south-east mountain ranges. Of course, you can expect to find the indigenous kangaroos, which outnumber people, and the koala. Australia also has the world's largest population of camels. They were imported mainly from India, but also from Afghanistan and the Middle East to help with the exploration of Australia's desert interior. Once motor transport arrived, these domesticated animals escaped or were released to become vast feral herds.

Crossing borders has always been difficult, especially with Lizzybus, but without her and only a rucksack each we're swallowed up in this enormous airport. There are more rows of manned kiosks checking passports than there are passengers. We're asked if we have any food stuff, to which we respond, no, and with no suitcase to collect, before we know it, we are here in Perth, Western Australia. What a huge milestone and achievement on our journey this is. Like every other milestone, it always comes with another issue and right now the issue is Lizzybus isn't with us.

Exchanging our Singapore dollars for Australian dollars, we take a minibus to Governor Robinson's Backpackers Hostel. It's hard to imagine now how important cash was back then - it was almost the only way to pay. I´ve struggled with how the world has changed, but also see the benefits and not needing cash is right up there. We arrive at this red brick-built house in a residential area of Perth at well past midnight. Apart from the light illuminating the key-coded lock, it's all in complete darkness. We have the code for this from our internet booking, which is all new to us and quite amazing when it works. Once inside, we find an envelope with our name on it pinned to a cork memo board with our dorm key. The magnolia painted dorm has three metal bunk beds, two of which have sleeping bodies in. We dump our bags on the empty third one as quietly as we can and head back out.

I'm hungry and thirsty, like the proverbial child, I'm grumpy, or as David says, grumpier, when I'm hungry. The only place we can see open is McDonald's, not the restaurant, but the drive through. Sitting on the pavement eating burgers, I remember the first time I was in a McDonald's, for my daughter's birthday party and the outcry it caused when our local Art Deco cinema was converted into it. How special it was at the Saturday morning cinema club. When the floor to ceiling red velvet curtains swished open the hairs on the back of my neck stood up in anticipation of the two hours of cartoons and films. As we didn't even have a television until I was fourteen, it was quite magical. The McDonald's 'golden arches', the most recognised brand by children worldwide, is a far cry from the sophisticated splendour of our old Art Deco cinema.

The dramatic change a border crossing brings has been diluted by the time we spent in the cosmopolitan cities of Kuala Lumpur and Singapore. I sit shivering, drinking the dregs of my coffee and smoking with a huge sense of anticlimax. Planes make me think of home; our home is Lizzybus, and she is not here with us. Many times on this journey, I've felt like the tiny speck of the nothing we are in it. We have driven round half of the world and are now in the southern hemisphere. Looking up into the vastness of an inky black moonless night sky I see the Southern Cross. I know this because David points it out to me, like he did the North Star, telling me they are not visible at the same time from any location on Earth. David and I are still struggling with intimacy since dealing with personal hygiene, grooming and living two feet away from each other. Sitting with David, looking up at the stars I feel a closeness I haven't felt in ages. It's a special moment and what is intrinsically tying us to each other more and more.

This morning the cheery owner of our backpackers arrives to inform us we are in a 'women's only' dorm. The other girls don't mind, nor do we. I was so cold last night, the single cotton waffle blanket reminding me of the one I was wrapped up in whilst in the sick bay at school. I was there after being force fed Irish stew which had gone so cold the fat had congealed forming a thick crust. When broken, it revealed the grey yuk inside of swede and rock-hard potato, making me violently sick. It didn't stop them force feeding me Irish stew, but for some reason, I stopped being sick after eating it.

It's so exciting today. We're on the train to Fremantle to meet

Graham our shipping agent. Passing through the suburbs of Perth, the houses are set in neat rows with façades of bluff yellow plastic brick. Each with the same square of lawn, they look like a scaled-up version of a developer's model ready to be presented to the city planners. In the boardroom, company director Graham listens with real interest to our escapades then reveals how complicated getting Lizzybus back is going to be. What? Doesn't he know what it took to get her here in the first place? How much more complicated can we take? It seems Lizzybus requires not just the AQIS (Australian Quarantine) inspection, but many more inspections and documents, from many different departments. We take a deep breath knowing it's just a process and at least we are in an English-speaking country.

Thirteen days later we're still living like students on a gap year in this pleasant, but cold and expensive backpackers. Most of the backpackers here are looking for work and the majority are Irish. Chatting distracts me from not being with my daughter today as it's her thirtieth birthday.

The other day we were re-united with Lizzybus at the docks. Having been driven off the ferry a week ago, she was the only one left in this massive runway-sized parking area. She looked magnificent in the sunshine, we felt a huge pride in her for keeping safe on her voyage across the ocean. I just wanted to get in and drive off into the sunset of my stolen life. We were there to have the dreaded AQIS inspection. Greeted by a young blond-haired inspector, who shook our offered hand, his 'sunnies' covering his eyes, it was only his mouth we could judge his mood from, and that remained rigid and professional.

In the run up to this moment, one of the many hold ups was that the Carnet had not been signed by us. This was something we hadn't realised was needed or had ever been an issue in the past. We'd Fedexed the Carnet to Graham from Singapore who, not wanting to delay this further, had signed the Carnet on our behalf. Looking through the Carnet now, the AQIS inspector tells us there needs to be a separate listing for our personal stuff. We offer to write one, but he says it needs endorsing by customs back at the airport, not the docks.

What? What can we do? We know for sure complaining about it would be futile and could even cost us this inspection. In our English way, we apologise for our oversight and ask if there is any way this could be overlooked. It can't. The vehicle-only inspection involves us lifting the bonnet, putting up and taking down the roof tent, and taking out all the equipment that cannot be inspected. Shinning his torch into Lizzybus and ticking the boxes on his printed sheet, twenty minutes later, almost under his breath, he says she'd passed. I forget for a moment that it's only part of the inspection and give him a hug and a high five. I see a small crease in his eyes behind the sunnies, wondering how his eyes could smile, even though his mouth did not.

A girl has arrived wanting a woman only dorm. As I don't mind where or who I sleep with, we're moved to a mixed dorm with seven men. Graham calls to say Lizzybus must be moved off the dock to a holding area to avoid fines and storage charges. We can't move her until she has her AQIS contents inspection, and even then there is a whole load of other requirements to get her legal.

In an attempt to avoid the cost of a flatbed to move Lizzybus tomorrow, we take a bus to the local transport office for a Temporary Transit Permit (TTP) which will allow us to drive her ourselves. The offices are closed. Having told Graham our intentions, he assumed when meeting him at the port we had one. David knows I will only keep shtum to the point I am asked outright. Despite my African training, I´m still a very honest person and a poker face is something I will never possess. One thing that helps to keep my gob shut is the feeling of being ripped off. Having to pay hundreds more in couriers and inspections and fifty dollars each time we enter the port, is focusing my mind.

Finally getting into Lizzybus, I realise how much I´ve missed her, not just her smell, but her sound. Starting up on the first turn of the key, I´m filled with love and a desire to just drive off into the horizon. We reach the manned security gates; Graham shows them the wallet of documents. The guards don't really have much of a clue what documents we need. I just follow Graham out without stopping. It's not quite how we wanted it to be; more like criminals stealing Lizzybus. It does feel, however, like sticking two fingers up to bureaucracy, and that´s amazing. Graham, having done his bit, drives off wishing us good luck. We're on our own.

The area for vehicles awaiting inspection and documentation is only a ten-minute drive away and doesn't seem to be part of any highway, just an access road to it. This little bit of activity gives us hope that this will all end sometime soon and that we'll have Lizzybus back and can go off to explore Australia, but it's false hope. Twenty minutes later, Lizzybus is once more parked up amongst a load of other vehicles awaiting inspection and more documentation. We're utterly despondent.

Whilst going up and down on this train to the docks and storage yard, we've been treated to the sight of leaping dolphins. We see them again today on what we hope is the last visit to the holding pen for Lizzybus. Graham has been invaluable in this process, like our secret weapon, personally picking us up and taking us to the places we need to go. We're not exactly sure how Graham wrangled it, but the sheet listing our kit, although not endorsed by customs, can be inspected once another fee is paid, of course.

It's a very different experience from the first one. The friendly jovial man apologises this was not done with the initial inspection. No kidding. He seems almost embarrassed to be looking through our kit, having neatly piled the items to be declared on a tarpaulin sheet. The wooden Ikea shower tray used at the foot of the roof ladder to wash sand, dirt and stink off David's feet. The spade with its wooden handle. The synthetic hair I use for plaiting my afro hair into braids. A pack of coffee and three tins of Heinz baked beans. The most focus was on our hiking boots and tent pegs. I'm so pleased with my anal approach to cleaning, having scrubbed them with a toothbrush and wrapped them in cling film.

Lizzybus has passed her vehicle and kit inspection. Halle-flippin-lujah - are you breathing a sigh of relief? Well do and don't. It´s not over yet. Tomorrow Lizzybus is booked in for her Vehicle Road Test (VRT), the equivalent of the English Ministry of Transport (MOT) to check exhaust emissions and roadworthiness. We know Lizzybus has new brakes, tyres and exhaust, but as for emissions and oil leaks - she's a Land Rover. If she stops leaking oil, it means she has run out.

Without the Temporary Transit Permit, Lizzybus is illegally parked on the street outside our backpackers. We failed miserably when trying to insure her and are now in the classic catch 22 situation. One thing cannot happen until the other thing does. Writing this is as annoying and confusing as navigating it, and we thought Africa was corrupt. Red tape is just a form of legal corruption. You have no voice; you just pay the charges heaped upon you. Oh, and did I mention, Australia being the most expensive country so far. At this rate we will both be selling a kidney.

Today driving Lizzybus (illegally) for her VRT we're unable to speak, as failing the VRT is a mechanical failing that a bucket of soapy water won't fix. Despite having an appointment, we join the long queue. Each inspection is taking over forty minutes. Three hours have passed when a sandwich board is put out announcing it closed for lunch. In our African inshallah life, this would not normally bother us, but it's Friday and we know all offices will be closed for the weekend. It will be bad if she doesn't get tested today, but even worse if she fails.

Leaving Lizzybus exactly where she is, we join everyone else at the cafe for lunch. I know David's anxiety levels are rising as he starts talking to me out of the side of his mouth, like he's passing me Russian secrets. I think it makes us look dodgy, filling me with worry I don't need. I leave him talking to himself and go for a walk. When I get back, David is deep in conversation with an English man living here- it's just the distraction he needs.

My euphoria when told Lizzybus has passed, lasts only seconds, as it's only the mechanical and safety part. She now needs a road test, which involves the examiner taking her for a drive. We are asked for the TRP which, of course, we don't have. Thinking we have failed at the last hurdle; the inspector says opposite is an office where we can get one. It's another twenty-five dollars, but they can charge what they want. Lizzybus is off on her road test, David and I are totally numb at this point.

The tester returns, saying what a privilege it was to drive Lizzybus, handing us a pass certificate. One last thing to get is road tax and insurance which is also available at the offices opposite.

The magnitude of this moment cannot be understated. Having got Lizzybus here to Australia, her fourth continent and forty-sixth country, through Africa, Asia, the Middle and Far East, this moment is pivotal. We did it. Lizzybus is legal, we can resume our mission of trying to get her around the world. A huge sense of relief washes over us.

Under a full moon we make our way back to the backpackers. I realise how hungry and in need of a beer I am. The gas to the cooker has been turned off and a notice put out stating no cooking between 21:00 - 09:00 hours. Knowing the owner lived off site, I just switch the gas back on and start cooking dinner. What we didn't account for was for free accommodation, some residents clean. This also seems to mean they are the enforcers of the rules, particularly this jobsworth old bag, who informs us of the consequences of switching the gas back on the most likely of being thrown out of the backpackers. Ugh! of everything we've been through, this petty ridiculousness nearly pushes me over the edge. She is lucky I don't give her a mouthful, but I choose to ignore her, cook our noodles and drink beer.

From the highs and lows of a trauma-filled day, we're utterly exhausted. After a gloriously hot shower, tucked up in our bunks sleep the sleep of the dead. That is until the early hours of the morning when the Irish men get back from the pub. Within minutes of getting into their bunks, the snoring, farting and burping begins. As the room fills with the stink of rotten eggs and stale beer, I understand why some women want women's only dorms.

Please let me be back in my roof tent.

CHAPTER 21

NO WORRIES, MATE

Our Australian adventure begins as our quest to drive Lizzybus around the world continues, three weeks since we arrived.

We leave Perth, the capital of Western Australia, following the inky blue Swan River to a backdrop of rolling hills and vineyards. The sense of wonder and adventure returns, having been sucked from us in the backpackers through the semi darkness of shuttered windows, and a television blasting all day. I'll miss the banter, I might even miss the beer breath and sulphur farts, but it's an open road and vastness of sky, it's becoming impossible to live without.

We're heading to Darwin at the top of Australia, over four thousand kilometres away along Indian Ocean Drive, a scenic coastal route of single lane tarmac through shrubby gorse, cultivated vineyards and vast cattle or sheep farms. Traffic is minimal with most vehicles towing boats or trailers. Road trains with multiple carriages, each up to thirty metres long, are something else. They just appear in your rear-view mirror from nowhere, sucking you into their wind vortex.

It's late afternoon when we reach the Pinnacle Desert, an exquisite area of eroded seashells, the sea and wind having formed them into pillars up to five metres high. These comical formations stand proud; some even have hats on, like a mushroom. It's a beautiful sunny day, the gentle breeze keeping it cool enough to wear a jumper - it's hard to imagine it as a desert. We see the many signs warning of kangaroos, ostrich and porcupine. The most worrying are the 'No Camping' signs. It's our first day back on the road; $30 to camp and a tank full of fuel is not good. Once the sun disappears, the temperature plummets. At least in our campsite there are hot showers and corrugated shelters to get out of the wind.

My euphoria at getting back on the road is tested. There's a nail in the rear tyre, and the water pump and head torches are broken. The mosquitoes are persistent bastards, even copious amounts of body-rotting deet doesn't deter them. It always takes time to settle back into the journey, to be at ease, to not panic every time you hear a clunk or a groan.

We hadn't realised how tough the last few weeks have been on us. The saying, "don't sweat the small stuff", is exactly what we're doing. Both so emotionally raw, having lived on our nerves, we have little left to give. Tonight, despite the no camping signs, we pull off into the bush. In the roof tent with new pillows and pillowcases, clean sheets, and wrapped up in my toasty sleeping bag gently rocked by the wind, I know I'm where I belong. I'm home.

This morning camped next to us is Roy Bartholomew, a silver-haired ex-pat from Middlesbrough, England, who's driving an impressive-looking Honda Goldwing and towing a little trailer around Australia - Jack Daniels in one hand, a pipe in the other. The sweet smell of tobacco mixed with eucalyptus is most pleasing.

David gets the water pump going and I try new batteries in the head torches. They are kaput, but it doesn't bother us, we can replace them. With the vast distances were having to cover here we're using a tank of fuel a day. It's the most expensive fuel, apart from Turkey, and putting a huge hole in our already stretched budget.

The road unfolds before us, cutting through this pristine landscape; we have yet to see a live kangaroo instead of the bloodied roadkill ones. Along with wallabies, kangaroos account for almost ninety percent of animal accidents on the roads. Another reason to avoid driving at night. There's a definite chill in the air, which I thought would be welcome after the blistering heat of Africa. Even with the windows closed, the pathetic Lizzybus heater doesn't help, we drive wearing coats. There's an army of 'Grey Nomads' who spend their retirement travelling Australia in luxurious mobile homes, towing cars. The wide-open endless tarmac roads with plentiful campsites make this a wonderful option. For the more adventurous like us, there are graded gravel roads to get off the beaten track. A true outdoor paradise for everyone.

Pressing on through the World Heritage Shark's Bay, straddling two peninsulas, we visit Hamelin Pool Marine Nature Reserve, a spectacular area and one of the reasons life on earth exists, with the stromatolites. I'm becoming more concerned at how interested in all of this I am - how this single cell organism converted gases into oxygen, three billion years ago. These submerged punk-haired grasses give the water a beautiful pinkie brown, yellowy hue. From the rickety wooden walkway, hovering over the pool, I see the tracks of carts from the early settlers. I imagine the daily grind in these harsh conditions of the men pushing heavy wooden carts with metal wheels, loaded with wool out to the waiting ships. Totally unaware they were wheeling them over one of the earliest forms of life on earth.

Further up the coast, we reach Shell Beach - when I say further up, I mean a day's drive away. Made from bleached cockleshells, it's like stepping into a massive bag of pure white pasta shells. I scoop huge handfuls of shells, throwing them into the air where they are caught by the wind and scattered like confetti over me. In places the beach is ten metres deep; compacted down it becomes hard enough to be cut into bricks, used to build houses. The beach is now a protected area and can only be quarried with special permission for use on historical projects.

We are beginning to settle into Australia and this journey. As dusk descends, we pull off the main highway down a dirt track to a secluded area high up on the cliff. With the roof tent up, a stew in the pressure cooker, we sit drinking beer. A white Land Cruiser with an official looking number on its door pulls up. Remembering the no camping signs we'd seen on the highway; we think they are rangers or police. They come over to us; I can barely speak. It turns out they're locals visiting friends and need to stop for the night. If locals are okay with camping here, we are.

Considering Australia is such a huge country, we're not feeling its remoteness. Pushing on from Sharks Bay to Caernarvon, we pay sixteen dollars each to visit the area of Monkey Mia where wild dolphins come to shore each day to be fed. Situated on the peninsula, it adds a three-hundred-kilometre detour to our journey north. What a disappointment, almost farcical, proving once more it's not the destination but the journey. The area as part of the world heritage site is pristine with pure white beaches and aqua blue lagoons. It's also full of tourist shops, restaurants, motels and hotels. It's true that the four dolphins, known by name, come to shore at set times during the day to be fed. They obligingly take the offered fish (and if you were a dolphin, why wouldn't you?), but corralled behind a rope, it felt staged and at odds with the natural wonders around us.

Pressing on we see a sign declaring the road ahead closed due to flooding. Knowing how far back the alternative route was, we carry on. The deep red mud splatters all over the places we had so meticulously cleaned, Lizzybus once more looks rugged and hard. A howling wind drives across this low-lying marsh, making it a desolate place. Totally alone, we pitch up for the night, with the tent acting like a sail, know it's going to be a stormy night. We eat the remains of last night's chicken stew around a campfire almost flattened by the wind.

Once in the tent it's not long before I need a pee, stepping down the ladder a thought crosses my mind: this might be perfect crocodile habitat. I don't know that much about crocs - and that's the way I like it - but for some reason I do know they are cold bloodied animals. Meaning their body temperature is not regulated inside, but by the outside environment. That's the reason you see them basking in the sun, not just for that all over tan.

It's ridiculous I know, but the thought they might be out there I pee hanging off the ladder. I'm impressed with how the wind blows away my pee and dries the drips. I'm thinking it might be the method to adopt on howling wind nights. I could never have dreamt of a life were hanging off a ladder, peeing in the wind drip drying, to avoid being supper for hungry crocs would be mine, but it is.

The temperature dropped to zero last night and toasty in our sleeping bags, we're reluctant to get up this morning. We're unable to shift this pit-of-the-stomach dread of possible issues with Lizzybus. With no phone coverage or the AA available on speed dial, recovery in this remoteness is not an option. Despite all the care and attention Lizzybus received from Alyna and Atick in Malaysia and not having had the starting issue since, it's an unspoken dread in us both. David spent most of the night asking what would happen if she didn't start. I spent most of it wondering where the gaffer tape was.

At the start of this journey, David's need to voice and regurgitate worst-case scenarios was making it impossible to enjoy this experience. We made the pact that he could vent his worst-case scenarios, list the options, decide on one, then shut the f***up. It would either break, get fixed, or never happen. David has forgotten this and is going on about it again. If I dismiss him, it means I don't care; if I admit how worrying it is, David panics more. I'm so resentful, feeling he is taking away from this incredible journey, bringing this doom and gloom upon us. Lizzybus starts, we drive back down the five-kilometre closed road to the main, open road.

Despite this, we both want and need adventure, otherwise what's the point? We may as well get a camper van and follow the tarmac. We head off to the Blow Holes, a rocky area adjacent to the ocean where we hear a haunting howling wail, then feel a wind, then see fountains of water explode through eroded holes in the soft rock. Its spectacular as the water cascading back down reflects the sun in all the colours of the rainbow. We sit eating our picnic lost in nature's wondrous spectacle, all anxiety gone, knowing sharing these experiences together is so much more than sharing them alone.

At Coral Bay, one of the big tourist hot spots, we find we are in the middle of the school holidays. I´m so uneasy here in our mud splattered Lizzybus. A huge wave of loneliness washes over me seeing all these families and people who all seem to belong. We just drive on through. Initially we take a graded dirt road, heading to Exmouth, but five kilometres in, David´s demons are back. He is worried about the starting issues and lack of decent maps, insists that we head back to the tarmac road. An hour later, to a setting sun, we pull off it into a lay-by. It's not a good place to stop as we can be seen from the road, but driving on is not good either.

Looking around I see a landscape of penis shaped red dirt termite mounds. All the trees and gorses are a uniform height, as if trimmed. Any tree that has the audacity to grow taller is bent over by the constant wind, its branches like flowing hair. I feel unsettled so close to the road, even though no traffic has passed for a while. I think of the book I read about a couple travelling through the outback of Australia in a camper van. The man was shot, she escaped by hiding out in the scrub. I wonder how much cover this low-lying bush would offer me in this situation. I force myself to imagine a different scene, one where I am safe. I´m in my sister's bed on the memory foam mattress with the softest pillows. If or when I ever make it back.

We made it to morning; David has not been shot and termites have not reduced us to skeletons. We head for the heart of Exmouth, looking for Whalers Restaurant as Andrew and Christina (a couple we met in Africa) insisted we say hello to the English owners. We find them, but it's awkward, almost as if we are expecting something from them. It's true, a coffee would not have been refused, but was never offered. We apologise for interrupting their busy day and leave. With travel, it's the people along the way who enrich your journey. Those moments of familiarity stay with you forever. When you feel overwhelmed, just to have the conversation lifts you. Life for them now is of making money.

One of the main attractions here is the solitary speckled plankton eating Whale Sharks. At up to twenty tons and eight metres long, they are the majestic gentle giants of the ocean. To see and, even better, swim with them would truly be the stuff of my dreams, but at over five hundred dollars, we just cannot justify or want to pay that sort of money. A little hurt that I will never swim with the magnificent Whale Sharks, I take comfort knowing I'm close to the ocean they swim in. It's quite ridiculous, but I feel like I've lost something I never had. I feel rejected, both by the friends of our friends and not being able to swim with the Whale Sharks.

Even though we're in an English-speaking country, I´m feeling more and more isolated. It seems all around me are families and groups of friends, all belonging to something, to someone. I´m repeating myself, I know, but since the intimacy all but stopped, or putting a comforting arm around my shoulder, or holding my hand, it's the physical touch I´m missing, the security and comfort it gives. From when I first met David, he refused to wear any form of deodorant, insisting his body needed to sweat naturally. This was not ideal even when hot water and washing was available. In our situation now I found myself wrapping my scarf around my nose, when David driving his arm resting on the window, his body odour was catching my throat. But desire is not just found in clean, it's also in words. Right now, there's nothing in any of David's words that is helping to change this.

A Dutch couple parked up with us last night at the end of their three-month driving holiday. They´ve also found Australia expensive, especially park fees and campsites. They tell us about the park pass covering most of Western Australia, at forty dollars, we have every intention of buying one. With parks here covering vast areas we'd be able to drive through them, rather than make long detours. Just their conversation cheers me up no end.

Although a sunny day, there's a stiff offshore breeze. Today we're going to have a beach day. In our neoprene shorties, mask and fins, we join the holidaymakers on the white sandy beach. Now hovering over coral pinnacles in crystal clear waters, I forget all about twenty-ton whale sharks. Children are doing what children do, building sandcastles and burying each other. Makeshift volleyball nets have been set up and picnics laid out. It's both a comfort and a distraction. But I can't help feeling trapped in this 'domesticity' of people's holiday life. David and I have never been beach people so why are we doing this now? As much as I've enjoyed it, I feel resentful to be wasting time like this.

Then I realise David is doing this for me. We have both always known, this is not a holiday; this is a mission. I need to make progress, not mess about on beaches.

Back at our illegal campsite, even the trees can't protect us from the wind as the roof tent acts like a sail. Our set-up has always been an issue, despite the new clam shell roof tent bought in South Africa it's still accessed externally. Not being able to shelter inside Lizzybus out of this chilling wind, makes it miserable. We end up sitting on the two front seats to eat, before getting into the roof tent.

I'm finding it hard keeping up with my journal; the days roll into one, as they happen, every day. When we first set off on this journey, progress was measured by the countries we got through. This country is one whole continent. It will take months, possibly even years to drive around it. I'm struggling to find the way forward, how to see or feel the reason.

To put it into some sort of order in my head, the states of Australia are:

Western Australia - the Northern Territory - South Australia - Queensland - New South Wales - Victoria - Tasmania

We are in Western Australia, heading to the Northern Territory. From now on, I will see each state as a country, each one as a goal, a target. Despite not having a flag to stick on Lizzybus, I will acknowledge it.

CHAPTER 22

ONE WORD – VAST

We press on and, thanks to the Grey Nomads, we now have a book listing all the official free campsites. The book itself was fifty dollars but it's paid for itself within the first few days. The campsites listed are basic, but all have access to water with long drop or flushing toilets. The biggest thing for me is their being legal. Without the possibility of hefty fines, I can relax. It's here we get to know, understand, and love Australians. Unlike the animated Africans, or the incredibly polite Asians, they are chilled to the point of being horizontal. Like coming to terms with the vastness of their country, it takes time to understand them.

The scenery changes to a rich burnt red earth, littered with honey blonde clumps of grasses. We could almost be back on the savannahs of Africa, minus the elephants, zebra or giraffe. Then we see them - kangaroos. Adult kangaroos are a lot, lot bigger than you expect, standing taller than a man. Despite their reputation, they are more likely to run off than attack you. Provoked, they become gladiators. By leaning on their tail, they kick out with their back legs, causing severe injuries. But it's a bite from a kangaroo that is most dangerous, as some carry rabies. Or running into one at night, which can destroy a vehicle. We're not wanting to pet a kangaroo anytime soon or have any intention of driving at night, so just seeing these iconic kangaroos is a thrill. We admire them from afar, giving them the respect they deserve.

We've arrived at the mining town of Tom Price. After several days' bush camping, we book into the local caravan park which has not just water, but hot water. First, we jump in and straight back out of the freezing cold pool. It makes the hot water of the shower sting my skin. My beautiful ochre coloured hair, after several washes, returns to grey. David works on Lizzybus, topping up oils, greasing nipples and u-jays and fixing the water pump, in the hope it will last longer than the day it lasted the last time he fixed it. I organise kit and cook food for the next few days on the road. Then we join our Aussie neighbours for a few tinnies.

Today, we visit Karijini National Park, the second largest park in

Western Australia at over one and a half thousand acres and included in our park passes. In the distance is Mount Bruce, another second, in being the second tallest peak in Western Australia. Of course, you're talking about a country that is a continent - a second anything here is colossal. The red earth changes to a white chalky dust, camouflaging the road. Bulldust coils up behind us as the wind blows it straight back in. It settles on us like icing sugar. I've started wrapping my sarong over my nose and mouth to avoid suffocating in it. Which pleases me as it has the added advantage of reducing other odours.

This park is famous for its gorges and waterfalls, pictures of which are used in all the tourist information brochures. We are hiking one of them, Joffre Gorge and waterfall. Having sat on our arses for most of this journey, a few minutes in and we're panting. The steps cut into the rock are close enough to the edge to make me close my eyes and not look into the abyss below.

The waterfall is not exactly cascading, more like slithering down the tiered rock, before meandering off along the valley floor. Rather than one crystal-clear plunge pool, there are several. I've long ago given up wearing underwear, being another thing to wash, another layer to chafe. I remember the time I wanted not just big breasts, but some breasts. Now I rejoice as those I have did their job of feeding my children, are not objects of desire and small enough to swing free without reaching my belly button.

I have a bit of dilemma though, as I want to swim. Should I do it naked or in my clothes? Having not seen a soul for the last few hours, I go for naked. Shit, it's freezing and takes my breath away, I feel a physical pain deep in my bones from it. Gritting my teeth to stop them chattering, I look over at David who is wearing boxer shorts. Totally unnecessary, as his bits have tucked themselves up by his kidneys. He is whimpering which cracks me up. My laughter echoes off the walls - the gorge is laughing with us. What an enchanting desolate place.

With our clothes back on our wet bodies, it's not long before they're dry, but with the physical effort of climbing, it's not much longer before they're wet again with sweat. We reach the lookout. Here in all her splendour is the breathtakingly spectacular curved cliff face forming a natural amphitheatre. In perfect solitude, we sit in silence eating our boiled egg sandwiches. Vivid emerald, green finches dive in formation below us, their happy chirping filling our ears. It's several hours before we make it back, physically knackered, but mentally rewarded by the scale and magnitude of this gorge.

Over the next few days, despite our aching bodies, we find and explore more, spending each night at the beautiful campsites included in the park pass. Notices warn of wild dingos and snakes and to keep all your belongings, specifically shoes, inside your vehicle. They are more than welcome to David's minging boots, but he seems to think he needs them. I insist he puts them in a plastic bag to avoid my asphyxiation.

Despite the need I have for progress, these magical few days give us, especially me, what is needed, a sense of reason and belonging. Driving on now through mile after mile gives purpose once more. We pass a sign for camping at a traditional working homestead, considered a real Ozzie experience. This one, with four hundred thousand acres and twenty thousand head of cattle, is apparently a small one. Due to a flu epidemic, we don't get to meet the owners or take part in any cattle mustering. There's just an honesty box for the camping fee. On the evening, we hike the small hillock built by the owners which gives them a panoramic view of their land. As the sun disappears we drink a tinnie, pondering the fact we have yet to see a cow.

We are becoming part of this vastness; the remoteness we craved is what we are now getting. We set up camp beside a watering hole, protected by towering silver gum trees, the soft sandy banks are trodden down by the illusive cattle. As cattle obviously feel safe to drink here, I think it´s less likely crocs might. Of course, the very fact that cattle drink here would make it a perfect place for crocs to hang out. Still, I´m unable to resist, I splash about in the shallows. The sun sets on another day, sat around a little campfire drinking a tinnie. Anyone would think we were in the Australian outback!

The termite nests are no longer stumpy red mounds but works of art in their formation. We're surprised to see the prehistoric baobab tree, common throughout Africa, known here as boab. Dubbed the tree of life for storing water in its trunk, its fruit provides food and fibres for making clothes, and you can even shelter in its gigantic trunk. It's such a comical looking tree; its branches look like its roots, as if planted upside down.

Despite settling into our journey, I can't shake this gut-wrenching feeling of loneliness. I know this has a lot to do with me, I understand that David, having been rejected enough times, would eventually stop trying. But we have gone past the point of it being just sex, it needs a conversation, something to bridge the gap to it. Something is broken, and I wish it was just a case of fixing it or replacing the part. Urgh! feelings and relationships.

Derby, a sleepy town astride the peninsula, surrounded by tidal mud flats is the habitat of the living dinosaur - top of the food chain, largest of its species, opportunistic predators, the saltwater crocodiles. This fact is brought to your attention by the many warning signs, making all thoughts of swimming, even dipping a toe in any water, a definite no-no.

Today, we are going on a real adventure, driving the six hundred and sixty-kilometre Gibb River Road, known locally simply as the Gibb. This true Aussie outback adventure takes you through the Kimberley, an untouched wilderness of dramatic gorges and cattle stations of epic proportions. Originally constructed as a Beef Road for moving and transporting cattle, it's a rough corrugated dirt road that will be tough for Lizzybus and us. What a challenge!

On the outskirts of town is the boab prison tree, with a hollow trunk so big you could hold a tea party in it. Said to be a thousand years old, it's where prisoners en route to the old Derby gaol were tied up. As it's our last stop before the Gibb, we stock up on food, water and diesel in town. We head off full of adventure and high spirits, totally oblivious to the disaster awaiting us.

We hear a loud bang, followed by a burning electrical smell. As I'm driving, I immediately stop and switch off the engine. David asks me over and over exactly what I heard and felt, to the point it feels like he is accusing me of having done something. Although on the outskirts of town, it's a desolate place. With no phone and not having seen any shops, houses or, for that matter, people for the last hour, the situation is bad. David lifts the bonnet, then assumes what has become his customary prostrate position underneath Lizzybus.

I feel desperately sorry for David. He questions his abilities, but the reality is, he is bloody amazing, but even bloody amazing can't always help. When nothing obvious can be seen, we try starting Lizzybus; she won't even turn over. Both now prostrate under Lizzybus, united in our uselessness, a vehicle pulls up. It's the minister of the local Baptist church, off to collect some of his parishioners for the Sunday service. He says he can't stop but will have his friend swing by. I'm comforted by this thought, so sit in the dust smoking as David continues his investigations.

An hour later, the minister's friend and two others arrive. We hang our heads in shame as we, the intrepid explorers are towed by a Toyota to the grounds of the Derby Baptist church. Once there, a group of worshippers help push Lizzybus under the shade of the gum trees. We're invited to join their Sunday service. We want to sort Lizzybus out but feel obliged to accept their invitation. In this sleepy little town, we think the whole population are here in this church. It's a gathering not just for worship, but to discuss the week's events and the upcoming ones. In the community hall, are tables with crisp white tablecloths, laden with homemade cakes and sandwiches, and a white crock tea pot full of tea. Like the Mad Hatter's Tea Party in Alice in Wonderland, or my Sundays at home, when Mom baked. The smell then and now is intoxicating, and the taste divine, very apt in this place of divinity. We are given an unconditional welcome and it's exactly what we need.

Behind the church is another building where we're shown a room with a bathroom we could use. Even having lost most of my English reserve, it's a little out of my comfort zone and I feel unworthy. We thank them saying we would prefer to sleep in Lizzybus so David can work on her. I've said before our beliefs are more about putting an extra 'o' in God and trying to be 'Good' people, rather than having specific beliefs. Know its people's interpretation of any religion that can cause great conflict, as well as great comfort, and personal to them. I smile at David, who is agreeing with the Minister that God will look after us. I'm just hoping Lizzybus can hear him. We've always felt we have a guardian angel. I like to think it's my mother lost to me in the fog of Alzheimer's, well before she died. For now, she appears in these people around us. We know Lizzybus tries her best to take care of us and is most considerate in her breakdowns. Imagine if we were halfway through the Gibb?

We wake in the roof tent, under the shadow of the church with heavy hearts, the challenge and adventure of the Gibb stolen from us. David focuses on the starter motor replaced in Malaysia. The call out for an auto electrician is a hundred dollars and that's without time or labour. I did mention Australia being the most expensive country ever, didn't I?

David takes off the starter motor with the intention of taking it to the electrician, but how do we get it there? This begins a chain of events where human kindness prevails, where strangers become friends, and beliefs can be admired, but not necessarily embraced. The man who towed us took us and the starter motor to be tested. It's confirmed as terminal. We're not convinced, but still a new one is on order. In England if something is flown in, it would be vitally needed organs or a pint of rare blood. Here in this country that is a continent, it's a starter motor, flown in from Perth where we arrived almost two months ago. A group of us try push-starting Lizzybus only to hear a high-pitched screeching noise.

Initial thoughts are it being the fan belt, but it's traced back to the locked solid alternator. My mechanical learning might have improved enough to be able to pass David the right tools, but the complexities of what drives what, are above my pay grade. My reporting and understanding of this little episode is not an exact science. To any mechanic out there, I'm trying my best. We will endure many more breakdowns on another continent before this all becomes clear, for now, we deal with what we are faced with in ignorance.

With the flown-in starter motor, the new six-hundred-dollar alternator and the burnt-out wires replaced, we fire her up. She starts immediately. I could burst with pride at my 'I'm not a mechanic' David and his temperamental mistress. We let her tick over for a bit before driving to the auto electricians who laughed at us when we mentioned Land Rover. On seeing Lizzybus and knowing of our journey, they are full of admiration and say jokingly that we may be driving round the world, but it will only be her number plate that survives. What is it they say? Many a true word is spoken in jest.

Finally, a week later, we leave this little community. It has become very special to us, especially Mary and Tony, once missionaries in Papua New Guinea. Life for them now is pottering around with the aid of sticks, in thier chalet in the grounds of the Derby Baptist Church. We're already missing the magical evenings we spent listening to them regaling us with the most incredible tales of their pioneering past. I wonder if David and I will make it together, to a place where we can potter and reminisce.

Gathered in a circle, Pastor Paul and his wife Laurel ask if they can pray for us. Of course, we respect their beliefs and are grateful for every scrap of help we can get, even in the form of prayers.

CHAPTER 23

THE GIBB

At the start of the Gibb is a sign stating that the route is suitable for 4x4 vehicles only. With what's just happened shaking our confidence, we question if we should take this route at all. But our desire for adventure is too strong - we're compelled to do it. The area is made up of Aboriginal communities, private cattle stations and national parks, with permission to go onto their land needed in some cases. We will bush camp or stay in the homesteads along the route. How I wish I could take part in a cattle drive; with my love of horses, this would be completely amazing.

To start with, it's a tarmac road, with some vehicles pulling trailers. Thinking if they can do it, we can, even in our fully loaded temperamental Lizzybus. It soon becomes a gravel road cutting through the red earth wilderness of the real outback. A fragile land where once yellow willowy grasses swayed in the wind protecting the earth's crust, as far as the eye can see now, it´s compacted, bare and barren, overgrazed by the illusive cattle. We arrive at Tunnel Creek, where the river cuts through the Napier Mountain Range.

Parking Lizzybus we walk through the knee-deep cooling water. Our voices echo off the cathedral high walls, bats dust our ears. We're looking for Aboriginal rock art, but an hour later at the end of the tunnel, we've seen no sign of any. Climbing up the rocks to a shady spot for lunch, we look down on a copse of trees, full of little tweeting finches. A kaleidoscope of butterflies flutter around them, David's pet hate, but being able to look down on them, he can at last appreciate their beauty. Then we see, on the walls behind the trees, the Aboriginal rock art we were looking for. David is convinced they are early pictures of Homer Simpson.

Where the sections of the Gibb cross the National Park, camping is in unmanned designated sites, with long drop toilets and fire pits. The twenty dollars a night fee is to be posted in the honesty box when leaving. We're still reeling from the cost of shipping, flights, and the latest Lizzybus parts. Having paid to enter the Park through our park pass, and the sites being very basic, we leave without paying. This bothers me and I decided I won't do it again. Driving under crystal clear blue skies, we see heavy clouds in the distance, when a few moments later, we're plunged into semi-darkness and choking acrid smoke. We're in a bush fire. Bush fires are not something we have experience of but know of their dangers. I just imagine the skeletal remains of a burnt out Lizzybus and us, found by hikers in the distant future.

This section of road is quite wide and surrounded by low lying scrub, as we know there's a river crossing a few kilometres ahead, we carry on. It seems to be more smoke than fire, until it becomes a hedgerow of flames. We feel the heat from it but are not exactly engulfed as the road is so wide. I imagine Moses parting the sea for the Israelites, but for us it's fire instead of water. I wonder if it's because of all the prayers we were given.

Bush fires are part of the cycle of life in the great outback and often its human carelessness that start them. They can destroy homes and habitats, at times even life. With the wind blowing across us, before reaching the river it stops as abruptly as it started. We exit through an arch of fire and smoke, back to the same blue sky we left. Magnificent birds of prey hover in the thermals, swooping down on escaping lizards and small animals. What an experience!

We reach the Pentecost River, grateful it's two months since the wet season when it´s over sixty metres wide and fast flowing. I imagine the struggles of the early pioneers in convoys of horse-drawn wagon trains. When breaking a wheel or tipping over in the strong current made them prey to the saltwater crocodile. The sweeping low-lying expanse of river has many grassy rocky areas ideal for a hungry croc to hide out in or bask in the sun. A weathered sun-bleached sign warns you of this imminent danger.

Normally one of us would walk a river crossing, but today neither of us volunteered. It's like a scene from Gone with the Wind, okay, a different time and place. But to me, horse-drawn wagons of people trying to make a new life for them and their families make it a 'Gone with the Wind' moment. I can hear the neighing of the horses, the groan of carriages, the crack of whips driving the horses on. I don't give a single thought to alternators, starter motors, or breaking axels. Water gushes in through the bottom of the doors, we lurch this way and that. It's just too exhilarating and romantic. Looking across at David, I love that he's loving this as much as I am.

Did I mention, I'm Jayne from a council house in Birmingham, driving across a croc infested river in Lizzybus in the outback of Australia, with effectively my Tarzan?

The Gibb is so much more than a road; it has many stunning gorges and falls along its way. These are graded in order of difficulty with walks from an hour to even overnight to suit all levels. Our favourite so far has been Bell Gorge and Waterfall. Just difficult enough to put most people off, but easy enough for our under-exercised bodies to tackle. A lazy river meanders along, cascading into a plunge pool. Smaller pools are scattered around, with smooth ochre red boulders. I dive off the boulders into the chilly water then bask like a lizard on them, soaking up their warmth. It's so perfect we camp overnight and stay another day.

All along this route we see signs for scenic picture spots, in truth it's all one big scenic picture. Meandering rivers nest in valleys, silver leafed trees shimmer, the rising and setting sun illuminates distant mountains. Tonight, needing fuel and supplies, we take a detour off the Gibb into a small town. A tour bus arrives and I see a man using his mobile phone. On arriving in Australia, we bought an internet stick, but so far have not been able to get connected. Tonight, after a hot shower, our dusty clothes washed, David cooking dinner, I manage to log on and get my emails from home. It's very, very special.

This morning, with the main and spare tank full of diesel, a gallon of unleaded for the cooker and a bag of vegetables and frozen chicken, we hit the road. Very few vehicles pass us, but when they do, they spray us with stones and a cloud of dust. Now when we see this cloud of dust ahead or in the rear-view mirror, in unison we close the windows. Seeing another cloud of dust ahead of us, we get ready to close the window. It's cowboys, real live cowboys on a cattle drive. It's simply timeless, with a wonderful mixture of mooing and clattering hooves. It could only have been bettered if I was on a horse driving cattle with them.

We pass El Questro Wilderness Park, a million acres of what was once a cattle station, now a privately run resort and homestead. The twenty-five dollars entrance fee does not include camping and a sign recommends booking online or at the registration station, open for limited hours. With no one at the registration station, and unable to log on, we just go in and park up. One of the attractions is Zebedee Springs, a thermal springs area of gurgling water and small rock pools. It's full of people but we find a little corner to soak off some of the dust.

Over the six days it took to drive the Gibb, we lose two wheel nuts, the bolt that held the sand ladders on, and every single orifice in Lizzybus and us is coated in red dirt. Were incredulous we drove and survived the Gibb and what an experience it was. Even better, our Lizzybus didn't let us down, she kept us safe. She showed us her strength and what she was built for. Despite the many times we despair of her, and each other, it's made up for in these moments, all part of Team Lizzybus.

We're heading for the UNESCO World Heritage Purnululu National Park and Bungle Bungle Range. It's sort of back on ourselves along the Victoria Highway. Going back on ourselves when we have a whole world to get around usually makes me most grumpy. But with confidence in Lizzybus growing, I'm bewitched by the magnificence of Australia. The distances are so great, we drive for many hours each day, bush camping, or, at the free public campsites from the camping book. Here we find a great mix of Grey Nomads and young people.

Talking to them, were told the most difficult part of their journeys has been adjusting to each other. Married, lifelong friends, lovers, or strangers, all feel this. When personal habits, opposing views, ideas of what the journey should be, or money, make it the nightmare, not the dream. I feel better that David and I are still managing to hold it together, to navigate our way through this, even though the cracks are beginning to show.

I understand why bush camping is not tolerated, specifically near towns, as some people's disrespect for this spectacular environment is shameful. They leave broken bottles, bags of garbage, even used toilet paper hanging from bushes. Burn, bury, or take it with you. Obviously burning with the threat of bushfires would not be an option, but burying or taking it with you is.

Such a shitty night, I have a stinking cold and I can barely lift my head off the pillow. The morning sun sends shooting pains through my pupils, every limb aches, even climbing down the ladder hurts my feet. I just imagine having a nice hot shower and wrapping my hands around a mug of tea, warm and snuggly in a dressing gown and fluffy slippers. David is frying bacon, it's making me nauseous, my mosquito bites are pulsating. I shove rolled up toilet paper up my nose to stop it dripping, full of self-pity.

We arrive at Purnululu National Park, which covers more area than

Australia's Capital Territory. I forget my aching bones and tissue stuffed snout, the focus now is getting through the deep creeks and the rock-strewn winding road. I can't believe in places it's tougher than the Gibb. The most striking feature of this park is the Bungle Bungle Range. Orange and grey-black beehive shaped sandstone domes, formed over millions of years, stand up to six hundred metres high. They are breathtaking in their beauty.

We hike along the expanse of dry riverbed to Echidna Chasm. At times it's only body width wide, the walls of layered rock soaring high above us change colour within sun or shade. By the time we get back to Lizzybus it's late afternoon and know it will take several hours to get out of the park. As the road was tough enough in daylight, we decided to camp in one of the official campsites. What a wonderful evening chatting into the night with people is so good for the soul.

It takes another whole bone shaking equally dramatic day to get out of the park. We pass an area filled with towering phallic-like protrusions of stripy rock. They look just like honey dippers, a wooden stick with spiral oval grooves used to get honey out of a jar. Winnie-the-Pooh from Hundred Acre Wood would have loved one, instead of his 'hunny' dipping twig. Like the finale of a fireworks display we finish at Cathedral Gorge, an almost complete circular arched wall, around a pool. It could only have been made more spectacular if we had been in the wet season, as then it's a complete curtain of cascading water. Of course, I´m grateful we didn't see it, with the many water crossings we're already facing; they would have been impassable in the wet season. David worries about water making its way into the axles, I worry about it coming in through the huge gaps in the bottom of the doors.

It's the times like this that are the toughest, to reset and get going again. These mini trips, whilst incredible, take a lot out of us. It is never an end, just another beginning, and the enormity of what does, and will go wrong hits us harder each time. Camping last night in the bush nestled by the river, eating a bowl of pasta, I realised it was David's birthday! With no internet or phone access, we didn't get any birthday messages or emails that might have reminded us. I figure just to have nearly forgotten it, made it extra special.

We have spent over four days here at Kununurra, a peaceful town built up due to the damming and irrigation of the Ord River. Mini-Me, my laptop, my confidante, for my ritual logging of this journey, has died.

When we set off, we had one laptop and one phone between us, it soon became apparent we needed one each, so I bought a small laptop and phone in Gibraltar. To have it repaired would cost as much as a new one here in Australia, we order a new one. Replacing and or repairing stuff like this when on the road has always been a problem. It being a weekend, it will not arrive until at least Monday, we have no option other than to wait it out.

To distract me, and knowing of my love of horses, David takes me to my very first rodeo. With our picnic lunch we join the locals in elaborately embroidered shirts, bell bottom jeans, cowboy boots, spurs and Stetsons. The crease in its top is called a 'reach and grab'. Every cowboy does just that, reaches and grabs the crease. The day progressed with children and their ponies in a gymkhana event and campdrafting, then the real rodeo began.

Sat around the metal-caged circular arena on chairs we brought with us, I notice pens holding bulls and horses. I thought it was just going to be cowboys, riding bucking broncos, I hadn't realised it was bulls. I begin to feel uncomfortable, seeing the terror in the eyes of the horses and the bulls. A terrified horse with its rider in a blind panic comes hurtling towards us. It crashes into the metal fence right in front of us with a sickening thud. The horse falls to the ground, quivering for a moment, then dies. I sit there in shock; blankets are thrown over it then it's scooped up on a forklift truck. I'm traumatised, David feels my distress, people assure us this has never happened before. It's happened now, and I just can't be part of it, we leave.

We spend the weekend at Swim Beach, an area on the edge of town, around a lake. Australia is set up for outdoor living, most places, like here, having picnic areas with wooden tables and benches, with free-to-use gas barbecues. Being a hot day, we're surprised no one else is swimming, but were soon in, swimming about. A boat pulling a water skier speeds past, then a seaplane lands, the passengers of which jump out, swim, then get back in before it takes off again. Getting out I notice the sign warning you to be aware of crocodiles. I remember being with my sister in the lake at our local park, we could paddle, swim, and never once did we have to watch out for water skiers, seaplanes, or crocodiles - what a simple life I had.

We're heading north along the Victoria Highway to Katharine, beside Lake Argyle one of Australia's largest reservoirs. It was formed by the damming of the Ord River. When full it holds around eighteen times more volume of water than Sydney Harbour. Its steep rich red banks plunge into deep blue waters. Its size and scale are disguised by its meandering contours and the seventy islands created, with homes and people living on them.

We have become so basic in our needs and wants on this journey. We don't have a bathroom cupboard full of lotions and potions to keep us young or aromatic. We have a bar of Wright's coal tar soap for washing us and a block of African yellow magic soap for washing clothes. My skin without any creams or moisturiser is okay, but my heels are cracked, bleeding, and incredibly painful. I have driven mostly barefoot or in flip flops. Putting my heels down now is too painful, I balance my foot on the pedals when driving. I do have a pot of petroleum jelly which helps a little, but with it smeared on my heels the sand and grit stick to it, causing more friction.

But it's the disappearing amounts of money we seem to have no control over that are becoming an issue. With the distances we're having to cover, we're using a tank of diesel a day, at eighty dollars a fill, it's crippling on our sixty dollars a day budget. We're needing to dip more and more into our savings to keep afloat. It's the first time we're not exactly worried about money but are aware of it. It makes me feel like the poor relation. It's crazy to think you could be poor with this priceless magical adventure. It's a pressure we really could do without, but it's the reality of travel for all of us.

Darwin, the top and tip of the Northern Territory. On Christmas morning 1974, Cyclone Tracy hit, levelling over half of its buildings. Now rebuilt, it has become a city of swanky apartments, restaurants and shops. Darwin is a milestone in that we have been heading towards it for nearly two months. Travelling for this long anywhere else, it would have been another country, but here it's just another city. Not for me though. As we arrived in Western Australia and are now in the Northern Territory, to me that's two of the six countries I have divided Australia into. Our next 'country' is South Australia. That will be celebrated only when we reach the middle of Australia, Alice Springs, as near as damn it one thousand five hundred kilometres away. Being the centre of Australia is quite apt as it is the middle of our journey through it.

We visit Fannie Bay Gaol, as it's free, then have our picnic in the local tropical park overlooking the Arafura Sea, a western part of the

Pacific Ocean. This sea or ocean thing confuses me; it's something to do with size and proximity to land. I just wished it was called one or the other.

We need to slow the journey down to allow the rental income to catch up on itself. But, having made it to Darwin, one quarter of Australia, with our three-month visa, we risk being overstayers. Our ultimate goal is Melbourne, the bottom of Australia, where we will ship Lizzybus to Buenos Aires and our next continent, South America. Our route along the Stuart Highway, also known as Explorers Way, passes through three time zones, the outback, desert and tropical rainforest. Almost three thousand kilometres long, it took over a hundred years to construct. It's a massive journey, putting huge pressure on us. We question why we came to Australia and didn't just ship directly to South America.

Because it's a continent and part of the whole world.

What I like is that we now have targets and goals, driving along the Stuart Highway, doesn't last long; we detour off to Litchfield National Park. David is never going to follow the quicker, more direct tarmac road, visa restrictions or not. We take the scenic route, highlighted in green on our map, David loves his maps. It's a sweeping picturesque road, taking us to Robin Falls. We see a good place to camp beside a stream shaded by eucalyptus trees, but it's only midday so we press on. With the light fading, just on the outskirts of a town, we end up in a lay-by.

In our hearts we both knew this journey would take as long as it took. What we never considered was the demands it would have, not just on us and Lizzybus, but also on our kit. Everything is wearing out; the difficulties of replacing or repairing anything magnifies their importance. Their loss gets taken out of context; it colours the mood. The latest is our Coleman cooker, spewing petrol from a cracked joint. We're now using our single burner Whisperlite, it's okay for a weekend camping, but not for us with our pressure cooker.

After an uncomfortable night so close to the road, we're up and off early, not wanting to be done for vagrancy. Litchfield National Park, formed on a wide central sandstone plateau, has four waterfalls and monsoon rainforest. Monsoon rainforest differs from a rainforest, in that it has a dry season followed by a monsoon season, rather than all-year-round rainfall. What's good for us right now is that Litchfield

National Park is, for Australia, compact and the road is tarmac. All along are signposts indicating the points of interest, like the Magnetic Termite Mounds (which still look like every other termite mound). Unique to the northern part of Australia, their thin edge points from north to south, minimising exposure to the sun to keep the termites cool. Termites are specific in how they use their nest: the top to bury their dead, the middle for the workers, and the bottom reserved for the king and queen.

It's late afternoon when we arrive at Sandy Creek campsite and dump Lizzybus to hike to Tjaynera Falls. It's magical in its isolation; the plunge pool has water cascading into it over pastel-coloured rock. We swim alone to the setting sun, reflected in the water. The next day we visit an abandoned homestead, hike through monsoon rainforest and climb the one hundred and thirty-five steps to Florence Fall, both breathless when reaching the top.

For some reason we end up back at Robin Falls, the camping spot we ignored two days ago. I paddle and play on the rope swing strung across the stream; David plans and schemes our route. We're back on the Stuart Highway, heading for Alice Springs and Uluru (Ayers Rock), the biggest monolith in the world. Along this road, we visit more National Parks - Elsey and Bitter Springs. Bitter Springs is extra special, as it has palm-fringed thermal pools and a lazy river. In its aqua blue, gin clear, warm as toast water, you float along amongst swaying grasses and turtles. It's an utterly enchanting and unique experience I never want to end. Tonight, we are camping on the banks of the Roper River in individual pitches. Paying for camping is usually in honesty boxes; here a couple arrives to collect the fee.

It's morning and we really should press on, but seeing the signs for Twelve Mile Yard Waterfall, think stuff it and stay another night. Hiking along the steep banks of the sultry green waters of the Roper River, it's hot, very hot, almost tropical with palms lining the banks. The Falls were underwhelming, but further on where the two rivers meet, are water holes that have created natural jacuzzis. We eat our picnic sitting in one of them, using a fallen tree with its pure white bark as our table. Hiking back to camp we see a floating wooden pontoon anchored just offshore. We know this is croc territory, from all the signs everywhere, but they also advise of daily inspections and traps to keep you safe. Come on, why would they put a pontoon there if not to swim out to it? I just can't resist, but once on it, the thought of swimming back freaks me out. I'm sure crocs can smell fear. I can't decide which would be best, to swim behind David, so he is croc bait, but then I could be picked off from the back. Finally, I insist we swim side by side, united in our fate, asking myself who's stupid idea this was anyway.

Back on the Stuart Highway, there's a routine to breaking camp. It seems my constant 'suggestions' about putting kit away have finally been listened to. It still needs a little tweaking as just shoving stuff in the right place all screwed up and dirty is still a little annoying. I´m also trying, in my map reading abilities, to see the Stuart Highway runs from the very top to the very bottom of Australia. David uses a highlighter pen each evening to chart our progress along it; he never colours more than an inch each day. An endless road, with just enough traffic to make you realise there is life on earth, and not just you rattling through it.

We call in at the iconic Daly Waters Pub which claims to be the oldest pub in the Northern Territory, and that Amy Johnson landed here on her solo flight from England to Australia in 1930. Inside this weathered, corrugated-roofed building, the walls are completely covered in foreign money, farming equipment, business cards, and even ladies' knickers. At nine dollars for a beer, we share one. I'm disappointed we don't stay the night as there is live entertainment, but a room with evening meal is a hundred dollars and that is a tank of diesel.

We see in the distance huge letters spelling out the name of the outback roadhouse of Aileron and statues of The Big Aboriginal Hunter and Anmatjere Woman and Child. The Hunter standing seventeen metres high, weighing eight tons, depicts a man from the Aboriginal Anmatjere tribe, the region's first settlers.

We arrive at Devils Marbles (Karlu Karlu), ancient granite boulders believed by Aborigines to be the fossilised eggs of the Rainbow Serpent. They got their name from a quote by British arctic explorer John Ross who said, "This is the Devil's country, he's even emptied his bag of marbles around the place." And that's exactly what they look like, a bag of marbles. Millions of years ago, water levels dropped and the ground lifted, forming these granite marbles which teeter precariously on each other. Around our campfire, as the sun sets, these granite marbles glow red, as if heated by the Rainbow Serpent.

Alice, Alice where the f**k is Alice?

CHAPTER 24

WHERE THE '****' IS ALICE?

We've made it! Twelve days after leaving Darwin, the top of Australia, we have arrived at Alice Springs, the middle. A once desolate telegraph station, we expected to find a dust bowl of nothingness, but it has everything a town could have. Best of all is the family run Land Rover specialist, a shop selling Coleman cookers, and a McDonald's, which to us means internet! Our first thoughts are for Lizzybus who is facing the huge maintenance issue of the timing belt. To all who don't know, including me, it apparently needs replacing every four years or sixty thousand miles. If it breaks, valves and pistons destroy the engine. The simplicity of getting into a car and driving around the world is a whole load of bollocks; the reality is, it's a whole world of pain.

Our first real mechanical breakdown of the water pump occurred on the Caprivi Strip, a desolate strip of land with a nothingness around it, when there was no option other than for us to change it (David had one in his spares). As it involved the taking off and putting back of a belt to get at it, I sort of thought the timing belt change would be something similar. But no, this belt is buried deep in the engine and requires major surgery. I can't get my head around that someone would put something so vital, that will at some point need changing, in such an inaccessible place. If I could get my hands on them, I would punch them in the face. They had no consideration to people like us, who are quite literally in the middle of a country that is a continent.

It's not just a belt but a complete kit that is needed, as getting at it means gaskets, seals, oils and so on are destroyed. Replacing a timing belt should take between four to six hours, depending on the vehicle and mechanic. I can't imagine for one minute Lizzybus will make this a straightforward operation. I know she will have plenty of surprises in store, from rusted bolts to sheared engine mounts. It feels good to know she will get a thorough check over and in a place that has, or can get, all the bits I know we will end up needing.

I feel blindsided by this and a lot pissed off. You might see that during this journey, I am beginning to develop a bit of a potty mouth. This I feel is more than justified with the constant challenges I am facing. Not least that it must be changed here in Australia, being the most expensive country so far. It won't just be the cost of the kit and the labour, but as our home is Lizzybus, we will have to book into a backpackers overnight. We're looking at around one thousand five hundred US dollars. It makes me breathless for all the wrong reasons. We have no choice; the consequences of not doing it would mean the end of our journey. As the only garage here is a one-man operation, and the timing kit needs to be flown out (of course it does), we're booked in for five days' time.

As we're still cooking on the Whisperlite since the generator arm cracked on our Coleman cooker, we hope the shop here has a generator arm. No, they don't. We both share the same sick lump in our stomach at having to spend more money, but decide to buy a new cooker. It's a vital part of our life on the road and we need a cooker.

With a five day wait we go off to explore starting with Uluru (Ayers Rock), the main draw here to Alice Springs. At just over 450km back along the Stuart Highway, it's a good day's drive. But we go in a huge loop via the MacDonnell Ranges stretching east and south of Alice Springs. What an amazingly picturesque area; when you expect a nothingness, it has an everything-ness, from rolling blond grassed hills, frosted white barked forests, to low lying shrub and desert. There are more magnificent gorges, where the sun never reaches, with ice cold swimming holes and challenging hikes. We hike a few, swim a few, and drive past a few. As the road changes from tarmac to corrugated dirt, Lizzybus leaves billowing clouds of red dust in her wake. We see herds of feral camels, but what is simply captivating is the flocks of different birds. They create vivid blocks of colour when flying over us, striking against the deep blue skies.

Two hours in, as we swap over driving, David notices a weep of diesel over the front brakes. Apparently it's not major, only a cracked diesel filter. It will get replaced when Lizzybus has her timing belt done, but it makes us both twitchy in all this remoteness. I question why we are messing about. Now I know about the timing belt, a destroyed engine is all I can think about. This is exactly why David doesn't tell me until he needs to.

We pull over for the night to camp in a dry riverbed. It's not the best place, but having been assured by the locals you can set your clock here for rainfall, we risk it. David is snoring, which is unusual for him

– I am the snorer – and this comforts me rather than irritates, knowing for now he is free of this constant responsibility and worry for me and Lizzybus. I hear a weird howling noise, between that of a pig and a dog in pain. Wild dingoes. We're so used to camping now, we never leave anything out, not even the rubbish bag. Being on top of Lizzybus we are safe; the worst they could do would be to piss up the tyres. Just like David's snoring, I find comfort in this too.

The locals were right, it didn't rain last night and we weren't washed away in a flash flood. Pressing on, we reach Kings Canyon where a signpost announces the four-hour hike around it. A canyon is a deep valley with steep sides, as opposed to a gorge which is a deep ravine, usually with a river running through it, but not always. You would imagine after all the canyons and gorges we have hiked, we would be getting fitter, and you're right – we are. It's great being able to do all this physical stuff. Kings Canyon starts with cut-into-the-cliff near-vertical steps, taking us to the yawning chasm of the Canyon. Standing like dots on its rim looking into it, we see a rock face as smooth as ice, with layers of what look like chocolate nougat. I want to cut a chunk off and eat it.

We know we need to get Lizzybus back to the garage in four days, but we can't leave without visiting Uluru-Kata Tjuta National Park, home to the iconic Uluru (Ayers Rock) and red domes of the Kata Tjuta (the Olgas). The area is one great big tourist destination and even has its own airstrip to bring the tourists in, but it's so vast it swallows everyone up. Entrance to the park or camping within it is not free and, as we know we couldn't possibly get around it in one day, we pay for a three-day park pass, even though we can only do two with our time limit.

Heading first for the sandstone-domed rock formations of the Kata Tjuta, we're confident, now that we're fitter, we can easily do the challenging hike through the Valley of the Winds. This takes us through the heart of these domed clusters and into late afternoon. We then drive over for the sunset over Uluru. We park Lizzybus beside all the other vehicles behind a fenced off area and sit on her roof. Uluru-Ayers Rock, at 3.6km long and 348m high, can be seen by everyone in all her glory, as the setting sun turns the biggest lump of rock in the world a glorious blood red. For me, what is so special is being with everyone else, each having had their own journey to get here, their own story to tell. We sit together with a bottle of beer, glass of wine, or mug of tea to experience this together as one.

It took two hours to get out of the park to the free campsite listed in our book, thus avoiding the camping fee. Today we're back, this time to climb Uluru, which is only allowed at a designated place and under guidance. Your to hold onto the rope anchored to the rock, which makes sense - you can't have a load of tourists climbing all over it, or falling off. Disappointingly, due to high winds, Uluru is closed. We make the decision to call the garage and re-book Lizzybus for the day after so we can come back tomorrow. For today, we hike around the base of Uluru, which is quite spectacular. The areas where wind and water have forced their way through have produced crested waves of rock, that fold over you as you walk through.

Returning today, the winds are still too high to climb Uluru so we head back to Alice to sort out a room ready for when Lizzybus goes into the garage. We have such a sense of achievement at having got Lizzybus to Uluru, and in good spirits, knowing Lizzybus is going to get the attention she requires. Driving along under a beautiful cloud-free sky, we hear an ear-splitting squealing noise, and unable to steer Lizzybus we veer off onto the hard shoulder. It's in this moment, the moment before you know what has happened, that you stop breathing and feel physically sick.

We totally understand and take seriously what we are putting our fully-loaded Lizzybus through every day, knowing that it would test any vehicle. But we want to just throw our hands up, surrender, and forget the whole f….g thing. It's not like we are blasé in looking after Lizzybus; every spare inch of space is jammed with spares and we spend more money on oil than we do beer. I realise I´m taking this as personally as David.

Once I've got over myself, in the warming up nicely, boiling hot sun, I put out warning triangles and we put on our high hi-vis vests. David diagnoses it as a seized back inner bearing. On the positive, David has had plenty of practice changing bearings and we have spares. A police car with two officers arrives. They are impressed with the efficiency of these 'tourists', not only in making the area and themselves safe with triangles and hi-vis vests, but at having everything necessary, like the tools, the spare parts and the knowledge to fix it. They laugh at us when we list all the food and water we have onboard, and the most important

Uhuru, Ayer's Rock, Australia

being the 'slab of tinnies'. With no phone service here, they give us their personal phone number, telling us to call them from the roadhouse fifty kilometres ahead when we arrive. If they don't hear from us by evening, they will come back to check on us.

I'd never even heard of a bearing in my old life, but now I'm sick of hearing about them. Being the inner bearing, it takes longer to get at and change. David again questions if it was his greasing, or lack of it, that caused this. I've just about had enough, as I know he is looking for reassurance from me in this. He knows that second to the love of his life Lizzybus, is his grease gun. It's given pride of place in Lizzybus and used, if not on a daily basis, definitely a weekly one. Surely to goodness sometimes, just sometimes, things just wear out?

Finally, we're back on the road and heading for the roadhouse. David pulls over to check the bearing. It's red hot which I didn't, but I do now, know is an indication of being over-tightened. Apparently, we need a torque wrench that allows you to accurately tighten bearings. It's not part of David's vast array of tools. Did I mention how big and heavy a Lizzybus wheel is with her steel wolf rims, and how precarious jacking her up is?

Once again, in the late afternoon heat, we puff, groan and sweat with the effort of it all. My nails have become as black, broken and grease-filled as David's, and as his body odour is not bothering me as much, I figure we must both stink. With the bearing released, I'm as determined as David to get a torque wrench added to our toolbox.

It's getting late by the time we're back on the road and we still haven't reached the roadhouse to call the police. I have visions of a full-on rescue party being sent out for us, helicopters and all. When we do eventually make it, as soon as we walk in we're greeted by the owners, saying the police had been calling to check if we had arrived. At the roadhouse we leave two West Midlands Police badges (donated by Mr T Senior) for the officers. As much as we want to, we can't stay - we have to get back to Alice for the timing belt.

At one of the free campsites listed in our book, a man we met somewhere on the road brings us a bucket full of hot water. I want to give him a hug, but I don't want to inflict my aroma on him. What a wonderful life this is when its value comes in a bucket of hot water. Its gift is most welcome, and not in the slightest bit odd or embarrassing. In the dark we strip off, wash our bits and pits, and collecting the used water in the bowl, I soak my feet. I'm not sure how much cleaner we are, but the feeling of hot water on my body and the smell of soap is comforting.

We're back in Alice. After dropping Lizzybus off with the mechanic for the one day it should take, we head to the backpackers. We both know that the 'one' day will never happen. We're right. It takes a day and a half, which means two nights in the backpackers at fifty dollars a night. Still, we make the most of the wi-fi and basic included breakfast - the hot showers are good too. Nothing will compare to my bucketful of hot water and the kindness from a person we met once. At the end of all this, we are almost two thousand dollars lighter. With the new cooker, two nights at the backpackers, a torque wrench, restocking of oil filters, bearings, and a box full of things I'm yet to learn about.

It's strange how okay we are at spending so much money, mainly because it has been spent on Lizzybus allowing us to have renewed confidence in her. This with being looked out for by the police and a bucket of hot water, we are feeling good. One thing that we had pushed to the back of our minds, but can no longer ignore, is having less than three weeks left on our visa. David has tried extending it online, but frustratingly was just getting error messages. We decide to ignore it, again.

In the past, when I visited my grandma's, in the corner of her room was an old, rusted bird cage. In it was a half bald budgerigar. This budgie could speak apparently, but never on demand. It was allowed out to fly around the room like a bomber pilot. You were to sit perfectly still and not scare it, although it scared you witless. You had to let it land on your head, where it would peck and poo on you. Before us now are wild flocks of the most beautiful fully feathered budgerigars. They fly past, not as bomber pilots, but like the Red Arrows aerobatic team. Sweeping this way and that, trailing lines of vivid green and yellow, quite exquisite. Not one of them wanted to land on my head or peck or poo in my hair.

From Alice, we're heading directly east to Brisbane and what I'm told is the Gold Coast, originally known as the South Coast (because it was south of Brisbane). Due to the high cost of houses, goods and services there, it was nicknamed the Gold Coast. To me this means expensive, well more expensive than Australia already is. It's decided to not exactly ignore Queensland, our fourth 'country' here in Australia, but to not explore it. With its sheer size and our visa restraints, we have to make a compromise - we will go in a straight line to it. I can't help feeling a little chuffed about this decision; as spectacular as Australia is, we have a goal, a purpose, that of getting Lizzybus around the world.

We're back on the road heading directly east through desert, glorious sandy desert, where you expect to, and do see, caravans of camels. In the immortal words of Michael Caine in the film Zulu, "bladdy thousands". It's a constantly changing evocative landscape, full of mystique and wonder. In the distance, rising fifty metres above the surrounding plain, we see Chambers Pillar, a landmark for early settlers, now part of the Chambers Pillar Historical Reserve. A naturally formed feature, this solitary sandstone column has been produced by wind, rain and erosion. You can admire it from a distance or drive to it on the unsealed old South Road, a submerged road of sand, notoriously difficult to navigate. With the angel and the devil sitting on each shoulder, the devil in both of us always wins.

Yes, it's tough, not just navigating in the deep sand and rock, but being a lot further than we imagined. Once there, we see the initials of the early pioneer explorers scratched into it. It's illegal now, but for some reason people still feel compelled to do this. We're content to just have made it here. I can't help feeling it looks like a gigantic rotting tooth. Sitting with our backs leaning on Chambers Pillar eating our picnic, not for the first time I feel a part of those earlier pioneer explorations.

In some sense, their struggles have been our struggles, and our spirits are their spirits.

Back now on the main highway, although tarmac, it is being swallowed by desert. I'm driving when I realise I have no brakes. I steer Lizzybus off the road into the soft sand to stop her. We see brake fluid pouring out from the cracked rear brake pipe, which over time has become brittle. David plugs it, but it's too late, all the brake fluid has drained out. Of course, of all the fluids David does have, brake fluid isn't one of them or, for that matter, a spare brake pipe. The decision is made to head back to Alice, using hand and engine braking.

Then we hear the familiar squealing of a bearing, bearings that had all been checked, greased and replaced where necessary in Alice. It's at this point, totally and utterly overwhelmed, we both lose the plot. All the beauty, all the adventure, all the joy gone, replaced with fear, anxiety and loathing. Loathing of this journey, of this constant struggle, even of Lizzybus. We cannot even comfort each other.

In this dusty nothingness, David, verging on insanity, takes out every tool, scattering them in the dust. I see it as his gung-ho way, but it's just him at the end of his tether. Having identified and removed the rogue bearing, David is now unwrapping the brand new one. To those who don't know, bearings are full of tiny ball bearings and must be lubricated, grit and dirt free. But its Murphy's Law that states, 'if anything can go wrong, it will', like in the buttered toast that lands butter side down.

We watch as, in slow motion, this brand new bearing slips out of David's hand, spins over and over to land face down in the sand. I launch a personal verbal attack, fuelled by the hurt, the pain, and the loneliness I feel. David total ignores me, as if I don't exist. Of course he does, he has to, he needs to. He also needs my support, but I´m totally unable to offer this right now. I think a little bit of me breaks each time this happens. I have tried so many times to talk to David about how I am feeling. How he makes me feel. How he feels. I always get the same response, "he has not thought about it".

Words are so powerful but left unanswered they are even more so. We're utterly beaten by it all, feel conspired against and completely betrayed, which of course we're not. Imagine if this happened on our way to Chambers Pillar?

David fits our last spare bearing; I clean and put away the tools.

We limp back to Alice for the third time to get the brakes sorted and some more bearings. It's Sunday, all the garages are closed, so we book back into the campsite we were at a week ago. The locals embarrassingly welcome us back, which is a distraction. I can't see how we can keep going, we're so overwhelmed. This roller coaster of incredible highs and lower lows is proving unsustainable. Even though we deal with things in different ways, we usually manage to keep it together, but there is a limit for us both. It's vital to be united, that we support each other, but it's getting harder and harder. We don't need to be lovers, which is a good thing because we are not, but we absolutely need to be friends. This constant stress of breakdowns, visas, and money, is taking all the joy and wonder out of the journey, replacing it with dread and anxiety. We both begin to question if we should, or if we can continue.

I've thought about how much I want, and how much I need, to share here, to be respectful of David, but also to be totally honest. To say David is a 'wham bam, thank you ma'am' kind of man would be true, as a lover and as a diner. Over the years, we have adjusted, both in bed and around the table. Sitting here now in my own thoughts, the devil himself is at play. I dismiss all the wonderful adventures, made possible by us both, but mainly by David, and what we have shared together. I can only focus on what is wrong with us. All I want, all I need, is meaningful to me, conversation. This is exactly what David wants, but his meaningful conversation revolves around Lizzybus and worst-case scenarios. Mine is about…. let's just say life.

I'm more upset with myself than with David, for how needy I am becoming. Emotions are a lot harder to deal with than breakdowns, you can´t just change the part. I make a pact with myself, to count to ten, but decide that's a bit ambitious, so settle on three, before I open my gob. To accept I never was, or ever will be, told how amazing, beautiful, or funny I am. How much I´m loved or receive a handwritten note declaring this. I need to focus on having someone beside me, who always puts me first, that is, of course, after his mistress and spare parts, and would give his life to protect me. One thing that has bonded us is our sense of humour, but the laughter is becoming less and less.

The next day, one hundred and fifty dollars lighter, we have new brake pipes, a bottle of fluid, a length of brake pipe, diesel, water, food, and beer. I kiss David, a proper kiss and we hold each other for a moment; being held is so powerful. It would have been wonderful for it to have been more. In this moment David's head is so full and focused on Lizzybus, he doesn't respond, but it's a start. United once more we head off. We need to believe we can make it, that we can do this.

We're now on the Old Ghan Railway, a disused part of it to be exact, which still runs a passenger service from northern Australia to southern Australia, from Darwin at the top to Adelaide at the bottom. At nearly three thousand kilometres, what an iconic journey that would be. How I would love to be lulled to sleep by the clickety-clack of wheels over the track, the chuff-chuff of steam, and the repetitive thumping of pistons. What! What am I talking about, pistons? What is happening to me, why would I even know about, or for that matter, find the sound of pistons comforting? What devilry is at play here? I want to go back to the ignorance of Jayne and enjoy nothing more than clickety-clacking and chuff-chuffing. But this is the me now, who takes comfort in not hearing any slapping or mechanical knocking from the Lizzybus pistons, safe in the knowledge that she has her new timing belt.

We're driving through the raw beauty of the true outback, the Red Centre Way, with its distinctive red soil and rock formations. Because there were steam trains with their need for water, there are many abandoned sidings with disused rusting water tanks. Amongst the remains of the early settlers' homes are old handmade tin cans, full of bullet holes. Along with the trash of modern man in the empty gas canisters and beer bottles. We realise how little Aborigines have been part of our journey, especially here where it has one of the largest percentages of indigenous peoples. In many areas, you need permission to enter Aboriginal Lands; the alternative is to visit one of the cultural centres where Aboriginal arts and crafts can be seen or bought, but for us that will never truly reflect this ancient culture.

Shit, what was that?

David 'I'm not a mechanic' discovers a sheared bolt to the track rod guard. With only one bolt holding it, it's being dragged against the underside of Lizzybus, resulting in this sickening metal on metal screech. David, having deemed it as unimportant, undoes the last bolt to take it off, throwing it in the back; we carry on regardless. We're not really talking, but after telling me what it is and that it won't affect us, David added that all our focus will now be on getting Lizzybus and us out of Australia. Not in seeing another gorge, another mountain, another waterfall. We are heading home. I like this, I like it a lot.

That decision was made at the end of a hard, chuck-it-in-the-back day of dust and pneumatic drill vibrations. Today, rested and refreshed we think sod it. We won't be beaten; we're not only on a mission but an adventure; we'll keep going until we can´t. Writing this now, I just can't understand why with so many more disasters than triumphs, we keep pushing. It feels we voice the 'let's call it a day' scenario like crying wolf, neither of us believe it, but in that moment, it seems to pacify us.

David has been talking to the locals, who have recommended a great drive on recently graded roads. A biro line is added to our map and we're off on another adventure. Half a day later, we reach Oodnadatta the site of Australia's first outback hospital. It's not exactly an oasis, but so remote I can only imagine the journey people would have to get help here and all those who died before reaching it.

CHAPTER 25

THE REALISATION

Initially on this journey, we had every intention of taking Lizzybus to New Zealand and from there shipping to South America, our next continent. None of this journey has been planned other than the general direction and what visas we would need, two to three countries ahead. With the sheer size of Australia, the cleaning, organising, and expense involved, we make the decision to not go to New Zealand. Although disappointing, it's such a huge relief. With what happened to us when getting Lizzybus into Australia, we just can't face it all again, emotionally, or financially.

Australia is, and has become, more and more magical; its people, landscape and sheer size is humbling. We are becoming almost feral, wanting, needing only food, shelter, water, and an ice-cold beer at the end of the day, the one part of the budget that is never questioned.

The days become one. I'm losing track of them and the exact route. We're sort of heading for Brisbane halfway down the east coast, Australia's third largest city and one of 'the' places to settle, due to its recent transformation into a sleek cosmopolitan city, whilst keeping its laid-back small-town attitude. We camp at Hookey's Waterhole, next to a barbed wire fence with a notice declaring it as Aboriginal Territory. No Name Creek - yes honestly, that is its name, No Name. We're in the real outback, a harsh, desolate, and completely flat area. Lizzybus struggles in the relentless wind, with her brick dynamics. Using her as a windbreak, we camp in this nothingness. A little campfire gives us the illusion of warmth, rather than actual warmth.

It's so flat we see the arc of the earth. The wind dies down allowing the smoke from the campfire to rise vertically, fizzling out in the dome of sky. We lie flat on our backs in the dirt holding hands. Looking up at the constellation of stars and moon, I feel connected. Not just to each other but to everyone we knew, know and love, as they are all under this same moon somewhere. If I say here that I reached out to touch Lizzybus, to include her in this moment, does it make me weird?

What makes the ancient Flinders Ranges with their jagged peaks and escarpments such a wonder is, having been in the flat outback for so long, they just rise up before us, and ever changing, from mauve mornings to midday chocolates, to ochre-red sunsets. The foothills have a real Alpine feel to them, reminding me of the opening scene to 'The Sound of Music'. I expect Julie Andrews with her arms wide open, to be running up them singing her heart out. I ask David to stop, so I can run up them with my arms wide open, not exactly singing, but squawking at the top of my lungs. "The hills are alive, with the sound of music". If only David had got out and ran with me. That thought makes me laugh. He can't sing a note, and as for running, were as bad as each other.

I can't remember when we last had a shower. I've moved on from Africa where we adopted the washing with your left hand and eating with your right. I've been buying kitchen towel, and use two sheets, with a squirt of washing up liquid for bits below, two more sheets with a mug of water for teeth, face and the bits above. It's surprising how clean I feel after this ritual. Is this oversharing?

I know my eyesight is getting worse, as when trying on some budget glasses, to replace my broken ones, I needed stronger ones. David, who always wore contact lenses, has given up on them with all the dust and grit. As he can see close up and I can see distance, we have one good set of eyes between us.

We move amongst people now who have no idea of who we are, or how we really exist in our life. Shopping in the supermarket, I get a once familiar waft of perfume. I stare at the fully made-up checkout girl, with vivid red lipstick that matches her painted fingernails. Australia is giving us what we need, seclusion, challenge, and people who speak English. The only thing we would change is its size because we have a whole world to get around.

The early morning sun is doing her best to return the colour back to a white frosted landscape, and the feeling back into my fingers, here in the heart of the New England Forest NSW. I'm on the verge of hypothermia; last night, driving sleet and high winds took the temperatures well below freezing. Even in our sleeping bags, I shivered the night away. I have succumbed, it's time, time to zip the sleeping bags together. For the smell of David's feet to be ignored in favour of their heat source. Time marches on, and with it our time at Menindee Lakes, a haunting area of submerged skeletal trees, with beautiful flocks of birds. We visit the Skywatch observatory perched atop a hill, driving on through routes listed as Star Way, Waterfall Way, all sorts of Way.

We detour on and off the major highways onto the more picturesque tourist routes. This of course means getting there in a few weeks, rather than a few days. The traffic is minimal but it's the road trains we hate. The length of six London double-decker buses, they just appear in your rear-view mirror. Leaving in their wake a wall of dust and tunnel of wind, pulling us this way and that. The 'Way' thing is here again, Lake Way. The road has sea one side and not one, but many lakes on the other, with imposing lakeside houses and sprawling shopping mall. Coming from the outback, with just a few roadhouses, it feels intrusive, just places to spend money we haven't got on stuff we don't want or need. We drive on through.

It poured down last night, our little campfire soon fizzled out. Sheet lightning captured the silhouettes of trees, freezing them in time like a Hitchcock thriller. David once more assures me our rubber tyres will keep us safe in our metal box. We're in the Hunter Valley NSW, the oldest wine growing area in Australia. We backpacked here for three weeks fifteen years ago, before our pound collapsed, their economy soared and we had no salary.

Mechanical issues cannot be ignored for ever. David is searching online for a Land Rover specialist in Sydney. Wow, you mean we are almost in Sydney, less than six hundred kilometres from Melbourne? Melbourne where we will ship Lizzybus to Buenos Aires, the Americas.

He doesn't find a garage, but he does find a Land Rover Expo in Sydney next week. I send them an email outlining our journey and immediately get a reply. We have been invited to attend and allocated a free pitch amongst the exhibitors for the three-day event. Knowing we will be as much an exhibit as Lizzybus, we head back to Lakes Way to the campsite which not only has hot water, but also a washing machine.

What a glorious thing clean is, with bedding and clothes smelling of chlorine, and hair of shampoo. Having abused the washing machine, we move from this expensive campsite to a picturesque one in the forest on the outskirts of Broke. Only three hours from Sydney where we are exhibiting Lizzybus in four days' time. A free campsite with flushing toilets and potable water, a large seating area with corrugated tin roof, and a fire pit with piles of wood you can use. In the roof tent I hear a low grunting sound, peering out I see a ringtail possum in the tree. It's the reflection of the full moon in its dinner plate eyes I see first, such shy little nocturnal creatures, a real treat.

The campsite is popular with the grey nomads. We have a steady stream of visitors which is most welcome, specifically the ones bringing beer. Regaling them with the trials and tribulations of our adventure and hearing about life for them as an Australian is wonderful. We also join them for potluck, where you all bring snacks and drinks to share. It took us a while to understand Australians as, unlike the English who need a formal invitation to join in, here you are just expected to.

The Expo is at Castle Hill, a sports complex just outside of Sydney. We go a day early to check it out. On realising you can park overnight on concrete hard standings in the wooded area behind the main buildings, with access to the showers and toilets, we do. It's an open-air arena, which transforms overnight with exhibitors and lots and lots of incredibly loved Land Rovers and overland trucks. Parked now in pride of place, we realise how woefully underprepared we and Lizzybus are. The other exhibitors erect impressive stands, with sailboat-size flags, and huge canvas billboards. We have a table with Sid on it - our black plastic mamba snake donated to us in Morocco, feared by black Africans and monkeys - a few of the business cards I had made in England, and the maps of our journey.

Today is the start of the three-day show. David spent last night drinking tinnies with the men from Modern Motors, setting up next to us. He brought me the cold remains of their pizza which was delicious.

Then it starts.

People are incredulous that we, two crazy 'poms' (a nickname for Brits with their supposed likeness to pomegranates and as rhyming slang), have driven alone in Lizzybus with such a basic set up all this way. There is a genuine respect for us and Lizzybus, with people wanting to know how she performed, what we faced. But it's the flags stuck in chronological order down each side of Lizzybus and the map on her doors, a visual record of our journey, that impress.

The show is over, the exhibitors have left, and we're parked back on the concrete pitch under the trees. As no one has said we can't or has asked for any money, we're going to rest up for a couple of days. People around us go about their daily activities of dog training, driver tuition, and various other club activities.

Sydney, surprisingly, is not the capital of Australia, that's Canberra. It is, however, the country's biggest and most diverse city. I dislike cities, but to have made it halfway around the world being here is such a thrill. So I allow myself to like this one … a little bit, especially on seeing the Sydney Opera House, said to resemble huge orange segments, snail palm fronds, or Malayan temples. Filling the skyline behind it is the instantly recognizable Harbour Bridge, affectionately called 'The Coathanger'. As a penal colony for early European settlers, there was a time when Sydney was filled with whalers, gold prospectors, and ex-convicts. Prostitution was rife and effluent ran down the lawless streets. That was before being recognised for its heritage; it got sanitised, some say modernised. Who cares, whatever it is, it is everything you would imagine one of the most expensive, cosmopolitan cities in the world to be.

As we drive Lizzybus through this sprawling city, the towering buildings block any signal to the sat-nav. The brakes are failing again, there's a loud clonking noise from the back end, and oil is spraying up and over the back door. When David, is betrayed by his mistress like this, it´s all he can focus on and wants to leave. I´m adamant. I have not driven all this way to not get a picture of Lizzybus with the Opera House and the Bridge. We see signs everywhere to register for an Emu pass, the same system they had in Singapore, where electronic number plate readers monitor your road use and charge you accordingly.

We have no way to register, were in gridlocked traffic, in a Lizzybus falling to pieces. I think stuff it, and park on the island with the Opera House and Bridge behind us to take our picture! The honking traffic stacks up behind and around us; David is ordering me to get back in immediately. Two traffic police walk over; I know they are telling us to move. I hug them, saying how fantastic it is to be here, how far we have come. They can't help congratulating us, holding the traffic back allowing us to pull out, shouting good luck. Finally, we get the respect and recognition we deserve. Next time I want a police escort!

I think there are many moments on this journey where if I was offered a tardis to transport me back to England, away from all this constant, I would take it in a heartbeat. The frustration we feel comes out in resentment towards each other, barely able to support ourselves let alone each other. After dumping Lizzybus on a side street we head for the Botanic Gardens. Having driven through the Northern and Southern Hemispheres and through their seasons, it is autumn in England but spring here. Sitting on the grass, we're surrounded by golden daffodils and the intoxicating perfume from pure white snowdrops. I lie back on the grass, looking up at the fluffy white cloud-filled sky, a magical moment all mine. In the middle of all this madness, it soothes me, giving me strength.

Tonight, we are going to a meeting of the Land Rover owners club, just outside Sydney, having been invited by one of the members we met at the Land Rover Expo. The guest speaker, Ross Charlton, was part of the Cambridge and Oxford teams, the first to drive to South Africa and back in Land Rover station wagons (same as Lizzybus). The idea formed from a drunken bet that driving across Africa could be done. The only real plan was that they would do it during their summer holidays. About as much of a plan as ours, our route being decided because I wanted to go somewhere hot. It is interesting that the idea, like ours, started from a throwaway comment, a drunken one in their case, making the insanity of ours even worse - we were stone-cold sober.

I feel an immediate connection to this gentle frail man, even though this happened two years before I was born. I was disappointed that although introduced, he was focused on preparing for his presentation, we never got to chat. I sat in admiration, mixed with a little envy at them being six people in two Land Rovers, the support and camaraderie they would have had. I did find myself wanting to wind him up, especially as I had not eaten all day and could see the huge pot of tea and homemade cakes waiting for us.

I daydream it's me up there, talking to everyone about our adventure, although I skip the thought of being eighty-two. It's almost midnight by the time he finishes. In the car park there is a big group of people admiring Lizzybus. These wonderful people give us invites to park on their drive, or sleep in their spare room. I can't understand why we didn't go with them, other than being so beaten and broken by Lizzybus, we want some space. We head back to Castle Hill and camp back amongst the trees.

It seems to me that every time we repair, replace, mend, or fix something, it is not the end. All I care about right now is brakes! I am adamant, whatever it costs, whatever makes brakes work, we are having it. In this case brake callipers, that since the new brake pipes, and brake fluid are now leaking. If I could scream right now I would. I know many don't give a stuff about the mechanics of this, and I apologise, whilst the mechanics out there reading this do.

David wants to strip down the brake calliper things and replace what would be the twelve seals in them. It's not a question of him being able to do this, it's a question of having a garage, the right tools, and the parts to do it. Driving now, I have constant instruction from David on braking and changing gear. I feel such an aggression towards him, something I'm finding increasingly difficult to control. It's said that given the right circumstances, every one of us is capable of murder, and I believe that wholeheartedly.

I've said that throughout this journey, we have been looked after by a guardian angel, today she delivers us to Daniel, a Swiss overlander we met at the Sydney Expo. Daniel, having overlanded from Switzerland with his now wife five years ago, settled in Australia and set up Mulgo, a company converting overland vehicles. With David still debating whether to rebuild the callipers, Daniel has offered us the use of his garage and all his tools. Still on my learning curve with mechanical stuff, to me it's simple. Whatever the hell these calliper things are, I want new ones, I need brakes. David is fixating on stripping them down. It fills me with frustrated despair, made worse by the ever-present issue of being overstayers. We're supposed to be driving around the world, but we are trapped in this cycle of mechanical breakdowns.

As Daniel will let us use his garage and tools, and any parts needed can be ordered through his company, it's decided David will strip down the callipers. I'm sulking because that's what I do when I don't get my own way. I want new ones. I'm told not only are they expensive, but we might not be able to get them. This annoys me even more.

I'm acutely aware in this moment that this is my story, about my journey. Despite it being a shared journey, I've always said our 'journeys' through it are completely different. I don't ever want to take away from David the massive achievement of getting Lizzybus this far, all due to 'I'm not a mechanic' David, but we both have a part to play. Decisions that seem black and white are not that simple here. It's factors like budget, knowledge, and the options available, that make the decision. To me though, it's pretty simple, I want new callipers as I'm sick of having at best dodgy, at worst no brakes.

On the way to Daniel's, we call in at BMI (British Motor Imports). My sparkle and enthusiasm have gone. I've always felt an ambassador of England, living proof that dreams can come true. Today I barely say hello. That is until the owner shows us his very own much loved Land Rover, covered in tarpaulin, out the back. He is so full of admiration, saying how he is dreaming of doing just what we are one day. I can't bear to crush anyone's dream, especially as we are what he aspires to.

We chat, drink coffee and eat biscuits whilst telling him all the reasons he should do it, but none of the reasons he shouldn't.

Whilst chatting, an ever-growing pile of parts appears on the table. Quite unbelievably, it includes a complete set of front and rear callipers. These, along with bushes, seals and oils, all charged to us at less than cost price. I try to convey the significance of this for us and our journey but can barely speak, in fact I´m sobbing. The pressure on David is immense, but it's a pressure on us both.

As we're about to drive away, he opens the back door and throws in a brand-new prop shaft. I´ve said before about emotions, the most common being anger, fear, disgust, happiness, sadness, surprise, or contempt, and how at times I've felt all of them in one go. Right now, there is only one, that of happiness. Not in the way laughter makes you happy, but in the joy and wonder that callipers and a prop shaft do. I recommend adding them to your Christmas list.

I don't think for one minute when Daniel offered us the use of his garage, he realised we would be sleeping in it. But as it's hangar-sized, with a shower, toilet and small kitchen, is dry and out of the elements, its perfect for us. This is where my admiration for David reaches new levels. Passing tools to him until way past midnight, my 'I'm not a mechanic' David fitted all the new callipers. I only lived with this wonderful feeling until morning. David, up early, starts work on replacing the clutch master cylinder, the bent-like-a-banana track road arm, and the new donated prop shaft, discovers something I am told is terminal. With play in the back axle, leaks from the power steering rocker thing and transfer box, Lizzybus is ready for the knacker's yard.

What David is unable to register right now, or take any comfort from, is that we are not stranded on the plains of Africa, or in the High Atlas Mountains, or in the middle of the Sahara. We are here in Daniel's workshop, with access to any and every tool or part we could ever possibly need. He mutters on about when we first bought Lizzybus and all the rot in her chassis (replaced before we left) for not 'getting rid!' then. What! How could he say that? I'm so in love with Lizzybus, she is my home, my life, my future and, despite everything, she got us here.

I'm so grateful Daniel is here to talk this through with David. He arranges for Sam and Rupert, the best Land Rover mechanics in Australia to come over tomorrow and take a look. I'm so broken right now, I can't even face writing in my journal. I take comfort in the possum looking down at me from the rafters; he looks as sad as I feel.

Today I go for a walk around the industrial estate, to a small park where children play on the swings. I lie down in the grass, listening to their mothers chatting away when something bites me on my inner thigh. I look at it, wondering if I am about to have another anaphylactic shock and die here alone. Within minutes it doubles in size, turning charcoal blue. I'm not panicked, just relieved rockers, shafts and transfer boxes will become irrelevant to me now. I drift off to sleep. I wake two hours later, disorientated but alive. Despite Australia having some of the deadliest insects in the world, my body, like Lizzybus, had looked after me.

I arrive back to find David walking like a castrated duck. He is in so much pain with his back from the hours lying under Lizzybus on the concrete floor. I don't mention my insect bite. He tells me that Rupert had said that the play, the leaks and so on, were all normal for a vehicle with two hundred thousand miles on the clock, especially a fully loaded one that had been driven off-road halfway around the world. With David, it's not so much that once his mind is made up it is made up, but he convinces himself it is. To me, I have been told she is normal for her mileage, age and the abuse we give her. That's all the confirmation I need. I want Lizzybus put back together and for us to get going. David is not convinced.

It hurts to see David in so much pain, but tonight, try as I might not to, I'm in hysterics trying to shove him up the ladder.

After eight days of living in Daniel's workshop, like a phoenix rising from the ashes, Lizzybus emerges into the sunlight. We are back to what is beginning more and more to feel like our self-imposed sentence of driving her around the world. Once more we dare to dream that we might even make it. We have been given a tub of melt-in-your-mouth, fat juicy slices of roast pork from the man at the garage next door. All the parts, oils, and seals we used, our incredibly generous, now good friend Daniel has given us at the discounted company price. I see in

Daniel's eyes a look of concern. I can feel the tug of resistance from something near her back end. It is what it is. I say nothing to David; he will find out when he drives her. I'm just ecstatic I have brakes.

We're heading for the infamous Bondi Beach where annually over two and a half thousand people are rescued from its lethal rip currents (not all successfully) because David's cousin Joel, his partner Charlotte and their four-year-old son Max live there. It's exactly what we both need, as life revolves around their pure blond, blue eyed chatterbox Max. They met whilst out here on working visas fifteen years ago and made Australia their home. We have magical evenings on the beach, barbeques with their friends, and watch Joel playing rugby to a backdrop of the Sydney Opera House and Bridge. Four days later, a sense of purpose and adventure returns, we hit the road with the glorious taste of last night's fish and chips supper in our mouths. We're heading now for the Blue Mountains which will test Lizzybus with its valleys, canyons and plateaus. A blue slate-coloured haze hovers over this area due to the oils emitted from eucalyptus and gum trees, hence the name Blue Mountains, and yes, they really are blue. There are three national parks within its area, popular with Sydneysiders seeking out relief from the summer heat.

Last night it was bitterly cold, even the roaring campfire couldn't keep the chill away. I wake in a coffin. The roof of our clam shell tent had folded down on us, it takes both of us to push it back up. Peering out, I see a magical winter wonderland. With it still snowing, it's like being in our very own snow globe. Climbing down the ladder barefoot, my feet compress the snow on the rungs. I'm so desperate for a pee, I put a pair of David's socks on, making a little V in the toes to get my flip flops on. My feet are blocks of ice by the time I get back and dig my boots out. Last night we noticed a wooden hut, in it we find a middle-aged American couple with their two teenage sons. They arrived late last night in a tiny rented Fiesta. Once the snow started, realising it was too dangerous to drive back, they set up their pup tents in the hut. A good idea as it had a fireplace with piles of dry wood, so they were able to have a fire.

Their little car is now buried deep in the snow. We help them dig it out, telling them to follow in our tyre tracks. It's quite surreal. Ahead of us is a mob of kangaroos; they disappear and reappear, hopping their way through the deep snow. A fallen tree, brought down by the snow, blocks the way ahead. We cut and clear it. In theory, they should be able to follow in our tracks, but the clearance on Lizzybus is a lot more than their car. It's not long before their front bumper is ripped off, splitting the plastic aerofoil. As a rental car, this is going to be expensive.

David and I put the bumper in their boot, secure the aerofoil with zip-wires and gaffer tape. Through all this, their two teenage boys sit in the back of the car, making no attempt whatsoever to help or, more to the point, enjoy the adventure. David and I love it - we work well together, like a team. We're at a point in this journey where putting the skills learned through necessity, trial and error, feels amazing, were confident in us and Lizzybus.

We reach Canberra (meeting place). Once nothing more than an outback sheep station, specifically designed to be the capital city of Australia. A city of importance as its where parliament sits, framed by the Brindabella Ranges and rugged outback. Its buildings are set back amongst wide open landscaping, with a war memorial, museums, and national galleries. More importantly for us, it's home to Rick and Ann who we met at the Expo and have invited us to stay at their 'shed' sitting in six acres. The main 'shed' has a wraparound veranda, looking out over rolling hillside; the other sheds are a collection of corrugated roofed buildings full of Land Rovers. I have come to realise that all men interested in Land Rovers have not one, or two, but sheds full of them, and all the parts you need to build one.

It's a home to them, Ann's sister and her teenage daughter and, just like them, it's full of organised chaos. Ex-military Rick runs a company providing defence systems, Ann works part-time and is also secretary to the Canberra Land Rover club; some of the members have been invited over tonight for a barbie. Our mouths water at the aroma coming off the barbie where half a lamb roasts. It's such a wonderful evening of conversation, finished off with a glass of aged port and chunks of proper cheese, delicious. We are invited to be guest speakers at their monthly Land Rover meeting in two days' time.

Today with Rick, we visit their neighbours to meet Frank their pet alpaca, who gives kisses, and to see the polystyrene house they're building. That evening more friends arrive as we tuck into huge bowls of spaghetti bolognese, garlic bread, salad, and generous amounts of fresh shaved Parmesan, a world away from the fried tomatoes, onion and clove of garlic we have on the road.

Tonight, we're sitting down to a three-course meal with all the club members. Seeing the area set up for us with a projector, I momentarily feel a little nervous. Now, stood in front of everyone, apart from an incredibly dry mouth, I can't wait to get going. Connecting our laptop to the projector, we show photos of our journey. With David dismissing the mechanical and security issues as 'nothing', I tell them about the time I was groped by our armed police escorts in Pakistan, the knife wielding robbers on the roof at three in the morning in the Congo, the constant breakdowns, even about the more personal issues around intimacy, loneliness and isolation. I admit to my naivety as to what the journey would entail. How living two feet from David twenty-four hours a day, when you can't slam a zip, like you can a door, or you can't drive to your sister's for a good old moan, was a challenge. How the sheer wonder, joy, and unconditional kindness of people whose lives touched ours along the way made it what it is.

Knowing I was only ever going to be honest; I knew I would be open to judgement and criticism. Talking openly and honestly, with no language barrier, was so good. Finally, having run out of steam, there was silence. A small ripple of applause became a resounding round of it. As Land Rover owners themselves they all understood, were genuinely amazed, interested and, most importantly, amused. I felt I'd had therapy, it was overwhelming and emotional.

Today we leave Ann and Rick's. Having said our goodbyes last night, the house is empty this morning with them having left for work. On the table is a tub of home-made chocolate brownies and the biggest chocolate cake, baked for us by Ann's sister and daughter, two to-be-treasured club T-shirts, and a handwritten note wishing us all the best for our journey. It's hard to underestimate the importance these moments are to us on our journey. We leave with heavy but contented hearts.

The Snowies form part of the Great Dividing Range, through which runs Australia's most iconic and majestic rambling river, Snowy River. In 1949, it underwent one of the largest hydroelectric engineering projects in Australia. Channelling its melting snow waters east opened vast areas of land for irrigation. A big success at the time, but leaving only one percent of the river's headwaters, the environmental effect was disastrous. Plans to restore some of its flow, balanced with the demands of a growing population, are ongoing. We visit the museum, showing the construction of the project over its twenty-five years. David remembers being taught about it at school, so it's quite a thing to be here now.

After all the snow in the Blue Mountains we wonder how wise it is to explore The Snowies, but it's sort of en route, or so David would have me believe. Through a twisting panoramic, at times sheer, dirt track following one of its tributaries, on the next bend there she is, in all her majesty. The Snowy River, a sprawling tangle of water, vegetation and boulders, flows over golden sand to a backdrop of soaring forest, and simply stunning.

For three days, we camp beside her in total isolation. The free-to-use campsite has a fire pit with a metal cooking platform and suspended hanging hook, a sheltered wooden seating area, and even a long drop composting toilet. Little wooden steps lead down to the river where we bathe in her ice-cold waters. Into the holes of a weathered fallen tree, I press some of my now not-so-precious cheese into its bark. Whilst swaying in my hammock I watch the prettiest tiny petrol blue wrens peck and squabble over it. The bush is far too thick to navigate so we walk along the track we came in on. We hear rather than see kangaroos thump thumping over the forest carpet of vibrant flowers, their faces wide open, inviting the dappled sunlight and pollinating bees.

Australia is home to some of the deadliest creatures on earth, snakes being one. Having already been bitten and survived a snake bite, I stay well away from the edge. We realise that what looks like a branch is not only a snake, but a snake with a lizard hanging out of its mouth. It's with a kind of revolting fascination we watch the snake's muscles convulse, as its body becomes a bulging lizard shape. Yuk, I'm just glad its mouth was full of lizard and no threat to me.

Heading now for Melbourne, the final destination here in Australia, I'm filled with both excitement and dread; excitement about having driven Lizzybus around Australia, but dread at being overstayers and the prospect of sorting out a container and a ship for Lizzybus for her six-week voyage to South America. And flights for us as we're not allowed to go with her. I have such a tangle of emotions. It's still weeks away, but already my heart is aching to be with my family, to see my grandson, son, daughter, and Jenny. It's been hard for them too.

David, wanting nothing more than to continue on like this forever, views the milestones very differently. He sees them as proof that one day this will end, our nomadic days will be over. I have never ceased to wonder how it's me here, privileged and humbled by it, but it doesn't stop my need and want for progress. To one day achieve what we set out to do, to drive Lizzybus around the world.

CHAPTER 26

THE CALM BEFORE THE STORM

Melbourne hits you full on, a city as big as London or Paris, with six lane highways, towering skyscrapers and what seems to be a million modern apartment blocks. In 1835, John Batman acquired 240,000 hectares of land from the Aboriginal Kulin peoples for little more than tools, flour and clothing. Five years later, more than ten thousand European settlers arrived. What scares me most are the sprawling docks which we must negotiate to ship Lizzybus to South America. We come up with a sort of plan, to concentrate on getting Lizzybus out of Australia then we will throw ourselves at the mercy of immigration at the airport.

It's strange to me now, having been so anal about visas, to have become almost blasé with it now. Once it was obvious we had overstayed, we justified it by the breakdowns, the outback, and the vast distances. We will accept whatever the consequences are, knowing we deserve them.

You would imagine that knowing this, we would book the earliest sailing possible for Lizzybus and a flight for us. We're only in November; if we did this, we would miss Christmas in England with family. We always said this journey was not at the cost of all else, or about ticking boxes. There were always going to be some compromises somewhere. It's decided, having set up a meeting with the shipping agent for four weeks' time, to wait it out. But not here in Melbourne; we head west along the Great Ocean Road from Torquay to Warrnambool - basically a bloody long way.

Driving along this great big bitumen sea snake of a road, it seems to be either uninhabited and desolate or populated with seaside resorts of uniform chalets and opulent houses. It is spectacular. Nature has modelled limestone cliffs into sculptures, not just on land but standing proud in the ocean. They're given names like the Twelve Apostles (only seven remain), London Bridge, Gibson Steps. We visit Loch Ard Gorge and blow holes; the noise and spectacle is something else. But my heart is no longer in it. It feels like killing time - which we are - putting off the inevitable.

Johanna Beach, where we will stay put for a week, as by not using any diesel and being a free campsite, it is good for the budget. Despite being amongst the dunes, we have little protection from the howling gales and constant rain. Using Lizzybus as a wind break, I set up the pup tent beside her. I remember the video I have, "All the Queens Horses", celebrating Queen Elizabeth's sixty-year reign. Inside this little tent, it feels like I finally have my own space. I love words, they are personal to each and everyone who reads them. Right now, I can't find the right ones to describe how watching this, hearing the music, the narrative, and seeing the pomp and ceremony the Brits do so well, transports me.

I'm finding it difficult to be present now. I feel we have done what we need to do in Australia. David, still in panic mode, wants to make sure we don't miss anything. We manage one night at Johanna Beach before heading off to the Grampians National Park, with outstanding natural features due to its unique rock formations. I'm sort of okay with this as I've had enough of the wind and rain, and it's in Victoria where Melbourne is. Going into summer is a good time to visit due to all the wild flowers, many species being unique to this area, and for now Lizzybus is behaving.

As usual, on all main highways you can detour off for the more scenic route, taking you through pine or native woodland, rolling hills, or majestic mountains. There are many State Reserves and Parks. We're at Rocklands Reservoir, with its protruding skeletal trees, a collection of weathered shingle-clad huts, and long drop toilet. Whilst we're setting up camp, a couple arrives, farmers from Victoria. Over a barbie and a few tinnies, we chat late into the evening. I love anyone with a passion; even if it's not your passion, it makes it interesting. They are curious about us and our journey, but passionate about farming, so conversation is focused on this. I love hearing all about the challenges and struggles they've had. They invite us to stay at their farm to help with the sheep shearing. This is something I´ve always wanted to do. What a fantastic way to have ended our time in Australia, but it's time to head back to Melbourne for the appointment with the shipping agent.

Picking up email in town, we find an invite to David and Rebecca's in Adelaide. They are building a truck for a trip to Africa and want some advice. It's sort of on the way back, but still I´m incredible grumpy. I wanted to go sheep shearing, not to look at a truck. We arrive at a vineyard with the usual collection of sheds full of the most amazing bikes, cars and tractors. Even though it was great - picnicking on the beach, walking to the pub for a beer, a full Sunday roast - it is not sheep shearing. We look on with envy at David´s (not my David) fully-prepared-by-himself Land Rover. With pop-up roof, an interior you can get inside of, heater and air con, it's a vehicle you would want to live in, whilst driving around the world.

The Grampians, bigger than most capital cities, is a vista of wild flower-filled forest and mountains. At only a day's drive from Melbourne, we will spend the last three days here. We trek, make fires, wash in the creek and pick the mould off the last of our bread, to fry with an onion, garlic, and tin of tomatoes for dinner. But it's when we run out of beer we head into the local town. David insists on taking the scenic dirt road when we get another puncture. During our journey, mishaps have only ever brought opportunity. Owen just appears, a real live gold prospector, in a battered old Land Rover. Clad in a check shirt, faded jeans and a wide-brimmed worn leather bush hat. Little wisps of white hair stick out of his hat, a thick silver beard covers most of his chest. From the back of his truck, he produces a plastic margarine tub full of gold nuggets. He gives me one the size of a coffee bean, which I gaffer tape to Lizzybus, making her as precious as gold! I forget all about my sheep shearing, I´m in the presence of tradition.

(I taped this coffee bean of gold inside Lizzybus, but the vibrations and the heat loosened it. My precious golden coffee bean was lost.)

With the pressure taken off, it being a waiting game, we begin to focus, even fixate, on each other's irritating habits. My constant need to pee means I disturb David through the night. My ongoing inability to read maps and smoking, not the fact of smoking, but of how much cigarettes cost here. For me, it's David´s unwillingness to shave, cut toenails, or wipe the tooth paste off from around his mouth. It's petty, I know. We do have funny, stupid, silly moments, conversations that make us laugh. But all too often we retreat into our own worlds.

Unzipping the roof tent on another glorious day, I rejoice on seeing mountains and forests, not to be woken by an alarm clock, but kookaburras and songbirds. As David makes coffee, I walk barefoot across the carpet of mosses with its sprinkling of delicate alpine flowers. Tomorrow, we will leave this woodland wonderland, the hikes up, and around Mount Difficult, Mackenzie Falls, and the Pinnacles. Its time to arrange shipping flights and face the consequences of overstaying.

CHAPTER 27

IT'S TIME TO FACE THE MUSIC

We arrive in Melbourne, at St Arnaud Guest House. Lizzybus is too tall for the car park so is parked on the street, which is not ideal with the two-hour parking limit. The grandeur of this three-storey Edwardian building almost lost in becoming a backpackers. The outside having a concrete rendering, and the inside partitioned off with plaster board to create communal rooms and dormitories. But it's the imposing central stairway, with seventies floral carpet, muffling the creaking groans of its ageing oak stair treads, that reveals its past. There is a sense of calm with piped music and cabinets stuffed with chintzy crockery and knick-knacks. We opt for a twin room, with a little balcony overlooking the rows of ornate metal filigree Edwardian houses opposite. It feels most genteel.

Sat on my little balcony with my morning coffee smoking, I look down to see David on the street below with a sponge washing Lizzybus in the rain. It makes me laugh. Having visited the shipping agent's office yesterday, Lizzybus is booked on a ship that sails in six days' time. Firstly, she needs to be 'stuffed' (secured in her container). This is not done at the docks, but in the depot of an industrial area, before being transported to the docks thirty kilometres away. We navigate once more across Melbourne, over the many suspension bridges with panoramic views of the dock and city, and through the long tunnels with bright neon strip lighting, to an industrial area on its outskirts. We are meeting the man arranging the container. For some reason, we both have a sense of foreboding.

Industrial areas are full of nondescript built-for-purpose corrugated buildings, and isolated places. We notice a tiny plaque on the hangar-sized building relating to our paperwork but can't find a door. Walking around a man appears through an opening we didn't even realise was a door. We're taken up the stairs, past a few offices with people at desks, until we reach one that he announces as his. Checking on his computer, he informs us that they have no information about us or any request to 'stuff' Lizzybus.

This is so typical of everything we have faced on this journey, be it in deepest darkest Africa, or here in the cosmopolitan cities of Australia. David panics; I go on the charm offensive. It sort of works and sort of doesn't. After a few phone calls, he confirms who we are and what we need, but he can't magic a Lizzybus size container. The earliest he can get one delivered is in two days' time. One of the biggest lessons we have learnt is to be there, be seen, and be early. And exactly why we came to this depot three days early. Making a friend of this man, we become more than an email or another job on his to-do-list, we become his personal project.

It's not just a case of 'stuffing' Lizzybus; we will need a customs officer on site to witness the sealing of the container, to sign and stamp the paperwork. Only then can she be transported to the docks. There is nothing more we can do for now; it is what it is. The pit of dread we both had has abated somewhat, but it will not go completely, not until Lizzybus is in the container, the customs officer has signed the documents, and she has been taken to the docks.

The weather, from downpours to bright sunshine, like our moods, is constantly changing. Today, the hottest day in Melbourne for ten years, is 'D-day'. Driving through the city streets, I want to shout and scream, to thank everyone for having us in their fantastic country. Cars pull alongside us, having recognised the British number plate, shout "Good on yer", "G'day". I shout back that we didn't just ship here, we drove here via Africa. Not one of them believes me. In the blistering heat, we pull up under the shade of a tree to take off the incredibly heavy top box and put it on the back seats. If we don't, Lizzybus will not fit into her container. A man from the factory comes out and gives us several ratchet straps and four wooden blocks. He even offers to give us a lift back to the train station when we have finished.

The lorry to take her to the docks, the customs officer to sign the paperwork, and the container are all there waiting for us. The simplicity of this is unsettling - we're waiting for something to go wrong.

With Lizzybus gone, the world - our world - seems silent. The last few weeks have been so focused on this moment, it's like a bursting bubble. We're momentarily lost in its puff. Although Lizzybus is not on her ship yet, there is nothing more David and I can do, she is on her own.

Today is the first of December, the festive season, a time for most to reunite with family and friends, and exactly what we intend on doing.

We can't wait to face the consequences of being overstayers, to no longer have the worry of it. Having heard back from the shipping agent that Lizzybus has been loaded and is on her way to Buenos Aires, we're ready to accept our fate.

Melbourne airport, as expected in this ginormous country, is a ginormous airport. We are tiny little dots in the tide of people, all going somewhere. At check-in, the girl is confused; we only have a ten-kilo bag. She is distracted by this whilst scanning our passports and asking the standard, "Did you pack your own bag?", "Has it been left unattended?" It's only us that initially hears the bleep signifying an issue. Scanning them again, she apologises saying there seems to be a problem. We're asked to follow her colleague to a small room. One of the two customs officers sat behind the desk asks us why we think we are there.

I immediately admit to it being because we are overstayers, even to the fact that it's precisely two months and two weeks over. I tell them how we had driven here via Africa, how massive their wonderful country is, not realising how long it would take us to drive around it. How we tried to renew visas online. David just sits there; he knew I would just admit it. Come on, we have passports full of countries, there is no way we would not have known about visas. I take a breath. In this moment of silence, one of the customs officers says, "Wow, no way, you drove here!"

Well, that was an invitation to tell them everything I had gone through. One thing about Australians, they seem to have all the time in the world. That's exactly what they gave me, all the time in the world. I regale them with tales of our journey, especially what we had done here in Australia; they were amazed, sitting open-mouthed. I become aware that, as wonderful as this little chat is, we have a flight to catch. They thank me for my honesty, but they cannot make the decision and need to speak to their superiors.

Firstly, we are going to be banned from Australia for three years. This is painless as we will be in the Americas. What we are waiting for is how much we will be fined. 'Nothing'. We are not going to be fined a single penny. The bureaucracy of life has been beaten by honesty and their admiration of us having driven halfway around the world to get here, that we had genuinely tried and not lied. Apologising at having to ban us, they assure us if we appeal it, it will be lifted. They stand up, offering us a handshake. I'm momentarily unable to believe this is the scenario playing out for real, and not just the one I had made up. When I realise it's real, I walk around the desk and hug them both, big bear hugs of relief and genuine gratitude. Australia, we thought we could never love you more, but you proved us wrong. We will be back.

I think about how I feel.

I will take with me a journey filled with humbling, exhilarating and, at times, distressing experiences. Of driving more than a hundred and thirty thousand kilometres, through forty-six countries, over three years, whilst eating, sleeping and occasionally making out, in an old Land Rover we call Lizzybus. I've learnt more about David than I ever wanted or needed, confirming what I already knew, that he is bloody-minded, determined and fair. I know there is no one else I would have wanted by my side.

For me, I wonder - have I survived this journey or thrived on it? Without a shadow of a doubt, I know I've done both in equal measure.

Survived because I am still alive and thrived because I have learnt not just new skills, but the true value of everything. Even to me, this seems a bit airy-fairy, as I've always valued my friends, my family, the simple things in life. I know the reward in giving blood, eating raw pig's eyes, or climbing mountains for charity. I wasn't looking to find myself; I knew who I was. The most difficult thing for me has been letting go of my English reserve, my need to form an orderly queue, and my sense of fairness. And to accept that for some people, giving is as important, even if they have nothing, as receiving.

I recognise that the most valuable and powerful thing we all have is time, not just in having it, but in giving it.

See you in Buenos Aires………..

www.ingramcontent.com/pod-product-compliance
Lightning Source LLC
Chambersburg PA
CBHW071655090426
42738CB00009B/1533